AGENT ROSE

AGENT ROSE

The True Spy Story of
Eileen Nearne, Britain's
Forgotten Wartime Heroine

BERNARD O'CONNOR

AMBERLEY

All illustrations courtesy of Odile Nearne.

First published 2012

Amberley Publishing
The Hill, Stroud
Gloucestershire, GL5 4EP

www.amberley-books.com

Copyright © Bernard O'Connor, 2012

The right of Bernard O'Connor to be identified
as the Author of this work has been asserted in
accordance with the Copyrights, Designs and
Patents Act 1988.

ISBN 978 1 4456 0838 9

British Library Cataloguing in Publication Data.
A catalogue record for this book is available
from the British Library.

Typeset in 11pt on 16pt Palatino.
Typesetting and Origination by Amberley Publishing
Printed in the UK.

CONTENTS

1 Prologue: 3 March 1944 & 2 September 2010   7

2 Growing Up in England & Escaping from France: 1921–42   14

3 Settling in London & Initial Interview with SOE: Spring 1942   24

4 Training for Work as a Secret Agent: Summer 1942–Autumn 1943   44

5 Preparations for the Drop into Occupied France: Winter 1943–Spring 1944   85

6 Working for the Resistance in France: 3 March 1944–24 July 1944   166

7 Arrest, Interrogation, Torture & Escape: 25 July 1944–25 May 1945   184

8 Life Back in England: 26 May 1945–2 September 2010   210

   Appendix   229

   Notes   233

   Bibliography   238

   Index   254

1
PROLOGUE:
3 MARCH 1944 & 2 SEPTEMBER 2010

In the early hours of the morning of 3 March 1944, a small, single-engine Lysander aeroplane flew low over northern France. The underside was painted black to avoid its being seen from the ground and the top painted grey and green to make it difficult for enemy night fliers to spot it. Flight Lieutenant Anderson used the reflection of the moon's light to identify rivers, canals and railway lines to help orientate himself, occasionally checking the folded map he had on his lap and consciously navigating away from the anti-aircraft sites he had marked. Behind him were two passengers, British secret agents destined to help the French Resistance prepare for D-Day. They were understandably nervous. Their flight had been cancelled twice during the last moon period so there was an urgency about completing this mission successfully.

It was a bitterly cold and cloudy night, and below them the passengers could not identify the settlements they flew over. They knew only that they were heading for an isolated field near the village of Les Lagnys, about eight kilometres from Vatan in the Indre department. Only a few hours earlier, in the warmth of Gibraltar Farm, the control room of the RAF's top secret airfield, they had pored over the photographs and sketches of the landing site and maps of the surrounding area.

Once past Vatan, the pilot dropped down and followed the line of the A20 south-west towards Châteauroux. Shortly, he circled the plane over a patchwork of hundreds of rectangular fields, searching for the red flashing light of the reception committee's torch. Then Jean Savy tugged on the other passenger's coat and pointed. He'd spotted it. So had the pilot, but he knew it wasn't from the field he'd been expected to land in. It was from one nearby. Nevertheless, as the torch flashed the correct identification letter, he decided to land.

Two more lights appeared, creating a letter 'L'. Knowing the two furthest apart indicated the wind direction, he lined up the plane and landed bumpily in the field. At the last torch he turned, knowing the third light indicated the width of the field, and taxied back to the first. Seeing a dark figure with the torch, he turned again, facing into the wind ready for take-off, stopped, pushed his cockpit canopy back and started lighting his pipe.

Several dark figures rushed across to welcome the pilot and help the passengers out. A young woman, twenty-three-year-old Eileen Nearne, known to her friends as Didi, but to her organisation as Agent Rose, pushed the passengers' Perspex cockpit cover back and climbed out. Using the ladder welded onto the side of the fuselage, she carefully descended a few steps so that her colleague could hand her their suitcases. One of them said, in a pure Parisian accent, 'OK? We have to act quickly to avoid being caught.' When he heard Didi talking, he said, 'Oh, a young girl. Go back. Go back. It's extremely dangerous. You must go back.'

It was indeed extremely dangerous, but Didi had not been told the full extent. Anyway, she was in no mood to go back. She had a job to do, to help liberate France from German occupation.

Working for a newspaper, you have to be prepared to respond to anything that you see happening that could provide a story. A reporter from the *Herald Express*, a South Devon publication, had been picking their son up from school in Torquay one Friday afternoon when they noticed two police cars following a hearse from flats in Lisburne Crescent, a row of whitewashed flats a few minutes' walk from the seafront. Thinking it slightly unusual, they alerted colleagues back at the office, who made a few enquiries.

They were told that an elderly, unnamed woman had died of natural causes, leaving no known relatives and that the council was arranging her funeral. The following day, two paragraphs appeared in the *Herald Express*, which started a chain of events reaching several continents.

They reported how, on 2 September 2010, the body of an 89-year-old woman was discovered in a small, rented flat. When she died was not certain, but a post-mortem examination revealed that the cause of death was a heart attack. When no immediate next of kin could be found, the town authorities were called upon to arrange a civic funeral.

One of the woman's neighbours rang the paper to say that the lady's name was Eileen Nearne and that council workers sent in to clean her rooms had found some old French currency, correspondence written in French and some medals relating to World War Two.

Glenn Price, one of the *Herald Express* reporters with a special knowledge and historical interest in World War Two, did some research and, according to the paper, 'the real Charlotte Gray' was revealed.

Charlotte Gray was the titular heroine of a very popular Sebastian Faulks novel, which was made into a film in 2001. After training as a secret agent, she was parachuted into France on a secret mission to help the Resistance. Disobeying orders, she used some of her time trying to find her boyfriend, an RAF pilot whose plane had been shot down and who had been reported missing in action.

As we shall see, Eileen Nearne was a secret agent, but she didn't parachute into France and didn't spend time looking for a missing boyfriend. Her experiences were a lot more stressful.

On 9 September the *msnbc* website ran a story titled 'U.K. recluse found to be war heroine after death'. On 13 September, *The Guardian* ran an article, 'Lonely death of a wartime heroine' and the *The Sun* had one titled 'Real life Rigby is WWII heroine'. The following day, *The Independent* had one named 'Eileen Nearne: Lonely death of a spy who evaded Gestapo,' and the BBC News reported 'War heroine found dead in Devon to have council funeral'. Word had spread across the Atlantic and the *Chicago Sun-Times* and the *Gulf News* reported 'Recluse found to be wartime heroine after her death'.

As no friends or family could be found, Torbay council planned to give her a council burial, which in the past was called a 'pauper's grave'. There was the suggestion in the *Paignton People* on 14 September that she was just like the Eleanor Rigby in the Beatles' song, one of the lonely people who died in the church and was buried along with her name – nobody came. They hoped the publicity would encourage those who knew her to attend.

On 14 September, Adrian Sanders, Liberal Democrat MP for Torbay, put forward a motion in the House of Commons with eighteen signatories recommending that the government should acknowledge Eileen in some way.

Plans for the funeral had to be changed when, on 15 September, research by Kin, a London-based investigation service, located and contacted her niece, Odile, in Tuscany, Italy. As her aunt's death was so sudden, Odile didn't know she had died and it was quite a shock for her. She flew over to

Britain straight away and was therefore able to attend her dear aunt's funeral.

Over the following three days, obituaries in *The Times* and *The Daily Telegraph* revealed more about Eileen's wartime past. Investigators had found that she had worked for the Special Operations Executive, a top secret organisation during World War Two, and, with a copy of her obituary, had managed to access her personal file in the National Archives in Kew. In fact, demand for it was so great that a copy was made available on their website.

The story was picked up on 15 September on *ABC News* in Australia, 'Death reveals secret of war heroine' and the *Taipei Times* reported 'Anonymous death reveals surprising heroine's tale'. The Australian *Fox Gazette* ran a story on her on 16 September: 'The secret life of a lonely old lady' and the following week the *Sydney Morning Herald* covered her story: 'Extraordinary heroism of "scatterbrained" Eileen – the spy who never came in from the cold.'

On 21 September, the story was reported in the *Daily Mail*, 'Charlotte Gray revealed – The Truth – British Heroine died forgotten.' The same day the *New York Times* reported, 'Eileen Nearne, wartime spy dies at 89.' The following day the *Irish Times* reported 'Hundreds gather for funeral of wartime spy'. On 23 September *CNN* ran an article, 'Secrets of British spy "Agent Rose" revealed in death'; the *Boston Globe* reported 'Eileen Nearne, unsung heroine of British Spy network in WWII' and the *Pittsburgh Post-Gazette* ran one 'Reclusive WWII heroine buried with honours'.

When links to some of these news items were posted on the Special Operations Executive user-group on *Yahoo.com* throughout September, my attention became focussed. Why? Because I had spent many years researching the women agents sent into occupied Europe during World War Two by this organisation, the Foreign Office's Secret Intelligence Service (SIS), General Charles de Gaulle's *Bureau Central de Renseignements d'Action* (BCRA), the American Office of Strategic Services (OSS), the Soviet Union's *Norodny Kommissariat Vnutrennich Dyel* (NKVD) and various other European government-in-exiles' intelligence organisations.

I already knew about Eileen Nearne and her sister Jacqueline and had researched their stories for a book I had written, so was keen to check the articles and update my accounts with any new information that had come to light.

It was not until a year later, in December 2011, when her story had disappeared from the headlines and Amberley Publishing had published my *Women of RAF Tempsford: Churchill's Agents of Wartime Resistance*, that Jonathan Reeve, their commissioning editor, contacted me and suggested that I write Eileen's story. Initially, I hesitated, thinking that others must already have written her biography, but he told me not to worry. There was nothing wrong with having several books on the same person. Anyway, my insight into the experiences of female agents would be valuable.

On checking what I had written on Eileen, I found that I had fewer than 4,000 words and my publisher wanted 60,000. Whilst I already had quite a library of SOE and SOE-related publications to search for additional information and numerous contacts whose knowledge and experience I knew I could draw on, there would be a lot more research necessary. Up for the challenge, I decided that it would help shed more light on the lives of some of the brave women who volunteered for particularly dangerous work behind enemy lines.

In particular, I need to acknowledge the assistance of Odile Nearne, Eileen's niece. Research by genealogists successfully located her in Italy and she very kindly agreed to help answer my many questions about the Nearne family's background in France. Sarah Pearson-Phillips, Elizabeth Bailey and Denis O'Connor provided valuable help in locating some of the family records in England. Rosie Greenham of ABC News provided details of Australian and American media reports on Eileen's death. Patrick Yarnold and Mark Yeats helped with information on the SOE training at Winterfold. Juliette Pattinson helped with Didi's time at Thame Park. Steven Kippax helped with obtaining copies of Eileen Nearne, Jacqueline Nearne, Francis Nearne and Jean Savy's personal files at the National Archives in Kew. Finally, Tim Sharrock helped with the editing.

2

GROWING UP IN ENGLAND & ESCAPING FROM FRANCE: 1921–42

John Nearne, Eileen's father, was of Irish descent on his mother's side of the family. Born in Birmingham on 8 August 1889, he grew up in the Midlands, but went to study medicine in London, living at 70 Margaret Street in Marylebone. On 6 November 1913, before he had finished his course, he married 26-year-old Mariquita Carmen de Plazaola. Known as Marie, the daughter of a Spanish count who had a house in Paris, she always considered herself Spanish. When the First World War broke out, he served as a private in the Royal Army Medical Corps. Wounded whilst in France, he was brought back to England and, after recuperating, worked as a dispensing chemist, living at 58 Perham Road, Fulham.

Their first child, Francis, was born in Hove, near Brighton on the English south coast on 16 July 1914. As John's father was an optician in Hove, it is probable Marie went to stay with her in-laws during the latter part of her pregnancy. Jacqueline was also born there on 27 May 1916. Frederick was born in the family home in Fulham in 1920, as was Eileen on 15 March 1921.

Two years later, the family moved to Marie's parents' home in Paris, partly because Marie wanted the children to have a French education and partly because Marie's family would be able to help her look after the four children.

It is thought that John found work as a chemist, but he must have had assistants as his French was reported to have not been very good. Eileen, known in the family as 'Didi', was looked after at home by her mother and grandmother whilst Jacqueline attended the Catholic convent of Les Oiseaux.

Two years later, her parents decided to relocate the family to the Normandy coast. They moved into 260 Boulevard Sainte Beuve, a seafront house in Boulogne-sur-Mer, which they owned. Both girls attended the Ursuline Convent and the two boys went to a Catholic college.

When Didi's Spanish grandmother died in 1928, her mother inherited a house in Nice. It seems the family house in Paris was sold and in 1931, when Didi was ten years old, the family moved to the Mediterranean coast, closing up their seafront house. They lived in a terraced property at 60 Bis Avenue des Arenes de Cimiez in Nice. This no doubt pleased the children as it was much warmer and Marie loved being by the sea.

The girls continued their convent education, but, according to Odile, they also received some private tuition. Jacqueline left the convent in 1934, when she was eighteen and took an unusual job for a woman at the time. She worked as a travelling commercial representative for a firm in Nice, selling office equipment and furniture, visiting businesses across the South of France. It was a job she found interesting and one which she did quite successfully. It also gave her extensive knowledge of French cities, towns and the railway system.

By the time the Second World War started in 1939, Didi was eighteen and bilingual in French and English, but there's no evidence that she found work. One can imagine the increasing concerns she and the rest of her family must have had as they read the French newspaper accounts of the deepening crisis across Europe during the 1930s. Very likely, with their English background, they had their ears glued to the wireless set, avidly listening for the '*Ici Londres*' that announced the start of the news on the BBC's broadcast to France.

After Hitler's armed forces invaded Czechoslovakia and Poland in 1939, 19-year-old Frederick decided to leave France and managed to reach England, where he worked for the Royal . Air Force. 23-year-old Francis would probably have gone too, but he stayed because he had recently married and his wife was expecting a baby. Although Didi by this time was eighteen and had left the convent, it is thought that she stayed at home, looking after her parents who were then in their fifties. One imagines that, being British, Francis, Jacqueline and Didi were very worried about their future, as would any other British citizen still in France at that time.

In April 1940, the Germans invaded Denmark and Norway, and, on 10 May, Hitler ordered the *Sichelschnitt*, an armed attack on Luxembourg, Belgium, the Netherlands and France. It was the Whitsun weekend when everyone was on holiday.

One wonders what Didi's reaction would have been when she heard that, on the same day, Neville Chamberlain, the British Prime Minister, resigned due to the clear failure of his appeasement policy. His replacement, Winston Churchill, a staunch proponent of rearmament, immediately ordered the British Expeditionary Force in France to advance north into Belgium to defend Britain's allies. They were supported by the French 7th Army.

Informed of his enemies' plans, on 12 May, Hitler ordered the start of a second front to the south. 136 German Army divisions pushed through the Ardennes, avoiding France's heavily defended Maginot Line. By 15 May, they had opened a fifty-mile (80 kilometres) gap in the Allied front and the Dutch government surrendered when faced with the threat of Rotterdam being destroyed and much of the country being flooded.

The speed and ferocity of German Panzer divisions in their push to the Channel ports caught the Allied military off-guard. Dutch and Belgian airfields were heavily bombed, giving the Luftwaffe, the German air force, control of the skies. Paratroopers rained down onto foreign soil and Stuka planes dive-bombed important transport links.

Despite bombardment by British, French and Belgian artillery, the German forces reached the Channel by 21 May, surrounding the Allies. When, a week later, King Leopold of Belgium surrendered, Churchill ordered the British Expeditionary Force to retreat, blowing up bridges as they left.

The Belgian artillery managed to hold off the full force of the Blitzkrieg until 28 May, enough time to allow the start of a major evacuation of 338,226 British, Canadian, Belgian and French soldiers and civilians from the beaches at Dunkirk in northern France.

Much of the Allies' heavy military equipment and supplies had to be abandoned. Some 40,000 Allied troops did not get onto any of the approximately 850 boats that had crossed the English Channel over the few days between 26 May and 4 June 1940.

Hitler's plans included utilising occupied airfields – from where the Luftwaffe could attack Britain – then using occupied factories for his war effort, transporting able-bodied men to work in Germany's factories whilst their own men were in the *Wehrmacht*. It was also vital for the Germans to secure transport routes across north-west Europe, particularly the Atlantic and North Sea ports.

During this Blitzkrieg, nearly a quarter of Belgium's approximately nine million inhabitants fled. Troop movements were impeded by escaping motorists and Didi and her family must have experienced the sense of panic when they learned of the *exode* – about two million people moving south through France in an attempt to escape the war zone.

Those that arrived in Nice would have told of how almost all the roads had been clogged with every kind of vehicle, from wheelbarrows, perambulators, pushcarts and farm trailers to lorries, wagons, buses, ambulances, limousines, hearses, cars and bikes. All of humanity was there, crying babies, toddlers, teenagers, young couples, soldiers, even struggling grandparents and invalids trying to escape the encroaching wave of what many in France called the occupation of *'les sales Boches'*.

There would have been accounts of how the rolling countryside blanketed with fresh green vines in hazy, warm, sunshine was regularly shattered by the roar of angry Luftwaffe engines; the staccato of their bullets and the explosion of earth and shrapnel, which tore through wood, metal and flesh as people struggled for cover beneath the plane trees that lined the roadsides.

By 5 June, German forces outflanked the Maginot Line and pushed deep into northern France. Italy declared war on France on 10 June and, within days, the French government fled to Bordeaux. Those British troops supporting the French at St Valery-en-Caux were surrounded and, on 12 June, eight to ten thousand Allied troops surrendered.

German troops marched into Paris on 14 June and three days later, General Philippe Pétain told the French people that he was seeking an armistice. When it was signed on 25 June, the Axis powers celebrated a spectacular victory, conquering four countries in six weeks.

After the fall of Paris, the Nearnes were given eight days to leave Nice. There was no alternative; they were forced to rent out their home and move to Grenoble, the capital of the Alps, where the Nazi invasion had been stopped by General Cartier in June 1940. There they found temporary sanctuary and, after living for a time in a hotel, the family moved into La Monta, an old, comfortless château on Rue Adolphe Muguet. Didi and Jacqueline had to collect firewood and saw it up themselves.

Francis, her elder brother, lived in Villa Picard, in St Egrève, a few kilometres north of Grenoble, with his wife Theresa and two-year-old son. According to documents in Francis' personal file in the National Archives, he was living under virtual house arrest, but the Italian authorities, who had control over that area of south-eastern France at the time, did not stop him travelling to work for a Jewish employer.

Whether Didi knew that Pétain was giving the Germans 500 million francs a day as well as supplying them with thousands of tonnes of food each week and hundreds of thousands of men for labour under the *Service du Travail Obligitaire*, compulsory work service, is unknown. It is probable that she would have known that, within a month of the Vichy government being formed, Pétain established a commission to review the naturalisation of Jews. He acquiesced to Hitler's demands and ordered that a register be taken of every Jew in France, whether they were born there or were refugees. According to Vichy, a Jew was anyone with three Jewish grandparents, or two whilst being married to a Jew. Almost all complied as law-abiding citizens. All schools and universities were ordered to provide lists to the local authorities of all students with foreign names. Living in Grenoble, Didi would have noticed the increased numbers of Jewish refugee families and, maybe knew teachers who were sacked for refusing to hand over such names.

She must have been aware of the widespread anti-Semitism in France. Most Orthodox Jewish communities were in the big cities within walking distance of their synagogue. Laws were introduced in October 1940, which barred Jews from possessing radios and telephones. Jews were barred from visiting public buildings like cinemas, restaurants, music halls, cafés, theatres, telephone booths, swimming pools, beaches, museums, libraries, schools, military installations and exhibitions. They were even barred from attending markets, fairs, public gardens, public parks, children's play grounds and any sports event. With such overt public humiliation, Didi must have wondered how this was possible in a France that believed in *'Liberté, égalité, fraternité'*.

Jews were not allowed to go out with non-Jews. It became an offence for a Jew to marry a non-Jew. One of her friends had told her before he was arrested that Jews would shortly be forbidden to breathe in case they polluted the air of the pure German race.

Legislation was passed requiring all Jews over six months old to be issued a six-pointed yellow star, which had to be sewn onto their clothes. Their *cartes d'identités* and food coupons were stamped with the word 'Jew' on them. Their children were not allowed to attend school. The adults were not allowed professions. They were not allowed to work in local or national government, whether in France or in the colonies. After they were banned from the professions, the list expanded to include the press, film and music industries. They were not allowed to run a business. Those in education, the media and entertainment were sacked. They were not allowed to leave their homes between 20.00 and 06.00 hours. Their bicycles and radios were confiscated and even their telephone services were cut off. They were not allowed to buy stamps and could go shopping only late in the morning, by which time the stores had little left. They could use the *Métro*, but only the last carriage. Some gendarmes were said to have demanded that suspected Jews pull their trousers down in public to check whether they were circumcised. Whilst some French people favoured these laws, many others opposed them and a brave few actually provided Jewish friends and neighbours with shelter, food and clothing.

Maybe Jacqueline had told Didi about Le Vernet, an internment camp in Pamiers in the Pyrenees where Jews were being interned. Maybe she had heard about Le Struthof, a concentration camp in Alsace, close to the German border, where Jews were being sent. Didi was probably aware of the revenge the Germans were taking on French citizens when any of their troops were attacked. Sometimes, fifty prisoners were executed. Other times, people in the street were rounded up and shot or hanged from lamp posts.

By 1942, Grenoble itself, particularly the university, had become a centre of resistance. During her travels, it is possible that Jacqueline had learned of the work of some resistance groups in the south of France who were running escape lines. Sponsored by MI9, a section of the British Secret Intelligence Service, they helped escaped Allied prisoners-of-war and downed RAF pilots to cross the border into Spain. From there, they made their way either to Lisbon in Portugal or down to Gibraltar where they could catch a ship back to Britain. If she had, maybe it gave her the idea of getting out with Didi.

Odile Nearne reported that Jacqueline had great difficulty when they eventually made up their minds to flee. They were turned back when they got to Marseille, presumably for not having the correct exit papers. There would have been no legal way that they could leave the country with papers identifying them as British. Anyone found to be an enemy citizen would be arrested, interned and sent to Germany.

One alternative was to hire the services of a *passeur* to guide them over the Pyrenees. The payment of 5,000 francs each was often asked, more than double most people's monthly salary, but there are reports of some demanding payment in gold, since it was such a risky venture. Keith Janes of *conscript-heroes.com* suggested that, with the right contacts, they would have been able to buy false documents and train tickets through Thomas Cook's travel company.

There was a resistance group within the University of Grenoble, which might have helped in providing false documents, but, according to some sources, they sought assistance from the American Consulate. There were two, one in Nice and one in

EDLC

Marseille. As the British Consulates in Nice and Marseille had been vacated, the American Consul was representing British interests at the time. Eventually, after trying again and again to get the necessary papers, Didi and Jacqueline were allowed to leave. How much money they took with them is unknown, but they must have had funds in a bank account that they could draw on.

In April 1942, after the Easter holiday when the weather was warmer, they left by train for Barcelona where, as other evaders have reported, the procedure was to contact the British Consul who provided papers allowing them onward travel to Madrid. There they had to contact the British Embassy, which would provide the necessary documents to exit the country. Little is known of Didi's and Jacqueline's experiences as they travelled through General Franco's Spain. They must have known that letters sent to their family would be opened and read and so did not want the French authorities to make life difficult for their parents or for Francis. He had remained in Grenoble, but, as we shall find out, he became involved in Resistance work himself.

Other evaders reported being caught by the Spanish police and imprisoned in a camp at Miranda de Ebro from where, eventually, the British Consul arranged their release. Odile was told after the war that, to avoid being sent to this camp, Jacqueline gave the authorities the name of a rich cousin in London who was going to look after them.

Eventually, they reached Portugal and lived for three weeks near Lisbon. With the help of the British Consul, they were introduced to the captain of a British merchant vessel who agreed to take the two girls to Gibraltar. Described as a bluff, hearty type, he had never had passengers on his boat before, but gave the girls his cabin and decorated the ship profusely with flowers. They spent three days in the British colony whilst arranging passage on a boat to Glasgow.

They got out just in time. On July 16 1942, only a few weeks after the Vichy Government introduced *la relève*, a relief scheme whereby one French prisoner-of-war would be released for every three workers who volunteered to work in Germany, Premier Laval ordered the arrest and internment of all Jewish men aged over sixteen. Those in Drancy were transferred to Vel d'Hiv in Paris, where it is estimated that more than 10,000 were brought by bus, truck and train and provided with little food and water until they were deported to camps in Germany and Poland. Trains, termed by some the 'Convoy of the Dead', took about 3,000 every week.

Next, all the Jewish women were ordered to be rounded up and interned and finally all Jewish children. Some watched in horror as the police arrested a woman in her apartment block in the Marais and led her away screaming and shouting that her three-month-old baby was still in its cot. There were some in the French *Milice* who showed utter and complete disregard of humanity.

It is estimated that over 75,000 French Jews were rounded up and deported. To avoid these *rafles*, some committed suicide. Some women jumped out of windows holding onto their children so that they both died. Some managed to escape and joined the Resistance who provided them with false *cartes d'identités*. With some more republican-minded Jews, they formed their own *réseau* called '*Organisation Juive de Combat*'. Other Jews joined the communists.

With no father, no mother and no adult relatives, many Jewish children were left to fend for themselves. Some managed to survive by being taken in by sympathetic French families who pretended that they were their own children. Others tried to survive by begging, borrowing or stealing.

3

SETTLING IN LONDON &
INITIAL INTERVIEW WITH SOE:
SPRING 1942

When the passenger ship from Gibraltar docked at the port of
Greenock, just down the river Clyde from Glasgow, the new arrivals
were ushered into the Immigration Office. Screened by Passport
Control, their identities were checked and their possessions searched.
Those arrivals from German occupied territories, even with official
papers, were not allowed onward travel to their destination. It was
wartime and careful scrutiny of new arrivals was undertaken to
ensure they were not Nazi spies. Armed police escorts accompanied
new arrivals by train down to London.

Didi must have recognised that there was something noticeably
missing in the atmosphere of the smoky capital. The sour *odeur
d'invasion* she had been used to in France had been replaced with the
oxygen de résistance.

They were not the only ones waiting at Euston station for
double-decker buses to take them to what was called 'The
Patriotic School'. Dozens of equally desperate passengers, mostly
families, but a significant number of single French men between
twenty and forty, were forced to wait for further questioning.

After travelling through France, Spain, Portugal and Gibraltar,
London was much darker. Although many buildings had

windows and glass-fronted doors criss-crossed with tape and with black-out curtains behind them, there were plenty of people on the streets, many in uniform. Piles of sand bags around doors of public buildings, many over head-height, probably made Didi much more aware of what danger the people of London were facing, as would the people wearing steel helmets and carrying gas masks.

Government propaganda posters were everywhere, interspersed with the more usual advertisement hoardings. The shop windows that they passed tried to look attractive, but there did not seem to be as much for sale since there was rationing in place. The requisitioned bus took them across the busy capital and over Wandsworth Road Bridge to the Royal Victoria Patriotic Building. It had a huge tower in the middle over the entrance and smaller ones on the corners. Like many continental buildings, its third floor windows were in the roof. There were forty-two windows on its façade. King George and Queen Elizabeth's Buckingham Palace had significantly more.

Inside, its flagstone corridors and high-windowed rooms reminded some visitors of a boarding school. The impression given by the enormous entrance hall, with its high, ornately plastered ceilings, towering columns and grand staircases was spoilt by the smell of carbolic, the cleaning fluid ordinarily used on toilet floors. Although originally built as a school for servicemen's children, it had been used as a hospital before being converted into an interrogation centre.

Visitors were shown to one of the dormitories to deposit their luggage. When they went downstairs, it would have been thoroughly searched and anything untoward noted. They were then taken for what was a thorough screening – termed by some their 'legalisation' process.

Plain-clothes officers from MI5, Military Intelligence, quizzed them about close and distant family and friends, making detailed notes. There was a great need to ensure they were not German or Russian spies who had had years learning their cover story. Photographs and fingerprints were taken.

As Didi and Jacqueline had just arrived from France, their interrogators would have wanted to know anything and everything they knew about conditions in both the Occupied and the Free Zone.

There was not just one interrogator. There were officers from the Navy, RAF and Army, each wanting up-to-the-minute details of German troop dispositions, what armaments they had seen and what coastal defences and military installations they had noticed. Whilst it may have been impersonal, there was more interest in their knowledge than their feelings. Grim-faced and unsmiling, the officials took copious notes of every scrap of information that they thought could be of use in the war effort. There would, however, have been friendly smiles from the women providing endless cups of weak, sugarless government tea.

They would also have been asked about their political persuasions. What did they think of Pétain? What did they think of de Gaulle? What were their views on Churchill? Did they support Roosevelt and, of course, what did they think of Hitler? They wanted whatever they knew about any 'Boches' they had ever come into contact with, and everyone they knew in England.

They would have been quizzed on the constantly changing papers people were expected to carry in France and every single one of the documents they carried in their purses would be photographed. They even wanted to know what food was available on the markets and in the shops and how expensive it was. They were interested in what procedures were needed when you travelled by bus or train and even what jokes people were telling about the Germans. The interrogators repeated questions in subtle ways to check and double-check the veracity of their stories.

Reports suggest they were not friendly chats, often overly formal, with the cross-examination being conducted without rest for hours on end, with nobody else to support them. The interrogation lasted at least two days.

Given that the British had rationing, the food provided was basic and served in a large refectory. One can imagine them being given a fried sausage, a dollop of watery potatoes, boiled cabbage and a spoonful of insipid pale grey gravy, nothing like French food, but it probably stopped them from feeling hungry.

Didi's and Jacqueline's interrogations must have convinced MI5 that they were *bona fide* evacuees, as they were then issued with their own gas masks and 'released'. Whilst one imagines they still had money left in their bank accounts after the expense of their trip, they knew it was imperative to find employment and accommodation.

As well as being issued with a gas mask, it was common for those visitors who succeeded in passing through the Patriotic School to be offered a new suitcase and a completely new wardrobe of British clothes – shoes, hats, scarf, gloves, umbrella, perfume and even toiletries in exchange for theirs. Why was this? The British government had a secret department responsible for building up a wide range of men's and women's clothing and personal belongings for their agents who were going to be infiltrated into occupied countries. Whether Didi and Jacqueline gave away what few possessions they had managed to escape from France with is unknown, but is very unlikely.

The refugees' belongings were stored in rooms in 'The Thatched Barn', a large, requisitioned hotel a few miles north of London on the A1 Barnet by-pass at Borehamwood. There, a skilled team of 'boffins' was working on 'ageing' various possessions to make them look more authentic. Agents would not be expected to wear their best clothes when they landed on a beach, parachuted into a field or got out of an aeroplane in a remote field in the middle of the night.

Other rooms were used for research and development of a wide range of what were described as 'Q' gadgets. These included camouflaged explosive devices such as cigarettes, stuffed rats, lumps of coal, logs and a range of animal droppings.

The people responsible for this work belonged to a top secret organisation set up shortly after Dunkirk. Before the war, the British government relied on the Secret Intelligence Service (SIS), spies working for the Foreign Office, as well as Military Intelligence. In 1938, Lord Halifax, Lord Hankey, Colonel Jo Holland and others formed what became known as Section D. The D was said to stand for Destruction. With the country facing the imminent threat of invasion, these men presented Winston Churchill, the British Home Secretary and First Lord of the Admiralty, with their plans for an intelligence agency, which was independent of the SIS and MI5. Churchill was enthusiastic about the idea and asked Neville Chamberlain, then the Prime Minister, to draft a charter for such an organisation. He did so and named it the Special Operations Executive, SOE.[1]

The SOE's function was to promote sabotage against the enemy by encouraging subversive activities, spreading political discontent and disrupting their means of transport and communication. In order to achieve their aims they needed to support the various resistance groups by dropping arms, equipment and agents and by lifting their important leaders out and bringing them to safety back in Britain.

Whilst it was possible early in the war for a submarine to disembark frogmen or a small boat to land people on the French coast, it became increasingly difficult once the German Todt corporation completed the construction of the Atlantik Wall. This was a series of concrete defensive gun emplacements along the coast from south-west France to Norway. Consequently, as the Norwegian, Danish, Dutch, Belgian and French airfields were under German control, the only way to help the various resistance groups across occupied Europe was clandestine night-time drops into isolated fields.

To do this, in August 1940 the Air Ministry allocated the job to No. 419 Flight, based at North Weald, about 20 miles north-east of London between Harlow and Chelmsford in Essex. Using the short take-off and landing Westland Lysanders, which were designed to carry two passengers, they started infiltrating agents into France and bringing people back. By August 1941, the renamed 1419 Squadron had landed twenty-five agents and picked up five, whereas the Royal Navy had infiltrated nine by boat and submarine.

Limited by the small number of available planes, SOE put pressure on the Air Ministry to create another flight. In response, 1419 Squadron was transferred to the heath at Newmarket racecourse, Cambridgeshire, where, supplied with old Armstrong Whitley bombers, Handley Page Halifaxes and Short Stirlings, it was renamed 138 (Special Duties) Squadron. By February 1942, it was separated into two Flights: 161 Squadron was responsible for landings and pick-ups, and 138 for parachuting agents and dropping supplies. The Halifax could carry up to eight parachutists, the Whitley ten and the Stirling twenty. They also carried containers and packages that were to be parachuted into occupied Europe. The pilots, crew and ground staff were given what they called the 'poison book', the Official Secrets Act, to sign. Under no circumstances were they to reveal the true nature of their work to unauthorised personnel.

As Newmarket had a grass runway, the larger planes needed concrete to avoid ruining the heath. So, in April 1942, the Flight was relocated to the newly completed RAF Tempsford, about fifty miles north of London between Cambridge and Bedford. It was described as the country's foggiest and boggiest airfield.

This airfield is said to have been designed by Jasper Maskelyne, a popular illusionist on the London stage during the 1930s. Described as 'The War Magician', he and his 'Magic Gang' were involved in numerous deceptions against the Germans. RAF Tempsford was built to resemble a disused airfield. Some of the farm labourers' cottages and farm buildings were demolished. The roof of Gibraltar Farm had part of its gable end dismantled, most of its slate tiles removed and windows deliberately broken. Sacks were draped across the inside of the window frames in front of the black-out curtains. Some of the doors were left rickety, hanging from only one hinge. Much of the black Bedfordshire weather-boarding was removed. The adjacent farm buildings got the same treatment and visitors reported seeing them mildewed, cobwebbed and covered in mouldering thatch.

Inside Gibraltar Farm, it was a different matter. The walls were reinforced to withstand bomb damage. It was said that the stairs, ceiling and first floor were removed to create a large control room and an office. A large table stood in the middle of the room on which different scale maps of Europe and aerial photographs of the proposed drop zones could be spread out. Map chests stood to one side and a green 'scrambler' telephone sat next to the black one. One wall had a huge blackboard on which one of the WAAFs (Women's Auxiliary Air Force) chalked up details of the night's missions. Another had an enormous map attached, which stretched from the Arctic Circle in the north to North Africa in the south and from Ireland in the west to Poland and the Soviet Union in the east. One of those wheeled step ladders, usually found in libraries to reach the books on the upper shelves, was used to allow another WAAF to stick different coloured little flags in to pinpoint the destinations of the planes flying each night. This was to become the airfield's nerve centre, where only authorised personnel were allowed entry.

All the aircraft hangars and administration buildings were camouflaged to blend in with the surrounding farmland and some new ones were said to have been thatched to give the impression that they were farm buildings. Nissen huts resembled pig sties or cow sheds. Some locals suggest that tarpaulins were draped over hangars and some of the administration buildings on which dilapidated buildings had been painted.

Outside Gibraltar Farm the pond was left with the odd few ducks. Genuine tractors were left, but moved occasionally in the fields and yards. The runways were painted grey and green in places to look as if they were overgrown. At one point, a thick black line was painted across the runway to give overflying Luftwaffe pilots the impression that it was the continuation of a hedge. Cattle were deliberately grazed on some of the fields when the runways were not in use to make the enemy think it was an old airfield now used for agricultural purposes. It succeeded.

Even though over two thousand personnel were eventually based at RAF Tempsford, it is said that the aerial photographs taken by German pilots who flew over were interpreted as a disused airfield. The local people knew there was an airfield, but they were not allowed access during the fourteen nights between the waxing and waning of the full moon. It was on these days, after darkness fell and weather permitting, that the planes took off. To reduce the chances of being attacked, they aimed to return before dawn. Planes dropping agents and supplies in Poland had a return flight of fourteen hours. Those destined for the Paris area might only be in the air for three or four, depending on the route taken to avoid any built-up areas and enemy airfields.

Although there were anti-aircraft guns placed at the end of the runways, the gunners were ordered not to fire at any overflying enemy aircraft except in an emergency. If Luftwaffe pilots were attacked and escaped, when they got back to base and were debriefed, they would have reported the location of any 'ack-ack', anti-aircraft gun batteries. This would have identified Tempsford as an active airfield and ensured it was subject to future attack. Throughout the war, not one bomb was dropped on the airfield and only one stick of incendiaries was reported dropped on a runway, luckily not during the moon period. Hitler was said to have known that there was what he called a 'viper's nest', but the Luftwaffe never managed to locate it accurately.

Chains were padlocked around the telephone boxes in the two closest villages of Everton and Tempsford to ensure that no-one made any out-going calls. Signs saying 'Road closed to the public' were erected at each end of the minor road between Everton and Tempsford and armed guards manned the barriers. For security reasons, many of those who were involved with the airfield called it 'Gibraltar Farm' or 'Tempsford Station'. This was because it was only a short drive from the station on the main railway line between London and Edinburgh. Locals reported that they never knew what went on there. They were not supposed to.

With three runways, it was much better suited for the larger planes. King George allowed his plane, a Lockheed Hudson, to be used. Able to seat twelve passengers, it allowed more people to be picked up, but the agent in the field had to find a much longer field for it to be able to land. They were later allocated Vickers Wellington bombers.

Both Squadrons had dedicated ground crews, also sworn to secrecy, who had to modify the planes for low-level night flying, removing extra weaponry and turrets, cutting a 'Joe hole' in the base of the fuselage for parachutists to jump through and installing equipment for carrying containers in the bomb bays.

It was to RAF Tempsford that SOE, SIS, OSS and NKVD agents were taken. Those who were to be landed in France were often flown in Lysanders from RAF Tangmere, near Christchurch on the South Coast. Sometimes they boarded the plane at Tempsford and the pilot flew to Tangmere to top up with fuel as the plane only had a range of about 500 miles (800 kilometres). Pilots landed there on their return trip if they were running out of fuel, and their passengers would then be driven up to London. In some cases, the plane flew back to Tempsford. As we shall discover, these airfields were to feature in Didi's adventures.

Evidence of exactly what Didi and Jacqueline did when they arrived in London is scarce. They certainly joined the SOE, which, over the following few years, built up a folder of forms, memoranda and correspondence relating to their time employed by the organisation, but there are documents missing that are present in other agents' files. Based on what evidence there is however, and the experiences of other SOE agents, it has been possible to recreate their experiences from June 1942.

Instead of going to stay with the imaginary rich cousin, Didi found what she and Jacqueline called 'digs', rented rooms in the house of an old friend of the family at 97 Darenth Road, Stamford Hill, telephone number: Stamford Hill 6895. It seems reasonable to assume that they tried to make contact with Frederick, their elder brother. Some sources suggest that he joined the RAF, but the organisation has no record of him. A note in Francis's personal file indicates that he served in the army.

According to Odile, the two girls registered with the Ministry of Labour and then spent weeks tramping around the various recruiting offices, trying to join one of the women's services. Didi very nearly joined the WAAF, manning the 'blimps', barrage balloons which dominated the London skyline during air raids. Floating above east London, they acted as obstacles to Luftwaffe planes flying on missions to bomb the city, the docklands and other industrial targets.

Jacqueline was refused a job by the Women's Royal Navy Service as a car-driver because she had no experience of driving on the left-hand side of the road or of driving in the blackout. The

Ministry of Labour however, noted that the girls were bilingual – ideal for espionage – and passed their details on to the SOE. The first form in Didi's personal file, dated 14 July 1942 and stamped SO2 (Special Operations), indicates she had applied for work as a driver/orderly. The tick beside it suggests she may have been successful, but, if she was, where she was based and what she did is undocumented. At least it would have provided her with some money.

What is not known is whether she or Jacqueline made any attempt to contact the *Bureau Central de Renseignements d'Action* at 10 Duke Street, just south of Manchester Square, close to Oxford Street. This was the Headquarters of General Charles de Gaulle's intelligence section. It is quite likely that the whole Nearne family had heard de Gaulle's appeal on the BBC Radio Service in June 1940 and was keen to help keep the flame of the Resistance burning. They understood that France had lost a battle, but she had not lost the war. Whilst they may not have heard Churchill's and King George VI's exhortations to help in the war effort, they must have been motivated to want to help France. Colonel Passy, the head of the service, was known to have turned down applicants who were considered to be too British. As the SOE had contacts in RF Section, they would have been aware of any volunteers offering their services.

Unknown to Didi and Jacqueline, in April 1942 the War Office had made a ground-breaking decision. In Kate Vigur's PhD dissertation into SOE's F section women agents, she states that:

It was decided women would be recruited by SOE for work 'in the field' providing assistance to local Resistance networks in Nazi Occupied territory. In a society where sexual equality was virtually unheard of, and where a woman's perceived duty was to raise the family or work in non-combatant areas of war work such as munitions or driving, official government permission was given to recruit and employ women to be trained to bear arms and to be infiltrated to work behind the lines as secret agents. MP Dame Irene Ward was present when the decision was made. Sometime after the event she stated that: 'the War Cabinet was [not] fully aware of what their decision involved. If they had been, permission would almost certainly have been refused'.[2]

Before this decision, SOE had already sent three women into France, including two Soviet agents who were reported to have been caught and presumed executed. The first, Giliana Gerson, was sent to Vichy to help her husband establish a network to help British troops escape over the Pyrenees into Spain. Reports from France indicated that there were decreasing numbers of young men being seen on the streets as they were being called up, forced to work for the Germans, either in France or in Germany. Consequently, male agents being sent in needed excellent cover stories and perfectly forged documents to avoid being caught in street searches. Sending women was seen as the logical solution. They would be able to merge with the local Frenchwomen and not be subject to so many searches. Their cover stories would be more convincing as they were not required for compulsory labour and because it was thought that they would be more successful in dealing with the French Resistance than men. Vigurs suggests that their presence might have helped:

> ...dissipate some of the 'macho' attitudes that may have arisen in an all-male environment, especially when adrenalin was high and the emphasis was on espionage and resistance. A woman's presence may have been viewed as calming, she might have provided an alternative perspective on issues or offered support in a way a male colleague could not.
>
> Whilst her English counterparts may have accepted the presence of a woman and treated her equally, in France her

presence and in some cases authority may have caused problems as: 'France in the early 1940s was a nation led by men, more so than Britain. French women did not have the right to vote; they were certainly not expected to take charge of anything, but the kitchen and the nursery.' The Resistance groups F section hoped to arm and co-ordinate were likely to be predominantly male, not to mention self-consciously masculine. They might agree to take orders from a British or Anglo-French envoy, especially if he provided them with weapons – but from a woman?[3]

To give them a better chance of survival, it was decided that those women who were not recruited from within the WAAF would be given an honorary commission in the FANY, the First Aid Nursing Yeomanry. This was the only female section allowed to carry arms. Sending them into France would allow them to defend themselves. Some in the upper echelons of the SOE thought that giving their women agents an officer status would mean that, if they were arrested, they would only need to give their name and number as required under the terms of the Geneva Convention and thus be treated as prisoners-of-war. As we shall see, Hitler disregarded such legalities.

Before Didi arrived in the UK, the SOE had already infiltrated sixteen women, including two Soviet agents, into France. As several had been caught, the rationale behind this decision was that giving women the right to 'bear arms' meant that they could defend themselves in the line of duty.

Mark Seaman, the SOE historian, considered that Maurice Buckmaster, the head of the SOE's French Section, arranged the infiltration of more than fifty women into France. His choice was inspired by France's strategic importance, the large number of French-speaking women available, the relative ease of inserting them into remote parts of France and the political dynamic of the British government to build up a resistance that was supported by Britain rather than by Charles de Gaulle's Free French Forces.[4] In order to identify potential recruits, the SOE used what has been described as an 'old boys' network'. Using their contacts in the RAF, WAAF, ATS (Auxiliary Territorial Service), FANY, their old schools, universities and company personnel officers, they passed on the names of any able-bodied, healthy people with language skills and experience of living overseas to Selwyn Jepson, the SOE's recruiting officer. British Customs and Immigration officials and those at the 'Patriotic School' also provided Jepson with lists of potential candidates. It is more than likely that it was the latter that led him to contact Jacqueline. Other agents reported responding to adverts in newspapers asking for translators or requests for photographs of a certain section of the French coastline.

According to Odile, one day, much to Jacqueline's astonishment, she received a letter from the War Office, saying they believed she might be of some use to the war effort.

Without saying anything to Didi, she went to meet a civilian who took her for a walk in Whitehall. He said bluntly, 'Would you like to go back to France'. 'As a spy!' said Jacqueline. 'Not exactly,' he replied. 'But how can I go there, by boat, submarine or parachute?' When he said, 'parachute,' she jumped up in the air in astonishment, but he told her that it wasn't as bad as all that. It was all very surprising to Jacqueline, but she said, 'All right, I'll go'. She told the man that her sister also wanted to get a job in the services and was told she could become a FANY de-coder or a wireless operator.[5]

According to Maurice Buckmaster, the head of the SOE's F Section, Jacqueline worked initially as a liaison officer at 64 Baker Street, his London headquarters. Later, she was sent to the 'Preliminary School'. This was Wanborough Manor, known as STS 5 (Special

Training School), a large country house with extensive grounds in the countryside south-east of Swindon, west of London. Here the recruits were given three to four weeks of physical training (PT), rope-climbing, jumping out of an aeroplane fuselage stuck up a tree, initiative tests, psychological tests, map-reading and basic weapons training.

Although there are no records of Didi or Eileen's interviews in their personal files, it seems probable that Didi was invited to meet Selwyn Jepson, the SOE's recruiting officer. Potential recruits to the SOE were sent a letter in a buff-coloured official-looking envelope from the Ministry of Pensions. It was headed the War Office, Room 055, with an invitation to attend a meeting in Sanctuary Buildings, Westminster, at a given time on a given date. It was signed E. Potter. There was no indication what is was about, but the embossed lion, unicorn and crown made it look official.

The SOE did not set out to locate people of a certain age, nationality or class. All Jepson wanted were men or women under the age of forty-five. Whether they were in the services or not did not matter. What was important was that they had to have perfect French, preferably without an accent, otherwise a cover story would need to be concocted to explain it away. They had to know France well, to be able to pass as a native, to look French as well as having all the other qualities needed for clandestine work. They also had to be sympathetic to the Resistance and the Maquis, those men who, to avoid compulsory labour, had gone into the hills and formed groups of saboteurs.

One can imagine Didi putting on her best dress, hat and coat, carrying her gas mask and getting a London cab to ensure she was there by the appointed hour. By that time, carrying a gas mask everywhere would have become second nature.

Sanctuary Buildings was a huge, rather intimidating, light-brown-and-cream-brick office block on Great Smith Street. A black-suited middle-aged man sat at the front desk reading *The Daily Telegraph*. What visitors reported as unusual was that he still wore his black bowler hat as if he was an absent-minded city gent.

When told that she had an appointment with an E. Potter, he folded his paper and bade her follow him up the elegant staircase, down a plush carpeted corridor, where he knocked on an unnumbered door. The room smelt strongly of tobacco.

An elderly, grey-haired gentleman welcomed her in French and invited her to hang up her hat and coat, put down the gas mask and sit opposite him on an uncomfortable chair. He said nothing until he had lit his pipe and then he stared hard at his visitor across the table.

His office, full of cupboards, filing cabinets and desks against the wall, seemed a busy place, but with no carpet or rugs. The walls appeared to have recently been whitewashed, but not very carefully as there were a few splashes on the blackout boards. The only decoration was a large calendar. He leaned back puffing great aromatic clouds towards the bare light bulb.

Unable to bear the agony of silence, Didi probably broke it, asking him in French if he was the Mr E. Potter who had written the letter. He would lean forward and, without confirming or denying his identity, fire question after question at her for the next twenty minutes or so. Throughout the interview, he would never move his eyes from the interviewee, as if searching for something.

Didi would have told him about her parents, brothers and sisters, what homes they lived in, what it was like growing up in Boulogne-sur-Mer, attending convents, moving to Nice, what other schools she went to, what conditions were like when war broke out, moving to Grenoble and then what arrangements she and her sister made to get out of France, what experiences she had getting through Spain and eventually reaching Gibraltar. She had probably had to answer similar questions at the Patriotic School as this was valuable information for the intelligence services.

If she had had an interview with Colonel Passy, he would have known. The SOE had its contacts in that organisation. He would have been particularly interested in why she wanted to help the Free French and what she felt she could offer de Gaulle.

No doubt he explained that his organisation needed people willing to go back to France and work for the war effort. He probably explained that it involved intelligence and could be dangerous. The organisation he represented needed people like her, people who spoke fluent French, people who had the special qualities needed to be trained to go into enemy territory and make life very unpleasant for the Germans.

If they questioned how they would go back, his response was they would have to jump. Depending upon the agent's age or health, in some circumstances they were landed in small planes, or infiltrated by boat or submarine.

If they asked whether they would be paid, his response was often, 'Of course, old chap.' He would not go into any more detail and finished the interview by telling them that, if they were successful, they would receive a letter in the post.

Whilst Didi waited, the SOE did background research on her family, wanting to double-check that she was not a double agent, working for the Germans or another enemy country.

Those who failed the first interview were informed and they went back to their previous employment. Those who passed received a letter with an invitation to another meeting, this time in Room 238 at Hotel Victoria on Northumberland Avenue.

Again, Didi would have worn her best outfit and made sure that she arrived for the appointment early. Walking through the revolving glass and mahogany doors, she would have entered into an ornate Victorian lobby with marble floors, oak panelling and oil paintings. All sorts of people in and out of uniform were scurrying around carrying official-looking files. At the counter, she would have been asked to fill in a form with her name and address, to give the name of the person her appointment was with and what time she had arrived.

A uniformed attendant took interviewees up an old lift to the second floor and told them to sit down on one of the fold-away chairs outside a door. The carpet was threadbare and stained. When the door of room 238 was opened, a tall, smartly-dressed, thirty-something woman in a twin-set suit and hair tied in a bun came out. She was Vera Atkins, the officer in the SOE's French Section with responsibility for agents. She would have invited Didi to go in and sit down. Who Didi thought must have been Mr Potter stood by the window smiling at her, pipe in hand, filling the room with white clouds. His assistant sat down beside him leafing through a file on what appeared to be a cheap trestle table covered by a green baize cloth. One of its legs had been repaired with pieces of Meccano. The secretary chain-smoked Craven A, fiddling alternately with a Zippo lighter and a rubber-ended pencil.

It was a dingy, bare little room, contrasting strikingly with the marble lobby. Maybe Didi's feelings of the 'romance' and 'adventure' of it all seemed to fade and the Spartan reality had none of the same appeal. A naked light bulb hung from the ceiling and, apart from the table and three fold-away chairs, the only other furniture was a grey filing cabinet and a green safe about the size of an oven. Some files rested on two plywood boards laid across a dirty sink. There were no pictures on the wall, no vase of flowers, just an empty fireplace, a black-out blanket and net curtains over a window, which looked across a grey courtyard onto the opposite building.

After a brief chat in French about the weather and the traffic, there would be questions about whether she was in a relationship, and what commitments she had. Eventually, she would be told that she had qualifications and experiences which could be of value to the war effort.

Questions included, 'What do you think could be the most useful or damaging work against the Germans in England and abroad?', 'What sort of contribution do you think you could make?', 'How would you feel about working against the enemy in France?', 'Do you realise what dangers you would face if you are caught?'

If she was prepared to join his organisation, she was told not to make a hot-blooded decision there and then, but to wait and consider it for a few days. She was then told that under no circumstances was she to tell anyone, not even her sister, about their conversation.

Jacqueline went through the same interview process and one imagines she was told not to tell Didi about it. Whether they followed instructions is not known, but Odile reported that Jacqueline was adamant that Didi did not train as an agent. She felt that a twenty-year-old should not be sent back to France and exposed to the risks of being a secret agent.

On the third visit the recruit was asked for his or her decision. As Didi must have said, 'Yes', Mr Potter told her that he proposed sending her on a training course, mostly physical training, but with some aptitude testing. He probably told her that if she was sent to France her work would involve military intelligence and it was vital that she knew at the outset that there might well be considerable danger involved. He added that the work had a mere 75 per cent survival rate and that, if she was not prepared to expose herself to danger in time of war, there would be no point in them continuing the conversation.

Once Didi accepted his offer, he would have shaken her hand firmly. Vera then told her that she would be spending four days in a country house on an assessment course. She would have to share a bedroom, not a double bed, with up to five men, so she would have to forget completely about being too prudish. There would be no women's toilets either, and there were no women instructors.

Under no circumstances was she to divulge any information about the interview or where she was going to anyone. She must also never mention anything whatsoever about her background to anyone. She was, as far as possible, to remain anonymous. She would be given a code-name, which had to be used at all times. This was to be her new identity. Whilst she was away, she was to behave in nothing but a professional manner.

Vera said that she would be in regular contact with the supervising officer who would report back details about her progress. Anything untoward would mean she would be withdrawn from the course and she would be returned to civilian life. As in the interview, she was only to use French, especially first thing in the morning.

Wishing her 'the very best of British luck', Vera saw Didi out of the building, probably waving as she sauntered down Great Smith Street. In the envelope was her code-name, Alice Wood, which she had to use from then on, an old five pound note and a slip of paper giving a rendezvous time inside Lyons Tea House on Waterloo Station on a specified date. There was also a list of suitable clothing for her to take with her.

4

TRAINING FOR WORK AS
A SECRET AGENT:
SUMMER 1942–AUTUMN 1943

It is highly unlikely that Didi and Jacqueline were assessed at the same time. It would have been too much to ask for sisters not to socialise together in such a way that the others on the course would recognise they were closely related, let alone recognise their facial similarities.

In the early years of the war, the SOE checked the suitability of its recruits by sending them to their 'Preliminary School' at Wanborough Manor. In Jones' *A Quiet Courage*, she states that Didi trained at Wanborough with Yvonne Baseden, but, by the time Didi was considered, they had introduced a much quicker and more accurate system of identifying suitable candidates for their various departments. In April 1943 they had allocated the task to the Student Assessment Board based at Winterfold.

New students reported being told to rendezvous at 10.00 hours by the clock on Waterloo Station. Maybe Didi tucked into a sugary doughnut in the Lyons Café beforehand. She would have been approached by a khaki-uniformed army officer who, on receiving the correct response to his question, would have given her a ticket for the 10.25 train to Guildford from Platform 7. There would have been no 'How are you?' or attempt to chat her up, just impersonal military precision. After telling her that she would be picked up by an army truck outside the station, he would leave.

Waterloo Station was dark and dirty. All the windows were blacked out with tar paper, even those on the roof. Listening to the noise of thousands of people, pigeons and steam engines and smelling the mix of sour coal smoke, steam, cigarette and pipe tobacco, Brylcreem and perfume might have evoked memories of her and Jacqueline waiting nervously for hours at the docks in Gibraltar.

One can imagine her sitting in a half-empty compartment, holding a small brown leather valise on her lap. Inside would have been just a few frocks, skirts and blouses, the odd cardigan, pyjamas and toilet bag. A note in her personal file described Didi as 'height 1.68m, brown hair, blue eyes, rosy complexion'.[1]

As the countryside flashed by, she would probably have been lost in thought, thinking about what lay ahead for her. Would she be able to remember that she was now Alice Wood, not Eileen Nearne? What sort of assessment would she be undertaking? What would happen if she was deemed successful? Might she be trained as a spy and sent back to France? Where would she be sent? What would she have to do? Might she be able to see her parents and Francis again? Or maybe she just read a book or magazine that she had bought at W. H. Smith.

She would have had to ask which station Guildford was, collected her belongings and got out when the train stopped. There were no station name signs. They had all been removed. She followed the other passengers out of the station and found the army truck waiting on the forecourt. A few men stood by the open canvas flaps at the back and, when the blue uniformed driver saw the new students, he checked their passes and told them in French to jump in. He might well have been pleased to give Didi a leg up.

In the back of the truck, there were benches along the sides, enough for sixteen people. Most would have been in their twenties, a few in their early thirties. Smiles and polite *bonjours* would have been shared. As Didi had been instructed to use only French, she knew that if she said anything in English she might fail the assessment. There were to be no first names, codenames only.

When they were all in, the back flaps were fastened so that they couldn't see out. Even if Didi did not have a good sense of direction, she would quickly have realised that the driver was taking them on a roundabout route, along the highways and bye-ways, up and down numerous hills, around endless and unnecessary twists and turns that were just an attempt to confuse them so that they wouldn't know where they were.

It worked. When the truck eventually pulled up and the passengers jumped out, they were on a gravel courtyard in front of a huge, three-storey country mansion, set in wonderful parkland below a wooded hill. Didi had no idea where she was, except that it was somewhere near Guildford.

The house was huge with accommodation in sixteen bedrooms for forty people. Usually there were up to sixteen students on each assessment. The other rooms were for staff. Although not quite as elegant as a French château, it seemed to be a wonderful stately home with several hundred years of history. Its tall, brick chimneys stuck out from the middle of a weathered old brick-tiled roof. Parts of it looked Elizabethan, but above the porticoed entrance was a glassed-in balcony. Outside, a terrace overlooked extensive grounds, dotted with shrubs, grasses and mature trees. Spoiling the view across the lawns were rows of Nissen huts sprawling all over the place.

Students were welcomed in French at the front door by the Commanding Officer, a tall, thin, black-haired army man who introduced himself as a Lieutenant-Colonel Charley. In his late-thirties, he sported a walrus moustache and dark, horn-rimmed glasses and spoke in a plummy, but rather squeaky voice.

Glasses of lemonade and plates of sandwiches were handed round.

The Lieutenant-Colonel's guests were taken into a large oak-panelled sitting room that reeked of polish, cigar and pipe tobacco. Its floorboards creaked as they were ushered in and directed to sit down. Beams of dusty sunlight poured in through two small windows onto a beautiful old Persian carpet. What stood out most about the room was the ubiquitous black-out curtains, which hung behind what looked like tapestry curtains, not the pin-ups that had been stuck on the different-sized spaces where the paintings would have been.

With his back to the window, the CO told everyone about the assessment and training course. He made it clear from the outset that it was not a holiday camp. He ran a military outfit. Rules were laid down, a bit like those at boarding school, but in a much grander house. For the duration of their stay, he insisted they used the appropriate military titles for their instructors. No English was to be used at all – only French.

Basically, he told them that they would be put through their paces to help them decide how their talents could best be used to help the war effort. He did point out, however, that they would be observed throughout their stay and reports written up on these observations. They would eat well, he told them, and, indicating a bell on one of the tables in the hall, said they could call a corporal who would bring them whatever drinks they wanted, whenever they wanted them. Didi probably wondered whether they kept a record to identify potential alcoholics.

There were six military staff – three captains and three sergeants – and four Royal Army Medical Corps officers – two psychiatrists who were both majors, and two psychologists, one a captain and one a lieutenant.

Didi and the other recruits were taken to a darker, similarly oak-panelled room in which there were several old wardrobes with dozens of army battle-dresses hung up on hangers. They were told to find one their size. Didi's must have been an easy choice – the smallest – but the smell of moth balls was overpowering. At just over five feet tall she was not an Amazon, but probably hoped that she had the strength and stamina to make a good warrior. They were then taken up to their rooms, told to change and meet on the gravel outside in five minutes.

Students had been warned that they would not be given a single room. They were all accommodated in the attic, a long dark room that had been created by knocking down the partition walls. The whole place creaked, owing to the uneven, terribly worn floorboards. It smelt of polish and wafts of boiled vegetables that reached up from the kitchen below. There was no four-poster bed, just rows of army cots, iron bedsteads, each with a folded palliasse, cotton-covered straw mattress, on top of which were a couple of blankets, a pillow, a clean, folded pillow case and, unusually, just one sheet. They were expected to fold it in half. They were to live a rather frugal life when compared to the previous inhabitants of the grand house.

For modesty's sake, the women on the course were provided with a wardrobe, behind whose doors they could change if they wanted to avoid the stares on the men in the room. Didi was probably more focussed on passing whatever test they threw at her than being distracted by men.

Once their battledress was on, they descended the grand staircase into the hall. No paintings hung on the walls. The owners must have put them into storage when the house was requisitioned. Beside an aspidistra near the door to the dining room there was a large blackboard balanced on a mahogany table displaying the following day's timetable. They didn't get a chance to look at it, since they were immediately ordered outside. A man with a shrill voice and what looked like a knife scar on his cheek put them through their paces. They quickly gathered from the other students' responses that he was the sergeant, probably straight out of Aldershot. He put his new students through a series of drills, shouting at them when they got anything wrong. Lying on their backs doing upside-down cycling was particularly awkward.

After half an hour of these exertions, they had a ten-minute game of basketball on a tennis court, minus its nets, before being taken indoors and issued with men's white singlets and shorts. They each then had to change out of their battledress and don a throw-over vest with a number on both the front and back, like a runner in a race. Their observers, and there were several, each carried a clip-board and pad of paper on which they made notes.

One of the first things they had to do was a cross-country run, not a gentle run, but a strenuous race around the perimeter of the grounds. It gave them their bearings. At both the main and rear entrance gates there were Field Security police armed with rifles.

After a half-hour run, they stopped at what looked like an army training field. The new exercise was an obstacle course, but with a difference. Each obstacle had a number painted on it, the easiest being five and the hardest ten. There was a choice of huge trees to climb, seventy-foot-long ropes to slide down, ten-foot walls to scale, four-foot-wide gaps to jump across, fifty-foot-wide rope bridges to cross, a fifteen-foot-high platform to jump from to catch dangling ropes, a fireman's ladder to climb and tens of square feet of rope netting to crawl under. There were eighty-five possible points available and they had to score as many as they could. Having been brought up in convents, it is unlikely Didi was a *garçon manqué*, a 'tom boy', so it must have been more of a challenge to get herself properly fit.

One student recalled being taken on her own to an ornamental fish-pond, about fifteen feet long and twelve feet wide. The instructions were to use her initiative and cross this 'sulphuric acid bath' without getting her feet wet. She walked around the garden looking for anything to use. There was no convenient ladder or builders' plank. There was, however, a pile of wood beside one of the sheds. She went back with a piece and tested how deep the pond was – just up to her elbow – so, taking a few at a time, she managed to make some wobbly 'stepping stones' to cross the narrowest part.

Another exercise involved a large sandpit over which stretched a wooden frame, maybe fifteen feet high. They had to cross what the instructor called 'the minefield'. The instructor hinted that this was a problem-solving exercise so students needed to work it out. The solution was using ropes from the obstacle course. Tying them together to form a loop, it was possible to throw it over a beam and, with a bit of energetic manoeuvring and your legs folded up, it was possible to swing across and jump onto the other side without their feet being blown off.

Then there was the wrestling. Whether Didi was embarrassed at being manhandled by fit sergeants and other recruits is unknown. All the time, they were told to 'land soft, roll backwards, sideways or forwards. Remember holds and grips'.

Didi must have ended up just as bruised and battered as the others. It was stressed that they had to use the element of surprise to their advantage. Later, they were given demonstrations of strangleholds and deadly grips and told that tapping the ground indicated surrender.

The bathroom didn't have a lock. They were told that there was constant hot water, but to use only five inches. Food was good. Although there was rationing, meals at Winterfold were generous, and students never needed to go hungry.

Morning reveille was at 06.00 hours followed by a parade and half an hour's PT before the choice of a full English breakfast or kippers, kidneys, toast and marmalade. Afterwards there was another run, longer than the first, which included a strenuous climb up a chalky track along the side of a grassy hill to the south of the manor. Push ups, leaping over barbed wire fences, scrambling over stone walls and wading through freezing cold streams well and truly woke them up.

The aim was to make them fit. By nine o'clock, lessons had begun. They always started with a lecture, followed by a practical session. Elizabeth Devereaux-Rochester, an American agent, recalled developing a good memory whilst there. They were shown a cloth-covered tray and told that underneath the cloth were some pieces of different coloured cardboard, which they had to rearrange to try and make a square in three minutes. When told to stop, they had to take the tray to the adjoining room, which smelt of stale coal fires. There, they were asked to show what they had done to a particularly odd-looking officer in battledress, waiting for them in one of those high-backed leather armchairs, puffing away on a pipe. Didi remembered being questioned about why the lavender and mauve pieces were where they were.

There were group exercises where pairs were allocated the task of carrying a sack of wet sand or an old barrel full of water over parts of the obstacle course in a set time. All of them had to cross the finishing line and the sack, barrel or a splash of water had never to touch the ground. If they dropped it, they had to do it again, with the sergeant haranguing them and abusing them like an officer in the Foreign Legion. It demanded discussion, suggestion, decision-making and giving commands. All the time, the instructor checked his watch and took notes. The session finished with yet another obstacle course – low level this time – with barrels, tractor tyres, nets and fencing. Each was marked A or B. Again, they were timed, but before they set off, the instructor whispered something in their ears. They might be told to go under the

As and round the left-hand side of the Bs. There was an opportunity to play tennis after tea.

There were lessons in Morse where, after being given the rudiments of the dots and dashes used to signify letters of the alphabet, they were allowed to practice tapping out messages on a Morse Code machine. Didi must have been quite proficient at this exercise, but it is not known whether she had learned it in France.

One morning there were individual interviews during which they were seated in front of a polished oak table with one of the male psychiatrists, called 'trick cyclists' by the students. He had the student's folder and studied its contents for a minute or so, occasionally looking at the students over the top of his horn-rimmed glasses as if checking its details visually.

Questions in French were fired in quick succession. The first ones were to check that their personal details were correct. They then veered towards asking them about their beliefs and opinions. He wanted to know about Didi's family and the relationship she had with them all, whether they were married, if not why not and whether they had had any relationships, and if so, with whom.

There were questions about her education and her experiences in France. He wanted to know what motivated her, why she was on this course. He wanted to know what she thought of Pétain, what she thought of de Gaulle, Churchill, Roosevelt and Stalin, and her political position and the reason for it. Students were asked what they would do if they were a criminal and the police had just entered the building or if they were a burglar and realized that they had left incriminating evidence at the scene of the crime. What would they go back and pick up? Some of the stranger things they were asked were whether they was afraid of heights and did they still wet the bed. All the time he would make notes.

The folder was then closed and he gave them a paper and pencil and opened another file in which there was a selection board intelligence test. Then he pulled out sheet after sheet with ink stains on, rather like those double images created by putting a blob of paint on a piece of paper and folding it in half. They were asked to identify the shapes and he made notes on their responses. Devereaux-Rochester suggested one looked like a dragon, but was told it was a bat. She persisted and at the end of the session, when he told her he thought it looked like a dragon, she thought he was 'bats'. Nancy Wake, an Australian agent, who adamantly insisted they were just blobs, described the place as a 'mad house'.[2, 3]

Another thing Devereaux-Rochester recalled was being told that she could smoke and the instructor studying how she took the cigarette, how she held it, whether she inhaled, how she knocked the ash off and how she stubbed it out, as if it might reveal something about her character.

Then came a word-association exercise in which he wanted her to come up with anything that came into her head when he called out a word from a list. When it was over, there was no feedback, just a thank you and good morning as he got up and showed her the door.

These were what the SOE called 'psychological screening' and 'psychometric testing', at that time used commonly in the armed forces to weed out anyone with lunatic, murderous, homosexual or extreme political tendencies.

All their lessons were held in the drawing room, elegantly furnished, but all the 'old masters' were missing. In the dusty morning sunlight their 'ghosts' could be seen in the rectangular shapes where they had once hung. It took some time to recognise that some wag had sketched in some caricatures in their place.

Outside in the grounds and inside the house, the students were kept under constant surveillance. Their numbered vest had to be worn most of the time so that their 'observers' could comment on their performance, to make judgements on their character and behaviour in a variety of difficult and trying conditions.

On some mornings they went on a forced march to a chalk quarry where a rifle range had been set up. Didi had probably fired a rifle before at fairs held in the summer or at amusement arcades. The Major gave them each a Lee Enfield rifle and a box of twenty bullets. After a brief instruction on how to load the weapon, they had to lie on their belly and shoot the first set of targets – a row of six tins balanced on a wooden frame. It was the shock of the recoil that took many by surprise.

With a few suggestions to improve their technique, those tins they had managed to knock off were replaced and they were given a second box of bullets. After the practice they were told that they would be assessed on the rest of the session. One hopes Didi eventually got a bull's eye and her instructor was pleased with her progress.

There were a few lessons given by a French officer on their platoons and arms drills. In particular, he wanted them to learn their command words. This was useful, invaluable for those whose cover story might include having once been in the French armed forces.

After the afternoon lectures, they normally had weapons practice with Thompson and Browning sub-machine guns, Bren guns and Sten guns, a French machine gun and a Schmeisser. They were shown how to take them apart, how to put them back together again and how to load them. Then they had to fire them, lying down, kneeling, standing up and then whilst running. One woman was said to have been an excellent shot as she always fired lower than the men.

In the evenings, they were given machine guns, the light was turned off and they were told to dismantle them in the dark. Having done that, they had to reassemble them. To speed them up one recruit recalled being offered a prize of a 'ten-bob' note. It is doubtful if Didi won it.

They also practised with revolvers, the Colt automatic, several Lugers, a small Belgian pistol and the .45. Her first attempt with this one probably knocked Didi over, but there was no question of her giving up. The .38 pistol was probably too heavy for her, so she would have used a .22. At the end of the session she was probably told to work on her reflexes.

There was a session in a chalk pit for grenade practice, which was jokingly called the 'Demolition Pit'. There were several mounds of chalk waste to shelter behind and a couple of badly pockmarked concrete bunkers at the foot of the chalk face. They were given an empty cocoa tin and told to put it down near the foot of the cliff and to find ten fist-sized chunks of chalk, walk back ten spaces, make sure they were well away from the others and then try to knock the tin over. Having done that they had to walk over and stand it back up, find ten more chunks and walk twenty paces back to try again and then do it from thirty. Tossing them underarm was not as accurate as throwing them overarm. Not having played cricket before, it must have taken Didi quite a lot of getting used to and she probably felt at a disadvantage when judging the weight, the distance and the amount of effort needed.

After the tins, they had a competition to see how many out of ten they could throw through a window of the bunker. They did a few hours on these exercises before being allowed to hold a grenade. Major went through the procedure; the correct way to hold it; how to pull the pin out; how to throw it and how to take cover. The grenades that he gave them to practice with were also dud, but, having practised with the lumps of chalk, it was not long before they could throw a hand grenade pretty accurately to within a yard or two of the target. Luckily, pin-point accuracy was not essential.

The live grenades were given a lot more respect. Major pointed out a rusty grain-threshing drum in another part of the quarry, which was ripped open by shrapnel in places. He told how one recruit wildly missed with his grenade and nearly blew up an estate worker who was relieving himself behind it. They had to stand behind another chalk mound and try to lob live grenades at one of the bunkers. It was one point for hitting the bunker, two if they got it through the door and five if it went through the window.

Other shooting practice included firing at moving targets using a pistol, a bit like a duck shoot or clay-pigeon shooting. Some would have preferred shooting partridges and pheasants. It might have added a little variety to their meals.

Nancy Wake, an Australian agent, recalled walking to the 'Demolition Pit' and stopping when they saw a branch that had fallen across the path. Kicking it out of the way, they were blown off their feet by a loud explosion. The others roared with laughter. It was a set-up. They had booby-trapped it. They were not hurt, but it was some time before they could hear properly again. At another time, they were stopped as they were running along a track in the woods and told that, in a few minutes, two men were going to run across the track in front and they would not see them. Suddenly, there was a loud explosion behind them and instinctively they turned round to see. When they turned back they were told the two men had just run across the track. They had been deliberately hoodwinked. They needed to be aware of that sort of thing and also to do it themselves, to create a deliberate distraction.

There were a few lessons on the rudiments of handling *plastique*, the French slang for explosives, nothing sophisticated, just explanations of the purposes of detonators and primers. The sergeant instructed them how to put the detonator into the primer and how to put the primer into what he called a 'six-inch brick', by which he meant a gun-cotton explosive. There was then a practical session where they were taught how much explosive was needed to bring down trees of different sizes and in such a way that they fell in whatever direction they chose. Subsequent demolition classes included getting to know the 'time pencil', 'instantaneous fuse', 'pull switch' and 'press switch'.

Another initiative test was to see if a team of two or three could get into a heavily guarded railway tunnel and lay a dummy charge without being spotted. They were shown on a map where it was and, after memorising its location and how to get there and back, they were sent out after supper. Getting there and doing the 'reccy' unseen was no problem. Their eyes quickly adapted to the dark and they managed to get quite close to the tunnel entrance and time the movements of the guards. Once every half an hour or so they walked from their hut to the tunnel mouth and stood having a smoke for a few minutes. Gauging the timing right, sometime after midnight they scrambled as quietly as they could down the side of the cutting and sneaked into the tunnel, laid the charge and made their way up the bank into the bushes. A firm hand on one of their shoulders indicated they had failed. A light-coloured trench coat and the noise they had made on the loose stones had attracted the guards' attention. They were told that they should have borrowed a black or dark-blue trench coat.

Initiative also helped in silent killing. A practice session for that involved disposing of an armed 'German' sentry guarding an ammunition dump. The 'knife' was, however, only a wooden spoon. The spot chosen was a sunken road in a wood. Creeping through dead leaves and sand trying not to attract attention to their presence when they were being accompanied by someone taking notes did not help to make it realistic. They had to inch their way to the top of the bank and spot the 'German' with his helmet and long grey coat. He was doing exactly what they hoped, standing at ease with his rifle over his shoulder. Standing up slowly to make sure of their balance, they had to jump on him, put one hand over his mouth, 'cut his throat' with the other and then grab his rifle to stop it rattling on the road. He offered no resistance, so it was a formality to remove his greatcoat and take it back as evidence.

There was a session of field-craft, where students were given an introduction into which plants, animals and insects were edible. However, the meals they were provided with were typical English fare, boiled vegetables and boiled or roasted meat with fish on Fridays, Grimsby fish they were told, with a whiff of sea air. There were fresh vegetables from the well-stocked garden. Food wasn't rationed whilst they were there.

What Didi would have found disconcerting was being observed eating. It was almost as if they wanted to know whether she was using the cutlery properly, whether she used the knife for eating peas or the dessert spoon for eating soup. She had to be seen to be eating the French way. Given that she'd grown up in France, this would not have been a problem.

At some meals, both beer and wine were served, lots of it! The Major was obviously trying to make them all drunk. He went on and on about how wonderful French cuisine was and how particular vintages of Burgundy Claret outclassed any German or Spanish wine. One student raised a laugh when she jokingly quoted General de Gaulle as saying the worst French cheese was better than the best English Cheddar. What they had not got to do was become too garrulous and give anything away about their real identities. To do so meant failure.

Pattinson's research into the SOE training addresses issues such as how agents were trained to 'pass' once in the field:

Instructors then, observed students' drinking, sleeping and consumption habits not in order to teach them to perform them better, but in order to test whether the students would be able to pass as ordinary French civilians once in the field.[4]

There was a billiard room, but whether Didi ever won a game is unknown. There was a bar too and drinking was encouraged. Singing raucous songs accompanied by someone on the 'joanna', slang for piano, helped raise spirits. Anyone with such dexterous skills would have been noted down as they could be potential 'pianists', the SOE slang for wireless operators. Maybe Didi played the piano.

Observers would have listened to their conversations and anything related to their real lives would have been a breach of security and they would fail the course. Maybe the others Didi was with were rowdy or mischievous, but given the circumstances, they probably played hard. Most likely the men would have been warned about trying anything on with the girls.

A common expression amongst Catholics was work hard, play hard and pray hard. One imagines Didi did all three, but, if the course at Winterfold was over a weekend, she might have found it difficult to attend mass. There was a Church of England church next door, which might have provided peace and tranquillity, a welcome alternative to the noise, excitement and commotion of Winterfold.

On one morning towards the end of the course they were woken from their slumber by the light coming on, their blankets being stripped off their bed and the radio being turned onto full volume. If they screamed and swore in English, they failed the course. The 'intruders' demanded their name and what they were doing. Keeping in role at four o'clock in the morning was a real challenge. They said it was preparation for being in the field. If you spoke in English, it would 'give the show away'.

At the end of the course she would have been debriefed, where her strengths and weaknesses would have been discussed. Then she would have been handed a sheet of paper and a fountain pen. It was headed 'The Official Secrets Acts, 1911 and 1920'. One expects that Didi read it several times before signing it. Under no conditions were they to disclose any official code-word, password, sketch, plan, model, article, note or document. Nor were they to divulge where they had been, who they saw, what they were told and what they did. The penalty for doing so was up to two years imprisonment with or without hard labour and a fine not exceeding £50.

Didi would have signed what others called 'The Poison Book'. Her signature is still there, dated 4 September 1942. There was a reward though. Students got paid leave – four pounds four shillings and sixpence a week.

Those who were determined to be unsuitable would have been transferred back to their previous employment. Whilst Didi was back in Stamford Hill, the final selection board convened. It was headed by the Commanding Officer, who was also the President of the Student Assessment Board, the examiners and representatives of the SOE's Country Sections. Each student's performance was discussed and suggestions made as to what tasks they would be best suited for. Although the final decision was the President's, it could be overturned by Brigadier Mockler-Ferryman, the SOE Council member with responsibility for training. Some student's personal files include the CO's report, but it is missing from Didi's.

A few days after getting back from Winterfold, Didi would have received an official-looking envelope. When she plucked up enough courage to open it, she would have read an invitation from a Major Buckmaster to meet him at Number 6, Orchard Court, Westminster. Checking on a map of London, she would have found that it was behind Selfridges, near Portman Square, just around the corner from Baker Street tube station.

It was an imposing seven-storey apartment building that must once have been a beautiful creamy limestone colour, but had been discoloured by many decades of smoke and smog. Once she pushed open the heavy front door she would have been approached by the doorman, who, in a well-spoken voice, informed her that he was Mr Park. In his sober dark suit and tie, he had all the mannerisms of – and looked just like – Jeeves, Bertie Wooster's valet.

He knew who she was, since her name would have been on that day's appointment sheet. Politely ushering her across the thick-carpeted entrance hall, through the gilded gates of the lift, he pushed the button for the second floor.

Once out of the lift, Park escorted her down the carpeted corridor along which luxurious ferns draped over side tables and pleasant watercolours hung on the walls. After he pressed the doorbell of Number 6, the green door was opened a moment later by a smartly dressed, stocky, middle-aged and almost bald gentleman, with piercing eyes, a droopy lip and a gold tooth. Behind him stood Vera Atkins.

Once the gentleman had confirmed Didi's identity, he thanked Park, ushered her into the hall and closed the door. Turning around, he introduced himself in perfect French as Monsieur Buckmaster. He took her proffered hand, didn't kiss it as some gentlemen did, but asked for her coat, which Vera hung on an ornate stand beside his black trench coat. The umbrella was placed in a brass pot beside it.

After congratulating her on passing the initial stage at what he called 'The Depot', he welcomed her to 'The Organisation'. He asked her if she needed the bathroom. Intrigued to see what it was like, Didi went in through the door that he held open for her. She was probably shocked by the extravagance: a plush pink carpet, jet-black bath and sink, an onyx bidet surrounded by peach pink mirrors and black glass tiles.

When she came out, he was standing by the open door of the sitting room, hoping that she was impressed with what she saw.

Just like the bathroom, it had rather expensive 1930s-style art-décor, apple-green wallpaper and lime-green woodwork. The net-curtained sash windows had heavy brocade curtains tied back with plaited ropes. Statues of stretching nudes draped with silk stood in the alcoves backlit in pink. Green round-armed settees and armchairs were arranged on a deep-pile cream carpet, which must have been a struggle to clean.

Once she was seated on a comfortable settee with a glass of sweet sherry, he sat down beside her and brought out from his briefcase a foolscap file with some reference numbers hand-written on the top right-hand corner. Pulling out a type-written form, he then spent about twenty minutes going over her Winterfold report, particularly emphasising her strengths in Morse Code. Having passed that assessment, he wanted her to consider taking a position as a wireless telegraphist. It was a vital post, which would involve communicating with men and women working behind enemy lines. Where it was, he did not say. Didi probably thought it best not to ask. Maybe Buckmaster had taken heed of Jacqueline's request that she was too young to be sent into the field.

Having agreed, Didi must have been pleased, knowing that if she had failed, it would have meant she had to find alternative employment, probably mundane shift work in a factory or working as a shop assistant. The prospect of working for the same organisation as Jacqueline must have been satisfying, but not being selected to be trained as an agent to be sent into the field may well have been a disappointment. Instead, she would be working as a wireless operator at one of the SOE's signal stations.

In preparation for her work for the organisation, Buckmaster told her that he had arranged for her to be given a commission in the FANY as a cadet officer. Maybe Didi did not feel brave enough to ask him what the initials stood for. Vera then gave her a letter formally welcoming her to the Inter-Services Research Bureau, the cover name for the SOE, and told her that her contact address for family and friends was 'Room 98, Horseguards, London SW1'. Any mail addressed to her there would be collected and then delivered by despatch riders.

As the formal part of the meeting was over, Vera ushered her into the hall, helped with her coat and told her that she was taking her out shopping and then for a meal.

The taxi dropped them outside Lilywhites Department Store, where every possible measurement was taken for her FANY uniform. The assistant told her that the women called it 'KD', khaki drill and that some in the FANY referred to its initials meaning 'First Anywhere' or 'Fun Anytime'. Lunch was commonly eaten in a secluded corner of Manetta's restaurant in Clarges Street in Mayfair.

A note in Didi's file in the FANY Headquarters gives two dates for her enrolling in the organisation, 12 July and 25 July 1942. It may be that the earlier date was her interview. She was recommended by Mrs Phyllis Bingham and Brigadier Gammel of the FANY and gave her mother as her next of kin.

The next morning, she turned up again at Orchard Court, where she would have met a group of other new recruits. When they were all assembled in the flat, Vera handed them a bulky parcel each, wrapped up in brown paper and fastened with string. It looked like a personalised parachute. Inside the parcel was the pristine, stiff FANY uniform, greatcoat and polished brown flat shoes. The right size too. Vera had done her homework. In one of the shoes was a Colt pistol. One can imagine Didi looking first at Buckmaster and then at Vera. Their eyes told her that she might have to use it.

After changing in one of the bedrooms, they shared the bathroom, admiring themselves in the mirrors. The FANY's outfit was khaki drill, a lightweight four-pocket jacket and divided skirt. The khaki service cap had a turned-up brim and a leather strap over the crown. There was also a khaki 'bonnet', a beret with a maroon flash and a bronze Corps badge of a Maltese Cross in a circle. Vera explained that the cross symbolised self-sacrifice to achieve unity and service. Lance corporals had one maroon flash on the side of their berets, Corporals had two and Officers had red, velvety buttons on their shoulders on stripes.

There was a wide Sam Browne leather belt. There was also a grey greatcoat with a double line of buttons up the front, fanning out from the waist to the shoulders with deep cuffs and scarlet lining. Didi would have looked very impressive when she tried it on.

Jane Buckland, an eighteen-year-old FANY and trainee wireless operator like Didi, said that, 'The nicest part of her uniform was the most beautiful Sam Brownes, lovely wide belts, which we had to polish all the time. It was just like the army — we were in the army, but special.' Attention to appearance was given great importance. As shoes, buckles and buttons had to be polished to a sheen, there was also a requirement that the lines down the back of their lisle stockings should always be straight.[5]

Before they left, Buckmaster gave them a lesson on military rank and salutes. They had to be able to identify from the number of stripes on military uniform the difference between Corporal, Lieutenant, Major and General. They also had to know how to salute them. Didi would have seen salutes being used when she was at Winterfold and occasionally out in the streets. The right hand had to be raised, palm down, and the first two fingers touched the right eyebrow.

At the beginning of the war, the main-line code room for communications between the British embassies and the intelligence service's base stations around the world was in Baker Street, London. As the SOE and SIS agents began being infiltrated into occupied Europe, they needed to be able to get information back to HQ. An organiser would have a courier to carry messages, important documents, explosives or other equipment within the country, but it was their short-wave wireless operator, sometimes termed telegraphist or radio operator, who kept in contact with London.

They had to encode the organiser's messages and transmit them back to London as well as receive encoded messages in return and decode them. Theirs was perhaps the most dangerous job of all the SOE's agents. It was said that the average life expectancy of a radio operator in the field was only six weeks. Francis Cammaerts, a French Resistance leader, said that, 'Without your radio operator, you were a pigeon without wings.'

With the SOE, SIS and the American Office of Strategic Services sending in an increasing number of agents, there was an increased demand for experienced wireless operators. As well the need for them to man the receiving sets in Britain, there was also a great need for wireless sets. Specialist wireless research and development was undertaken and factories and workshops were taken over for wireless set production.

As the premises in Baker Street were not big enough to cope with the extra sets needed, specialist listening stations were needed. With the Luftwaffe's bombing raids on London, premises needed finding outside the capital. There was also a need for buildings to be used for training wireless operators.

Consequently, the SOE's property section requisitioned large, secluded properties in the English countryside within easy reach of the capital. By the time Didi and Jacqueline arrived in England, the SOE had several wireless training schools and listening stations. They had also made arrangements with the FANY for some of their girls to be transferred to wireless training. With the increased demand for wireless operators, Buckmaster must have decided to send Didi to STS 54.

A number of accounts of Didi's life mention that she was sent to Thame Park in Oxfordshire. This was one of the SOE's establishments, where students were trained as wireless operators. There are no documents in her personal file that confirm that she did, but Maisie McLintock, her supervisor, provided details of meeting Didi and becoming friends at Thame Park.

On the back of Didi's signed Official Secrets Act was the section 'Joining', after which was written 'STS 54'. This was Fawley Court, near Henley-on-Thames in Buckinghamshire, an elegant seventeenth-century mansion set in parkland that ran down to the River Thames, gardens designed by Capability Brown and views north to the Chiltern Hills. Designed by Christopher Wren, it is claimed to have inspired Toad Hall in Kenneth Grahame's *Wind in the Willows*.

Requisitioned in August 1942, batches of up to 150 FANYs at a time were sent to master Morse at Fawley Court under the instruction of experts in the Royal Corps of Signals. Their chief instructor was Mr S. H. Gray, who also worked at Thame Park, the SOE's Base Signals Station. He probably had most success with those women who had been in the Girl Guides or men who had been in the Boy Scouts. They fared better as they had some understanding of Morse code. For the others it was a matter of rote learning, something Didi must have done particularly well in after the nuns' teaching in French convents.

One recruit recalled having to sleep in a freezing attic and learning to send and receive messages in Nissen huts in the grounds. Once they reached the required speeds, they were posted to either Grendon Hall, (STS 53a) off the A41 between Aylesbury and Bicester, Poundon House (STS 53b) near Bicester or Thame Park, (STS 52).

Situated a few miles south of Thame, between Oxford and Aylesbury and thirty-seven miles south-west of London, Thame Park was originally a Cistercian Abbey. Before the war it was the home of Sir Frank Bowden, heir to the Raleigh bikes fortune, but it was requisitioned for the SOE's wireless school. The seventeenth-century mansion was a palatial building with a grand staircase, built it is said for one of Charles II's mistresses. It had a large conservatory with huge peach trees inside and Didi may have bought some from the gardener who sold them at half a crown for a dozen. Set in 250 acres of parkland, Thame Park had secluded gardens, large areas of woodland and a large duck pond covered with water lilies and a punt. She would probably have been shocked if she had gone into the private chapel, as there lay the embalmed body of a former countess.

Its remote location made it an ideal base for the SOE's wireless school, but it was also the 'Holding Station' for SOE's Spanish section. Communist soldiers in the International Brigades who had escaped from Franco's Spain after the Civil War were accommodated there whilst waiting to be sent on missions. Consequently, there was a military feel about the place. So, as well as their wireless training, the women had to do PT and drills. There were two twenty-mile route marches each week through the Oxfordshire countryside and night exercises, where they were taken in a truck and dropped miles away and left to find their way back. Although there was no assault course, they were given some practice at demolitions, just to keep their hand in. The public were told that the people staying at the house were repairing the roads inside the estate. There was also a small firing range for hand guns.[6]

As well as these exercises, the sixteen-week course included mastering Morse Code, typing at between eighteen and twenty-two words per minute, using, diagnosing faults in and repairing a variety of wireless sets, learning how to encode and decode messages and memorising all the security checks necessary during transmission.

Didi had three WAAF instructors who were said to have put new recruits under pressure with a steady efficiency and a ruthlessness which would stand no slacking. Their pupils were there to learn and learn fast. If they could not take the pressure or their work fell below what was expected of them, they were sent to another unit with a strict warning not to say anything about what they had been doing. They had all signed the Official Secrets Act.

It is quite possible Didi and the other new recruits were briefed on security by Leo Marks, an officer in the SOE's Signals section. In his book, *Between Silk and Cyanide,* he detailed such a session. The group had been deliberately kept waiting for over an hour in a freezing window-less basement with no chairs or other 'creature comforts'. When he eventually arrived, he walked to the far end of the room and flicked a switch, which started a replay of the young women's conversation, which his assistant, Sergeant Blossom, had recorded:

The ill-lit room was rapidly illuminated by a corporate blush. As the recording progressed, it became clear that we had a most promising intake. The free-flowing language, scatological humour and picturesque imagery promised well for the agents' ditty box. They looked everywhere but at me, which was in every way understandable – and suddenly seemed reluctant to look at each other. Sensing that their embarrassment was about to peak I turned the volume up.

We then listened to a lengthy debate concerning the nature of the commitments, which had made me late. The consensus was that I'd been 'having it off' with the FANY supremo in a variety of positions (specified) though they were by no means unanimous as to whether she had kept her brigadier's hat on. They would decide when they saw me whether the transpositions had been single or double.

The next dealt with the state of the 'piss-house' in which they found themselves waiting. They blamed the lack of chairs on my failure to realise that FANYs had fannies – which one of them proposed to remedy in a time-honoured way. If it were the beefy one against the wall it could prove a terminal experience.

This account was detailed in a chapter entitled 'The biter bitten' as he went on to give his lecture on security, only to discover afterwards that it too had been recorded by Sergeant Blossom. Didi therefore heard something like this:

You've been waiting in a cold room to make you tired and irritable because when you're tired and irritable you grow careless, and when you're careless you're talkative. I promise you that, before you've been with us long, you'll be limp – but next time you feel like talking, remember that the Germans have recorders too – where even you wouldn't think of putting them.

Each of you has a crowd of admirers you've never met. Don't get excited – they're Gestapo admirers and they welcome you today just as much as I do. They hope you're green enough to want to boast. You'll have plenty to boast about. You're important people. You're going to be told about things you shouldn't know – but can't help ourselves, we have to trust you.

Every department has its secrets – you in Codes will read all the secrets of the departments. If you talk about any of them, a man will die. It's as simple as that. Now, I'm never going to mention security to you again. You think you're tired, don't you. Then imagine how tired an agent feels who's had no sleep for three nights and has to encode a message. The Germans are all around her so-called safe house. She has no supervisor to check her coding. All she has is a vital message, which she must transmit. Now, I'm going to put a question to this house. Hasn't that agent got a right to make a mistake in her coding? And, if she does, must she pay for it with her life? Must she come on the air again to repeat her message, whilst German direction-finding cars get her bearings?

You look puzzled. Is there something you want to ask? No? Perhaps no one's told you that many of our agents are women, members of your corps and about your age. I'm thinking about one in particular. Last week the FANYs at Grendon tried four thousand keys to break one of her messages and succeeded on the four thousandth and second. You'll find that double-transposition is easier to joke about than to crack.

There's an indecipherable down there with your names on it. It's from a Belgian agent who's completely blown. He sent us a message telling us his co-ordinates – that is, where he can be picked up. A Lysander is standing by to get him out. The message won't budge. At ten o'clock this evening he's due to come on the air and repeat it. If he does those cars will close in. we will lose that man – just as a few weeks ago we lost a young Norwegian named Arne Vaerum, code-named Penguin. The SS shot him while he was retransmitting an indecipherable message.

Must that happen tonight if there's any chance that you can help us to prevent it? Well you're going to have that chance! You will be told what to do by your colleagues. You will find that they are tired, tense, sulky – and the salt of the earth. None of them is quite sane – but don't worry, you'll soon be like them. Sleep in the train going down – sleep in the coach that waits at the station – but don't sleep in the code room.

If any of you finds the key that breaks this message, you all will have broken it. You're part of a team now, an indispensable part. Sorry about the recording – if you can think of a better way of reminding you never to talk about your work please tell me now.

I'd like to end with a word of advice. Don't grow old too quickly and don't stay young too long! Good luck – good coding, and remember ... you're the only hope that agent's got.[7]

To give you an insight into what Didi was doing at Thame Park, it is worth including a few paragraphs from Margaret Pawley's

In Obedience to Instructions as she provides fascinating detail of exactly what their work entailed. Each agent's codename and call sign were chalked up on a board and beside them was stuck a coded message, which had to be sent immediately after their call was heard. Once contact was made, the agent's message was transcribed. Accuracy was of vital importance. One false letter or figure in a code could make all the difference to the meaning of the message when the decoders had to decipher it.

This knowledge needed to be transferred to operating a special key, which represented the dots and dashes in terms of short and long sounds. When proficiency was attained, the mock practice key became part of a B2 radio set, which relayed the sounds into the atmosphere and could be captured at a distance on a specified wavelength, previously determined.

> A group of twelve girls ... sat at a series of wooden tables, practicing their Morse on a dummy key day after day. As it became possible to speed up, one moved to the next table, with an instructor sitting at the end. Most trainees would stick at one letter and not be able to overcome the resultant pause for a short period. There was a test once a week, when the atmosphere was really tense. Ann Bonsor recalls going to the cinema and quite involuntarily turning the sign EXIT beside the screen into morse. Probably on this account, radio operators, like coders, became obsessional; many FANYs have never lost the skill, only some of the speed, fifty years later.[8]

Ron Brierley, a wireless operator who trained at Fawley, admitted in an interview for the Imperial War Museum that coding was quite a laborious business:

> Quite obviously you can't send messages in clear, not only would they reveal the point of your transmission, but clearly

give the enemy exactly what you were talking about and what you were doing, so everything had to be in code. The system under which we trained was basically the commercial Q code, which is the normal system used in radio communication work by ships and sometimes aircraft, where you used a standardised system of calling. For example, you send out a signal 'QRK IMI' to enquire whether base is receiving you and at what strength. Base would reply, 'QSA 1, 2, 3, 4' or '5', according to the strength of your signal. That's known as the international Q code and there's a whole series of three-letter combinations of letters, all commencing with Q, which indicate short messages like 'Send faster', 'Send slower', 'I missed that', 'Send me a bit more'.[9]

Every operator had to master coding, a language with its own grammar and syntax. The operators at the listening stations were given a code pad identical to the one that the agent had in the field. This was five blocks of five letters printed on a pad in random fashion. You had a row of letters across the top and you wrote your message underneath. If the first letter along the top was an A and the first letter of your message was an L, you took the A and the L to what the coders called a silk, a piece of silk five inches by four inches, on which the alphabet was printed horizontally and vertically in upper case. Beside each letter, printed in lower case, the letters of the alphabet were printed in a random fashion. You would look for A along the top row and look for the L down the column and where the two intersected, you took the lower case letter beside it for your message. For security reasons, messages to and from the field had to be at least 200 letters long.[10]

Each SOE Section had its own team of wireless operators. For example, France's was F Section, de Gaulle's was RF, Holland's was N Section and Belgium's was T Section. When Leo Marks joined the SOE's Signals Section, he discovered that some

Country Section officers sent the same message to all their agents so, should one fall into enemy hands and be broken, they would know what to look for in any future intercepts. As Marks said, it would be an 'anagrammer's delight'.

In his autobiography, he noted how the SOE's first agents were sent into the field in early 1941 using a code poem, one that they knew off by heart. The most popular were from the Bible, Keats, Molière, Poe, Rabelais, Racine, Shakespeare and Tennyson. They were scheduled to transmit at certain times of the day or night on a given radio frequency. The home station knew when each agent was expected to be 'on air' and what frequency they would be using. To let the decoder know which five words they had chosen, they inserted an indicator group at the beginning of the message. The problem was that the agent's transmissions were sometimes recorded by Gestapo wireless listening stations and, if they managed to break just one message, the cryptographer would be able to mathematically reconstruct the five words and immediately try to work out the poem. If they managed that, they would be able to 'read' all future transmissions.

Agents were also expected to insert security checks to let HQ know if they were transmitting under duress. These were dummy letters in the body of the message. For example, the letters CAU inserted in one place and GHT in another. Their absence or alteration was the alert that something was amiss. As an added precaution, they were expected to make deliberate spelling mistakes at prearranged places. However, when Marks examined this method, he pointed out that it took no consideration of an agent's code having been broken or tortured out of them. They could work out the security checks themselves. It did not make allowances for what was called 'Morse mutilation', human error by the sender or the recorder or atmospheric changes, which may have affected the quality of the transmission.

On the wall of the room where their operators had their sets was a large poster with the words: REMEMBER THE ENEMY IS LISTENING. On another was a large board on which each of their agents' codename, call sign and scheduled time for transmitting were listed. Didi would only have known the codename of the agent whose traffic she handled; the operators were never allowed to meet them.

Once the message to the agent was encoded, it was attached to a board beside their codename. Didi would have to wait until the agent made contact, collect the message from the board, transcribe the incoming coded message and then tap out the encoded message for them. The transcribed message had to be passed on to the relevant Country Section.

Accuracy was of vital importance. Any mistake in numbering and any misspelling would produce gibberish and make the entire message what Marks called an 'undecipherable'. A dedicated team of FANYs was trained in unravelling the meaning of these.

James Gleeson, a *Daily Herald* journalist who wrote about women agents, described it as:

> A difficult, tantalising and unenviable job for the FANYs – their average age was nineteen to twenty. Sometimes the agent would be late, sometimes due to raids and arrests by the Germans, she would not transmit at all. The FANY in Britain sometimes had to wait fruitlessly with her head-phones on, hearing nothing but atmospheric noises for hours on end – it might be days, once there was nothing for six weeks. Still she waited.[11]

It was not all work and no play. There were weekend excursions to pubs and dance halls in Thame, less than two miles away. The first port of call was usually 'The Spread', the Spreadeagle Pub, where they undoubtedly met the 'Ox and Bucks', men from the Oxfordshire and Buckinghamshire Regiment. The

Spanish soldiers, using the cover as being Mexicans, had a fierce reputation and were reported as often being involved in fights. To defend themselves, they carried lemonade bottles filled with sand. One imagines Didi avoiding such fracas and spending the evenings enjoying herself with friends.

Hit tunes at the time included recordings of Glen Miller, the Ink Spots and the Andrews Sisters. She would have listened to them on the wireless or on an HMV (His Master's Voice) wind-up gramophone. At the dances, she probably mastered the tango and the 'glide'. Maybe there were days when she felt she had to go to confession or to mass. St Joseph's Catholic church in Thame was within walking distance.

One of Didi's training instructors at Thame Park was Sergeant Maisie McLintock, who had joined the FANY in December 1942, aged 26. As she was paid £1 a week, one imagines Didi would have received less, as a volunteer FANY. In an interview with Juliette Pattinson, lecturer in Modern British History at Strathclyde University, Maisie, known to her students as Mac, reported there being very tight security at Thame Park. On no account was she to let anyone in the training section know that she worked on the operational station at Grendon Underwood, and, if she recognised anybody, she had to look right through them. She had to never tell anyone where she had been. When Bunty Mackin, one of Didi's instructors, was ill, Mac was sent from Grendon Underwood to cover for a fortnight. As she was able to speak French, she got on well with Didi. In fact, she commented that Didi deliberately disobeyed rules like having baths after hours.

When Didi was training, she didn't have any shorts or tennis shoes so when Mac went home, she found some to lend her. When her mother asked about it, she said, 'Oh, it's a girl that I know who is wanting shorts and tennis shoes', and Mother, because clothing rationing was on by that time, Mother was a little cross that I'd given mine away, but I said 'Oh, it's all right,' … I don't think I can impress sufficiently upon you how terribly security conscious we were. Really, if anybody was ever there the one day and out of there the next, you never said where are you going, and if anybody came in from somewhere, we never said, 'where have you come from?' Just people were there, and then they weren't, and you never knew what had happened. So, Didi was there the one day, as large as life, and the next day she wasn't.[12]

When Mac mentioned Didi not being there one day, it is possible she had been posted to Scotland. There were occasions when wireless operators were sent to what was called an 'outstation' at Dunbar (STS 54b), near North Berwick, to take part in a scheme called SPARTAN. This involved three two-week trials, where they practised transmitting messages back to Thame Park. It allowed their instructors to ascertain their accuracy, identify weaknesses and give them an opportunity to overcome them.

It also gave them experience of the difficulties they might experience should they have to operate in areas of higher altitude. The nearby Lammermuir hills interfered with their transmissions, giving the operators difficult conditions to work in. Didi recalled, 'It was terrible interference, awful. I could never get the messages and I was very worried about it. But that was done a bit on purpose to see how you coped under pressure'.[13]

Pawley commented that, whilst in Scotland:

FANYs would be based in a mobile signal station, to which agents in training, dispersed throughout the countryside, would work back their sets. Before proceeding overseas, most coders and radio operators received some experience on an operational station, dealing with live traffic from the field. This would be at

Station 53A, Grendon Underwood, or Station 53B, at Poundon. Messages came in from Holland, France, Denmark, Norway and so on. During their earlier training radio operators would have become familiar with the Q code and the sending and receiving procedures based on this international method of communication; no other means were allowed, never plain language, though some agents in distress, anger or jubilation, might sometimes resort to it.

A FANY operator on duty at her set would be allocated to what was known as a 'sked' (terminology for an expected message at a previously defined time from an agent), with the appropriate frequency, codename and call sign, by the signal master, or other authorised person. She would listen for the three-letter particular call sign of the out-station, which should be calling at intervals of one minute, and then listening for one minute. If contact were established, the home operator would send the call sign, followed by QRK 'How are you receiving me', plus IMI 'Question mark'. The field would answer QSA 'Your signal readability is', followed by a number from one to five. If it were over three, and therefore fairly audible, the home operator would wait for the field to send QTC 'I have a message for you'. Field messages were always sent first. With numbers less than three, each group of five letters (the invariable number in which signals were sent) would be repeated. The base operator then took down the message in pencil in block capitals on special forms, and then waited until QRU appeared 'I have nothing more'. If the base operator had messages, the procedure would be reversed. To ask for repeated groups, or QRS 'Send slower', was not well regarded, unless interference was particularly bad, since it would expose the field operator to danger. At the end of a transmission, the base would send VA 'Close down'. In the event of sudden enemy attack, the field could send QUG 'I am forced to stop transmitting owing to immediate danger', whereupon a FANY operator would report this at once to her senior officer. In the event of gross inaudibility, it was possible to ask for help from a second base operator, but this was an exceptional measure in particular circumstances. 'Listening watches' were set up when a field mission failed to respond at its allotted time according to its signal plan.

A specialised training was given to become a signal planner. A small group of FANYs learnt to provide a signal plan for every mission, which went into the field. It included a call sign by which to be recognised by the base station, an allocated frequency, obtained by the supply of the appropriate crystals (two slices of quartz cut to a precise wavelength, which determined frequency, about the size of a postage stamp) and specific times on a regular basis at which attempts to transmit to the base station were to be made. Trained signal planners who undertook this skilled technical work were given the rank of Lieutenant.

Another technique in which the FANYs were instructed later in the war was that of 'finger printing', i.e. the recognition of morse-sending methods. All who learnt to send Morse developed their own individual style. If an agent in occupied territory were captured, attempts would be made to work the radio back to base in England. A FANY operator who could detect a change in field operator would prevent unwise future communications, drops, or reinforcements to that mission.[14]

Not everyone passed the four-month wireless course. They had to reach at least twenty words a minute, much higher than the peace-time requirements of the services or Post Office. Those who failed to get the hang of it dropped out. There were many who were transferred to become coders, registry clerks, copy clerks, signal distributors, teleprinter or switchboard operators.

Didi was one of the successful ones. Whilst she undoubtedly played an important role at Thame Park, she was part of a much larger operation. According to Cliff Lord and Graham Watson, in their *History of the Royal Corps of Signals*, there were 250 personnel in 1942 and 1,220 in 1944, including 350 Americans. Worldwide, the SOE had about 5,000 wireless operators.[15]

Jones claimed that, as soon as Didi realised the nature of the agents' work and the qualifications needed to do it, she volunteered to be sent into the field. Still being so young, her 'reserved personality' and 'unworldly air' mitigated against her, but the SOE contacted Jacqueline, her next-of-kin, to see if she would agree. Much to Didi's annoyance, she refused. She maintained her opposition for several months, but, for some undocumented reason, possibly SOE's need for more agents, she changed her mind.[16]

Mac did not question Didi's absence from Thame Park and it was not until much later that she knew where she had gone. The SOE had an important job for her. With so many organisers being sent into France to co-ordinate the French Resistance prior to D-Day, she was needed to act as one of their wireless operators.

Whilst Didi was training as a wireless operator, Jacqueline was undergoing the SOE training in preparation for being infiltrated into France. Having attended the preliminary course at Wanborough Manor, Jacqueline joined the second group of women to be sent on the SOE's three-week paramilitary training course in Arisaig, north-west Scotland. She was one of the first women to undertake the five-day parachuting course at Ringway aerodrome (STS 51), now Manchester Airport, before going on a four-week course in clandestine warfare at Beaulieu, an isolated estate in the New Forest. Details of her wartime experiences will be found in a subsequent book.

Having been briefed for her mission, on 25 January 1943, hardly six months after her arrival, she was driven up to Gaynes Hall (STS 61), one of the SOE's 'Holding stations', to await a flight from RAF Tempsford. In an article entitled 'Travelling Saleswoman', Buckmaster provided an account of Jacqueline's wartime experiences:

In a room in a country-house a girl was sitting alone. The blackout curtains were drawn back, and the only light, that of the moon, nearly full and serene in a clear sky, fell upon her face. It was a young and beautiful face, in which courage and steadfastness showed clearly, but a close observer might have noticed traces of stress.

As on previous occasions, she was spending her leave in this country-house. To her hostess she was just a F.A.N.Y. on leave from the daily round of normal and perhaps monotonous duties. But in the girl's mind thought followed quickly upon thought. The moon will be full tomorrow night, and the weather should be clear. Shall we take off, and will the flight be successful this time? Her thoughts returned to those other flights, fraught with danger, when she had set out, strung to concert pitch, to fly over France and descend by parachute upon enemy soil, only to suffer the dreadful anti-climax of the return flight because conditions had proved unfavourable for her descent. That long cold wait in the aircraft; that return to another spell of waiting in England; how many more times must I endure them? Thought ran on unceasing.

It was the winter of 1942, and France was occupied by the Germans. The only convenient way for British liaison officers to get there was by parachute. And even this way was not, strictly speaking, 'convenient'.

In the early years of the war few aircraft were assigned to special operations of this type, and the weather, especially in winter, was not often suitable for landings by parachute. Liaison officers might have to wait for weeks, possibly months, before their hazardous journey could be undertaken. Even then the pilot might well be unable to find the small field perhaps 400 miles from his base, where the 'reception committee' flashing feeble torches, awaited his passenger.

False alarms, abortive and dangerous flights menaced by enemy night-fighters and 'flak' were even more unnerving for the passenger, who had his mission before him, than for the crew of the aircraft. We used to reckon that three months waiting or two abortive attempts were about as much as an officer could be asked to endure, unless he or she had particularly strong nerves. But Jacqueline, the girl in the moonlit room, certainly had strong nerves. She had to wait from September until December and make several unsuccessful flights before the night arrived on which she made her parachute descent, yet she remained as calm and collected as one could wish. Jacqueline's name was given to me because of her perfect knowledge of French; after a brief interview she was enrolled in the F.A.N.Y., and seconded to my department for special service. She quickly obtained her commission and started training. But her French education and long residence made difficult to her problems which would have been easy for a girl with English upbringing. She became nervy and depressed; whereas at the first interview she had been confident of her ability to go back to France to live an underground life, now the very complexity of her training shook her self-confidence. She became thinner, and was obviously worrying about her ability to take on the job.

It was at this stage that I saw her for the second time. The training authorities had just issued an unfavourable report on her, and I thought that perhaps I had been over-optimistic about her qualifications. I went to see her at the school. There was no doubt about her being worried; but in the course of half an hour's talk she unburdened herself of her worries, and when I realised that her preoccupation was purely with the mechanics of what she was learning, I had no hesitation in advising her to go on with the course. She worked fantastically hard; she was determined to master the theoretical as well as the practical side of the job. That she succeeded is proved by her magnificent record, which owed much to the high standard of security, which she maintained throughout her area of operations.

During the last and successful flight there came again that tense feeling, those speculations upon the immediate and perilous future. Now they were near the place, and she made the final preparations; the green light indicating that she should leave the aircraft showed; a last contact of friendly hands helping her out of the aircraft, and she was falling ... She thought: 'I must make a good landing, I hope I don't get caught in a tree. Who will be there to meet me? Have the enemy been warned?' She landed, and as she collected herself perceived a shadowy figure approaching. Was it a German? She drew her pistol and waited.

The figure approached, also with drawn pistol, but all was well, and she was welcomed, and taken to safety for food and rest.[17]

Jacqueline parachuted from Flight Lieutenant Prior's 161 Squadron Halifax with her organiser, Squadron Leader Maurice Southgate, codename Hector, into a field about a mile north of Brioude, in the Massif Central. Southgate's mission was to take over the leadership of a new STATIONER network, which stretched from Châteauroux to the foothills of the Pyrenees. She must have had her heart in her mouth when, very shortly after landing, Southgate asked a woman cyclist the way to Brioude – in English!

Codenamed Designer, Jacqueline worked as a radio operator using a suitcase radio and went on to become a courier between several SOE groups operating around Paris. Her cover was that she was a chemist's sales representative. Her life as a secret agent was filled with constant danger. The threat of being exposed as an SOE agent or betrayal by a comrade must have created tremendous tension. Despite this, she travelled on long and arduous train journeys to maintain contact with agents, radio operators and the neighbouring HEADMASTER network run by Sydney Hudson, forming a vital link between several other SOE networks operating in Paris, Clermont-

Ferrand, Toulouse, Pau and Poitiers. She also carried spare parts for radios and organized reception committees for newly arrived agents. In Pattinson's book, *Behind Enemy Lines*, she included a transcript from the film in which Jacqueline starred after the war:

> Cat – The police were searching luggage at the station. They made me open my suitcases.
> Felix – Gosh – what did you do?
> Cat – I tried sex appeal.
> Felix – Did it work?
> Cat – No, it was a complete flop! I had to open it.
> Felix – What about the WT set?
> Cat – I told them with a sweet smile that it was an X-ray machine.
> Felix – It must have been a very sweet smile for them to have swallowed that![18]

Part of her work included escorting downed British airmen along the escape line south to the Pyrenees. 'Were they pretty glad to see you?', Buckmaster asked her on her return to England. 'Well yes, but of course they had no idea I was English; I didn't tell them who I was.'[19]

In May 1943 she made contact with her brother, Francis, in St Egrève. To avoid him being called up for compulsory labour by the Germans, Jacqueline recruited him to work as a courier, presumably funding him from the money Southgate brought with him for his network. Using his wife and child as a cover, Francis travelled by train between Grenoble, Vichy, Clermont-Ferrand and Lyon carrying parcels and letters as directed by Southgate or Jacqueline as well as suitcases containing explosives and wireless sets that the 138 Squadron had dropped.

Following the arrest of the family whose house he stayed in in Clermont-Ferrand, his life was in danger. There was worry that they may be forced to talk. A flight was urgently arranged to lift him out and bring him back to England. His wife and son returned to St Egrève and he made his way to a field, codenamed Achile, one kilometre north of Soucelles and one kilometre north-east of Angers in the Maine and Loire department. In the early hours of 20 October 1943 a Hudson landed, four passengers disembarked and he, Jacques Frager, an F Section agent codenamed Louba, Alexandre Lévy and M. Leprince, a Giraudist agent, were flown to England.

After going through the same intensive interrogation sessions that Didi and Jacqueline had when they arrived in England, Francis was sent on the SOE's preliminary assessment course. Despite the Commandant's report not being very impressive he was sent on the paramilitary course in Scotland, but was returned to London early. There were concerns about his state of health. Rather than continuing to employ him in the SOE, he was transferred to an army unit at the beginning of 1944. Whether he met up with Didi in London before she went back to France is unknown.

5

PREPARATIONS FOR THE DROP INTO OCCUPIED FRANCE: WINTER 1943–SPRING 1944

With so many arrests in France, SOE was desperate to send in replacements. When they decided to choose Didi to go in as a wireless operator is not documented in her file. What is known is that she was to accompany Jean Savy, one of their organisers who had recently returned from a mission in France. When and where Didi first met Savy is not known, nor how much, if anything, he told her of his background. One imagines that he would have briefed her about his time in France.

Research in various SOE histories, biographies and autobiographies of SOE personnel, Resistance-related websites and his personal file in the National Archives reveal that Savy was born on 4 December 1906 in Sarcelles, Seine et Oise. After attending the École libres des Sciences Politique, he graduated in law from the University of Paris and, from 1933, worked as a solicitor in the Civil Tribunal. He was married to Suzanne Hirtzman and had a house at 12 Rue de Villefort, Paris. His office was at 6 Rue d'Alger, close to Tulieres *Métro* station and rented from Robert Gieules, an administrator at the Compagnie Générale des Conserves.

By the end of 1940, Savy was helping the Allied cause by supplying valuable military intelligence to the American consul in Paris and was described as playing an important part in helping the French to resume the fight against the Germans. Exactly how was he was involved over the next few years has not come to light, but by 1943 he had met 38-year-old Lise de Baissac, one of the SOE's organisers.

Lise was born to French settlers in Mauritius, but she and her brother Claude were working in France when war broke out. Like Didi and Jacqueline, Lise and Claude escaped through Spain and Portugal and came to England. Both were identified by the SOE as potential agents and trained. Claude was parachuted south of Nimes on 29 July 1942 with Harry Peleuve, a wireless operator, with a mission to set up the SCIENTIST network in the Bordeaux area. Lise trained with Jacqueline and, on 24 September 1942, was parachuted from a Whitley with Andrée Borrel, a wireless operator destined for the PROSPER network.

They landed in a field, codenamed Bois-Renard, near St Laurent Nouan between Crouy-sur-Cosson and Nouan-sur-Loire, eight kilometres north-east of Chambord. Part of Lise's mission, codenamed ARTIST, involved finding volunteers to form reception committees to receive supplies from the Special Duties Squadrons, locating what the RAF called DZs (drop zones or landing grounds in isolated wheat fields and vineyards), making arrangements for the infiltration of the SOE agents into the area around the sleepy university town of Poitiers, capital of the Vienne department, and finding them safe houses. She also had to rendezvous with contacts in Paris as well as with her brother in Bordeaux, providing them with information that their wireless operators would transmit back to England, and receive any messages they had for her.

Through Lise, Savy made contact with Major France Antelme, a wealthy, aristocratic 43-year-old businessman who had sugar, tobacco and coconut plantations in Mauritius and had undertaken daring exploits for the SOE in Madagascar. Lise may well have helped arrange his arrival. On 18 November, 1942, he was flown out of RAF Tempsford by Flight Sergeant Wheatley and parachuted into the same field Lise used. Accompanying him was Captain Victor Hayes, a sabotage instructor. Using Reynaud as a codename, Antelme's mission was to establish contact with Éduoard Herriot, a former French prime minister, and Gaullist and anti-Gaullist resistance groups in the hope that they could accept SOE support. He also was to make use of his contacts in the civil service, banking and business with a view to supplying the planned arrival of Allied expeditionary forces with food and financial support.

Over the following months, Savy helped Antelme with this mission. Lise in the meantime arranged for thirteen SOE agents and many tons of arms and explosives to be landed on her fields to join her brother's network. Their missions included the destruction of the radio station at Quatre Pavillions – from where Admiral Dönitz coordinated the Atlantic U-boat attacks – along with the power station supplying the Luftwaffe airfields near Marignac and the electricity transformers at Belin, which powered the radar station at Deux Poiteaux and anti-aircraft batteries. As a result, the Germans intensified their efforts to destroy the SCIENTIST network. Knowing that Claude and Antelme were wanted men, a double Lysander operation was arranged to take them back to England for debriefing and a rest.

On 17 March 1943, Flight Officer 'Bunny' Rymills and Flight Officer Vaughan-Fowler flew out from Tangmere on Operation Trainer and landed their Lysanders safely in the early hours of the morning in a field 4.5 kilometres north of Marnay, south of Poitiers. On board were four SOE agents, Francine Agazarian, John Goldsmith, Pierre Lejeune and R. Dowlem, all destined for the TRAINER network in Paris. Antelme returned with Claude, Raymond Flower and his wireless operator.

After being debriefed, he spent two months working for the SOE under the name of Joseph Antelme and preparing for another mission. On 20 May 1943 he was flown out of RAF Tempsford in a 138 Squadron Halifax and parachuted into a drop zone, codenamed Marillion, near Chaumont-sur-Tharonne, twelve kilometres south of La Ferté Saint Aubin. Codenamed Antoine, his new mission was to take Winston Churchill's invitation to Herriot and Paul Reynaud, the new prime minister, to come to England. As Herriot was old and in bad health and the Gestapo had them both under surveillance, this part of Antelme's mission was unsuccessful.

However, Savy introduced Antelme to many of his political and official acquaintances in and around Paris, from whom he collected useful economic intelligence, which Lise encoded and sent back to England. From time to time Savy, given the codename Alcide by the SOE, provided Antelme and other Resistance members with a safe house in Paris. He also loaned Antelme 1,150,000 francs, a very considerable amount in those days. The agreement was that the SOE would put money into a bank account for him in London. Antelme also managed to provide safe houses and false papers for newly arrived SOE agents. One was Noor Inayat Khan, a wireless operator, codenamed Phono.

On 23 June 1943, following a successful Gestapo infiltration of an escape network in northern France, Francis Suttill, organiser of the PROPSER network, and many hundreds of Resistance members were arrested. After interrogation and torture, it is likely some talked and the Gestapo started searching for Savy and Antelme. M. R. D. Foot, the late SOE historian, mentions the Gestapo having obtained copies of Antelme's communications with Herriot.

Early the following month, Monsieur Gieules, Savy's landlord, spotted the Gestapo waiting outside his office. Knowing Savy was planning to visit him, he rushed to meet him at Tuilieres

Métro and told him to make himself scarce. Savy immediately left Paris and, with Lise's help, laid low for a while in a safe house in Poitiers. Aware of the arrests and that Savy was a wanted man, Henri Dèricourt, the SOE's Flight liaison officer, agreed that a Lysander pick-up be arranged to lift him out.

On the night of 19/20 July, Flight Officer 'Mac' McCairns of 161 Squadron left RAF Tangmere on Operation Athlete. After fifty minutes of very tense flying through a thunderstorm, he landed safely in a field, codenamed Grippe, 1.5 kilometres east-north-east of Azay-sur-Cher, thirteen kilometres east-south-east of Tours, in the Indre-et-Loire department. Two SOE agents – one of which was Isidore Newman, a wireless operator destined for F Section's new SALESMAN network in Rouen – were met by Lise's reception committee. Once they got out, Savy and Antelme were brought back to England with Déricourt and Mme Felix Gouin, the wife of a French politician. It must have been a tight squeeze as there were only two passenger seats in a Lysander.

Known in the UK as Jean Millet, Savy was introduced to Maurice Buckmaster who arranged employment for him and Antelme working in the SOE's false documents section.

When Lise discovered her network had been penetrated, she feared for her safety. Even though the other network she had established in Ruffec was still secure, SOE ordered her to return. Accordingly, Déricourt arranged a Lysander pick-up for 16 August 1943 for Lise, her brother and Nicholas Bodington, an SOE agent who had been infiltrated on 22/23 July, to clarify the circumstances of the collapse of the PROSPER network and investigate claims that Déricourt had betrayed several agents.

Squadron Leader Hugh Verity landed in a field, codenamed Torticolis, two kilometres east of Couture-sur-Loir, seven kilometres west of Vendôme, and returned them safely to England. After her debrief, Lise was given the role of conducting officer for Buckmaster's F Section, which is where she met Didi and Jacqueline.

Marks reported that, in preparation for Antelme's return, Buckmaster sent in four young agents on 8 February 1944. Two days later, the wireless operator's message was received, but his security checks were incorrect. When a test question was sent to which the answer should have been 'Merry Xmas', the reply came back, 'Happy New Year'. Something was wrong.

Marks was concerned about Antelme returning to France. Captain George Noble, his colleague in the SOE's coding section, was worried about Noor Inayat Khan, one of their few remaining wireless operators in Paris. The omission of her security checks suggested she had been arrested, but messages were still being received from her set. In the circumstances, Antelme was recommended to be dropped blind, without a reception committee. As he had so few contacts left, he had no alternative but to trust the PHONO network and ignore the SOE's advice.

On the afternoon of 29 February 1944, Antelme, Lionel Lee (Daks) and Madeleine Damerment, two more wireless operators, were driven up the A1 to Tempsford. Once checked and kitted out in their jump suits and parachutes in the barn on Gibraltar Farm, they were taken to Flight Lieutenant Caldwell's waiting Halifax. He flew them into France and they parachuted to a drop zone at Sainville, thirty-three kilometres east of Chartres, closely followed by thirteen containers. Foot reported that Antelme's mission was to investigate the security of the network operating around Rennes; arrange a double Lysander operation near Le Mans; look into the affairs of the BUTLER network, and set up his own in the Paris area.[1,2,3,4]

As soon as the three agents pulled in their parachutes, they were welcomed by the PHONO reception committee, which, unbeknownst to them, had been taken over by the Gestapo. Taken unawares, there was a brief struggle; they were handcuffed and driven away for interrogation and torture at 84 Avenue Fochs, the Gestapo HQ in Paris, less than an hour away.

According to Marks:

On 2 March [the day before Didi arrived in France] Noor sent a message confirming that arms, radio equipment and money had been successfully dropped, but that Bricklayer had severely damaged his head on landing. She amplified this a few days later by saying he'd been taken to hospital, that he was in a coma, and that, according to his doctors his condition was critical.

Nothing yet had been heard from Daks, and London demanded to know why he hadn't reported the accident himself.

After another week of radio silence (an awesome sound) Daks sent a message in his one-time-pad explaining that his WT set had been damaged on landing, and this accounted for the delay. He confirmed that Bricklayer had been taken into hospital and was still in a coma.

So were Daks's security checks: the code room supervisor had marked his message 'security checks incorrect', but hadn't given the details.

Knowing that he was an erratic coder who'd frequently omitted his security checks in training or substituted those of his own making, I sent for the code-groups so that I could examine them myself. Like all WOK/LOP users, he'd been taught never to transmit the indicator groups exactly as they were printed, but to change them by prearranged numbers. He was to add 4 to the second letter and 3 to the third. If he changed them by any other numbers we'd know that he'd been caught. The indicator of his first message was DBOPR and he should have changed it to DFRPR to tell us he was safe. But instead he'd inverted the last two letters of DBOPR and transmitted DBORP.[5]

Marks admitted that, when the supervisor at Grendon Underwood informed him on 8 April 1944 that Daks's messages now included the security check, he didn't bother to double check. Noble queried this as there had been no replies to his personal questions. When Marks did the double-checking, he noticed the last two letters of the indicator group had been inverted, but 'he had made no attempt to change the second and third letters by the requisite numbers'. On checking with the supervisor, he discovered Daks had not been given any secret numbers to add – an error Marks well understood:

All he had to do to tell us he was safe was insert three sets of dummy letters at the beginning, middle and end of every message. He'd failed to do so in his first message, but had inserted them correctly in the two we'd just received.

We'd sent the station the wrong code-card. The one she believed to be Daks's was a copy of the conventions he'd used at training school before his checks had been finalised. He'd been taught to insert three sets of dummy letters as an additional check, and this was all that he'd remembered. I asked what significance she'd attached to the inversion of the indicator groups.

She replied, 'None at all.' She then reminded me that I'd warned the girls that many agents found their silks difficult to read, and that their indicators were often Morse-mutilated, and she'd assumed that either or both of these factors accounted for Daks's inversions. She also thought I'd given him a special check as I had to Noor, and that it consisted only of inserting dummy letters.

But the Daks disaster didn't end there. I discovered that his real code-card was nestling in his training file and had never been dispatched. I also discovered that a trusted member of the typing pool had misspelt two words of his poem.[6]

This was the beginning of what Marks called 'The Decline and Fall of the Holy Coding Empire'. He then had to try and convince his superiors, Colonel Ozanne and Captain Claude Dansey, that, following the Gestapo breaking up the PROSPER network, they had captured several of the SOE's wireless operators with their sets and, sometimes, their codes. Under torture and, possibly with the offer of financial reward, some must have revealed their codes and security checks. Gestapo-inspired messages were being encoded and transmitted back to London asking for weapons, ammunition, money, supplies, wireless technology and more agents. As the Gestapo arranged the drop zones, they knew exactly when and where the Special Duties Squadrons' planes would arrive, even the correct code to flash the pilots. Once new agents were in their hands, they might be able to extract from them information about D-Day.

Research shows that the Germans had been playing what was called '*Englandspiel*' in Holland since 1941. Exact figures are understandably difficult to ascertain, but, according to Foot, they ran 18 wireless lines ordering 190 drops to 14 locations. They picked up 570 containers, about 150 parcels, arrested 46 British and 51 Dutch agents and up to 350 Dutch Resistance members. They got 15,200 kg of explosives, 3,000 sub-machine guns, 5,000 pistols, 2,000 hand grenades, 75 wireless sets, 100 torches, 6 silent pistols, 3 wireless direction finder sets, 3 S-phones, 2 infra-red torch-lights, more than 500,000 cartridges and more than 500,000 Dutch Guilden. 138 Squadron lost 12 planes and 87 personnel, shot down once they had completed their drops.[7]

There are some today who argue that the SOE was playing the same game back to Germany, lulling them into a false sense of security so as to distract their attention away from the true location and timing of the D-Day landings. The full details of the radio games played in France have yet to come to light. Needless to say, it was into this very dangerous background that Didi was sent. Marks had to ensure that subsequent wireless operators underwent a special intensive security course. A document in her personal file indicates that she attended a W/X course at Beaulieu in January 1944.

In Foot's account of the SOE in France, he reported that Antelme was in a huge rage to have been tricked in this way, but, although the Germans knew who he was, he stuck to his new cover story. He, Lee Daks and sixteen other SOE officers were subsequently sent to Gross-Rosen concentration camp in Upper Silesia and were executed in July or August 1944. Damerment was executed at Dachau on 13 September.

Didi was probably unaware of these radio games and would very likely not have been told of agents' arrest and capture. As she had had to examine the agents' messages to ensure their security checks were included, anything dubious would, in theory, have been noted and reported to her supervisor.

On learning that Antelme had been arrested, Savy volunteered to return to France. Whether Lise de Baissac recommended him taking Didi or whether the SOE chose her, is unknown. With so many wireless operators being captured, there was an urgent need for more, given that D-Day was fast approaching. Described in his personal file as 1.76 m, 70 kilos, dark hair, brown eyes and with a withered right arm, the SOE decided that it was best that he should be taken back in a Lysander operation. Hence, there was no need for Didi to undergo the parachute training course at Ringway.[8]

Didi was very likely surprised when she learned she had been chosen to accompany Savy. She would probably have received a letter from Vera Atkins, informing her that she was to meet her at Orchard Court on a specified date at a specified time. Her valise had to be packed, ready for the last part of her training. What this entailed was not mentioned.

On arrival, Park, still with his bowler hat on, probably recognised Didi. Students reported him being particularly observant of visitors. Once credentials were checked, Didi would have been ushered upstairs. Buckmaster welcomed visitors at the door, took their coat in exchange for a half-full schooner of sherry and whisked them into the sitting room. If Lise de Baissac was Didi's conducting officer, she would have been there to greet her, as would other students selected to go on the course. Once comfortable on the armchairs or settee, Buckmaster congratulated them on successfully completing their course at Thame Park, acknowledging the contribution they had made to the war effort. Having been chosen to be sent into France as a wireless operator, prospective agents needed to attend a four-week course at the SOE's 'Finishing School'.

Despite some students being given negative reports from their training courses, Buckmaster is known to have overruled them and sent the student anyway. Sarah Helm, who wrote Vera Atkin's biography, said many of the trainee's assessments were wrong. 'Most of these reports were proved completely meaningless later because when these women were in the field, what they needed was determination, know-how, common sense and bravery – and they had all of these in abundance.'[9]

As the war progressed and plans for the D-Day landings took shape, there was an urgent need for wireless operators. Buckmaster would probably have known, but wouldn't have told Didi that their life expectancy in the field averaged only six weeks.

Whether students asked him if he could shed some more light on the organisation they were now working for is not certain. If he did it is unlikely he went into the fine detail, but may have briefly explained how it had been set up after the evacuation from Dunkirk, to provide help and assistance for the various resistance movements in occupied Europe. Some people had been deliberately left behind to try to support and encourage resistance groups. Thousands of tons of supplies and dozens of agents were being parachuted in under the cover of darkness almost every night of the full moon. Planes were parachuting or landing agents on remote fields and often picking them up again after their mission. Downed pilots and aircrew, VIPs and vital documents were also being picked up and returned to 'Blighty'.

Maybe he told them what these agents were doing. They were helping the war effort, either directly themselves or training others in sabotage. Cutting telegraph wires was one example. With communications down the Germans could not be warned about the RAF bombing raids. Telephone workers were being recruited to intercept German military messages and pass them on to members of the Resistance so they could be sent on to London. Postal workers intercepted important military communications, opening, copying and then resealing letters or copying telegrams. French railway workers had their '*Fer Réseau*', diverting freight trains from their designated destinations, not operating points correctly so as to cause derailments, destroying railway lines, demolishing bridges and tunnels. They needed the organisation's help to undermine the enemy's war effort.

Others were sent as couriers, carrying messages from their organiser to other members of the Resistance, sometimes taking parts for wireless transmitters, explosives or money. As Didi would have known, some were sent as wireless operators, picking up encoded messages from HQ, decoding them and passing them to their organiser. They would also receive messages in clear from their organiser, which would need encoding and transmitting back to HQ.

After these preliminaries were over, they were told that they were going to be sent to an exclusive finishing school. To ensure Didi and other 'students' were up-to-date in the work of wireless operating whilst in the field, the SOE decided they needed to attend a two-week 'W/X' course. Whilst there was no details about it in her file, it would very likely have also included several weeks of training in clandestine warfare. She was attached to a small F Section group that was there between December 1943 and January 1944.

Buckmaster is reported telling women agents that the first female group sent on this course had successfully overcome some of the opposition in the training staff to female students and proved that women could cope with the physical, emotional and psychological pressures of an intensive paramilitary training course. Theirs would be similar to the preliminary training at Winterfold, but different.

Most students sailed through the course with flying colours, he told them, and he expected them to do the same. But, he pointed out, there were some instructors who still had reservations about women. It was going to be a demanding few weeks and the future of the increasing number of women who were joining 'The Firm' would depend on how well they did. There was a major difference between the work they would be doing and that of a soldier. They would be able to rely on their comrades for some support, but mostly, they had to rely on themselves. Once out in the field, in all likelihood, they would be on their own.

After taking them out for lunch in an Italian restaurant in the Trocadero, near Piccadilly Circus, Buckmaster made his farewells and they would have ambled back to Portman Square. Waiting outside Orchard Court was a large black Wolsey. With all their valises stowed in the boot, Vera drove them down Park Lane, over Vauxhall Bridge and south out of London. Even though all the road signs and street names were down, Didi would probably have known that they went down the A3 and into Hampshire.

After about three hours, they were driving through a forest of ancient oaks and beech trees, interspersed with open, sandy heath of gorse and bracken on which wild horses and ponies grazed. Vera often stopped in the late afternoon in an attractive village somewhere in the New Forest, where they stretched their legs and were treated to sandwiches and a beer or shandy in an old-world pub, the Turfcutters Arms.

When they came out, an army truck was parked beside the Wolsey. Vera wished them well and sailed off back to London. She had work to do. Like at Guildford Station, they piled into the back with their little valises and were driven around the highways and byways.

Didi would have had no idea where she was being taken. When the truck pulled up at a check point, maybe she expected another 'Stately 'Ome of England', like Fawley Court or Thame Park, but it wasn't. A high, barbed-wire gate barred their entrance and it was only when the driver showed his pass to the guard that he lowered his sub-machine gun and let them through.

When the flaps were opened, Didi would have seen a drive lined with rhododendron bushes, which led to a gravel terrace in front of a very nice, but modern, 1930s brick-built house called 'The Drokes'. It had three floors and numerous bedrooms. Extensive grounds stretched down to the banks of the River Beaulieu and mature trees hid the house from any local's enquiring eyes, should they cycle down the quiet country lane. A small pond lay hidden in the bushes.

Inside, it was light and airy, with similar art-décor furniture to Orchard Court. French windows from the huge sitting rooms opened onto a mossy patio with a long, well-kept lawn. There were no hills, just a rather low, undulating horizon, disappointing after months in Oxfordshire, but probably heavenly after war-torn Central London. It was quiet too.

The officer in charge of the house introduced himself in fluent French. Maybe he had taught Jacqueline, who was one of the second groups of women to undergo this training. Didi would have used her cover name, Alice Wood, as in Winterfold. The women shared rooms with their conducting officers. They were large and airy with a single bed each, a wardrobe, chest of drawers, a mirror and a washbasin, but no en-suite bathroom and toilet. The view out of the window was of a traditional English country garden, looking across the river to low-lying woods and farmland.

After freshening up they went downstairs and sat around the dining room table, where tea was waiting for them. The house was managed with military precision. They were told that French had to be spoken at all times, morning, noon and night. All their instructors spoke French. The more practice they got in using it the better. Responding to someone's knock on the door with 'Come in' would have drawn a reprimand. It would be a dead give-away if they were to do that in the field. In the evening, sometimes they tested themselves on specialist vocabulary.

Didi's conducting officer would still have accompanied her, all day, every day, except for a few days towards the end of the course when the student was expected to go off on her own. Carrying her note book and pencil with her, she would jot down any points which Didi would find useful, any strengths and any areas of weakness. Part of her brief was to report back to HQ on how well she did in each course, how she coped under stress, how her behaviour changed, whether she was able to take the teasing and what made her lose her temper.

From experience, Didi would have been very wary when offered drinks, probably well aware of what her limit was as far as alcohol was concerned, and would say no when already tipsy. Conducting officers were instructed to find out how talkative they became under the influence.

Using the knowledge and experience obtained from debriefing returned organisers, couriers and wireless operators as well as from the 'boffins' working on the latest radio technology, the SOE felt it was essential that new operators were 'au fait' with the equipment as well as with agent security. The course would have included more practice in coding and decoding messages, sending and receiving radio messages on the latest wireless sets and mastering Leo Marks' latest coding system. There was also practice in how to repair wireless sets and other household electrical equipment.

Whilst it is likely that she had to use her cover name, Alice Wood, the code card in her file identified her as Miss Eileen Nearne. Going into France at this time of intense Gestapo efforts to destroy the Resistance was a highly dangerous mission. Sue Ryder, one of the FANYs, mentioned that the men and women who were successful in their training as radio operators included the bravest:

> For if they were caught with a set they knew they faced death. To escape detection they frequently had to change the place from which they transmitted messages and, to avoid capture, they often had to disguise themselves – sometimes at barely a moment's notice. German radio-telegraphists were on duty at their listening posts twenty-four hours a day. The Gestapo always had a flying squad ready to go into action immediately to hunt and seize these Bods.[10]

Escott mentioned in her *The Heroines of SOE* that part of the wireless security course included the dangers of being detected. There were staff employed at the Gestapo Headqurters on Avenue Foch who were on shifts keeping a continuous lookout for wireless operator signals.

Relays of about thirty German clerks gazing at their cathode ray tubes in every available frequency, searched for any new blip to appear on their tube. They would then telephone the Direction Finders at Brest, Augsberg and Nuremberg, giving the reading of the new frequency, and ask for cross bearings. These found, the Direction Finding vans, full of the most sensitive equipment, would take up the hunt, forming a triangle within a triangle, until they were within a mile of their quarry, and moving slowly along the lanes and streets. Finally, men on foot in long raincoats, their earphones hidden by their high turned-up collars and hats, read off the distances by miniature metres, on what looked like large wrist watches. In this way they could pin-point the very house from which the signal came.

In Vigurs' research into the SOE's F Section women agents, she stressed that the work of a wireless operator required someone with mental stability and the ability to work alone:

The wireless operator would be known by as few members of the network as possible and would keep a very low profile. They would pick up messages from 'letter boxes' or have them delivered by a courier. A wireless operator would change location as much as possible to avoid detection by Nazi Direction Finding (D/F) mobile equipment and the maximum time for a live transmission would be 20 minutes, as any longer and the wireless operator's location risked compromise. This was often problematic as messages could become garbled or they could have an awkward signal caused by jamming or a noisy frequency. All messages were sent and received in unique codes that the wireless operator was required to memorise.

The work of the wireless operator was fraught with danger and if they were caught an entire network could fall apart as the operator was needed to ask for supplies, pass intelligence or relay other important messages such as arrest updates or requests for more agents. Wireless operators had the most dangerous job of all agents, as they risked detection whilst transmitting or moving about the country with their wireless sets. They also knew details about other members of the network and its activities that others did not. Training a wireless operator was time consuming and they were difficult to replace due to their specialised skills.[11]

One of the code instructors was Captain Drake, another University-educated, well-spoken Englishman who spoke excellent French. His were the probably the most useful lessons Didi had at The Drokes. Whilst for many, coding seemed like an interminable alphabetic juggling, for others, like Didi, the message jumped out as if by magic. One minuscule error would completely destroy the whole structure. What Marks' Code Department in Baker Street had done by early 1944 was to identify the most common phrases like 'all's well', 'arrived safely' and 'thank you very much' with coded numbers. It saved time. Hundreds of them were printed on silk.

The SOE had inherited the well-established poem code, where a message was encrypted through a unique key poem that the agent had to learn off by heart. They had discovered several fatal drawbacks to this code in the early years of the war. After sufficient traffic passed on the same poem, a Nazi crypto-analyst could mathematically reconstruct the poem itself, opening all previous and future traffic to direct reading. More commonly, it was believed that the Nazis had tortured the poems out of agents. To counter this and reduce the risk of capture in the first place, Marks had invented worked-out keys (WOKs), letter one-top pads (LOPs), memory one-top pads (MOPs), and a host of new codes to enable operators to never have to remember their cypher keys due to their randomness and to transmit messages with a very short length. These cyphers they had to use. He showed them what looked like a handkerchief. It was a sheet of silk on which had been printed lines of random upper case and lower case letters. The bottom line was the 'one-time code'. Use it, tear or cut it off, burn it or swallow it. Whatever else, it must never be allowed to fall into enemy hands.

Cyphers were complex. It took students a while to master them. They were a means of sending information in such a way that only the sender and receiver would recognise. But you both needed to know the code. One of the first lessons was to listen to the BBC *messages personelles*. These were pure nonsense to the vast majority of listeners, but to those who were in the know, they meant a lot. Each *réseau*, or resistance network, had its own code message. If it was read out by the BBC after the 19.30 news, it meant that a mission was planned for that night. If it was repeated after the 21.00 broadcast, it was confirmed. The 'op' was on. If it wasn't, then it had been cancelled. That meant someone in the network had to listen to the BBC at least twice a day. They were told that having a wireless was illegal in France and being caught listening to the BBC risked death. Many people were risking their lives daily to be kept informed. Remember that, and they would save lives.[12]

The other important message he wanted them to remember was that, by altering words and their place in the lines when they transmitted home, the Code Department would know certain things about their mission. In particular, they could let them know if they were compromised, whether they were transmitting under duress. Accuracy was essential, not just in tapping out messages in Morse, but also in any coded communication.

As Didi would be working in France, it was vital that she understood more than just the rudiments of wireless communication. Wireless operators needed to be experts, not just in using the set, identifying and repairing faults and coding and decoding; they also needed to be aware of the security needed to survive. Messages sent back from the field and accounts by returned agents made the SOE aware that many wireless operators had been caught. The hundreds of arrests that followed gave rise to the suspicion that some must have talked under torture and either agreed to relay German-inspired messages or gave up their codes and security checks so German wireless-operators could use their sets.

Marks reported how one Canadian wireless operator, caught and imprisoned, had become so bored that his guard gave him a Morse set to keep him occupied. Whilst he tapped away in his cell, he was unaware that a German expert sat in the adjoining cell listening in. This allowed him to learn his personal style, the so-called 'fingerprint', and send messages back to England before the SOE eventually realised.

Marks acknowledged that the Germans, like the SOE, made recordings of their operators' transmissions and used oscilloscopes for comparing the style. The SOE parlance for this style was a 'fist'.

> To an outsider this seems rather incomprehensive, after all it is only about dots and dashes. But one operator explained it to me. This was rather easy and came quick during training. They soon recognized the 'fist' of everyone they trained with. You get a very characteristic way of your transmissions – it could be the length of dots and dashes, the pause between them and the interval between letters; every letter had a characteristic style. And as you write, it became music for them; they didn't hear the dots and dashes, but the actual letters.[13]

Didi would have been pleased to hear that the traditional system of telephones and the Post was still functioning in France, but she was warned that it was very easy to intercept mail. Telephone conversations connected via the operator could be listened in on. Whilst at Thame Park, Didi would have been accustomed to using a transceiver, a wireless set which could both transmit and receive Morse messages, and one imagines she would have been encouraged to suggest any modifications and improvements to her equipment. This was where the 'boffins' came in. These were the 'back-room boys', the scientists working specifically on military technology.

The early wireless sets were huge and needed at least two people to transport them. It would have been explained that, by using smaller and smaller parts, the portable sets sent to France were reduced from 26.5lbs to only 14.5lbs. Even so, a stone is still heavy – about seven bags of flour, and, once fitted inside a small valise, really made your arm ache. They were told to carry it in a bike basket – or get a man to help. They showed them examples of everything that the sets could be hidden in like vacuum cleaners, gramophones, sewing machines and X-Ray machines.

The case was quite small, about eighteen-by-eleven-by-five inches, a bit like an attaché case, made of fibreboard with reinforced metal corners and a black enamelled fastening. They were told it was waterproof. The set was powered by electricity and therefore needed batteries or, for when they ran out, access to a power socket in someone's apartment. The signal, they told her, was quite weak, only 20 watts.

The interior was lined with baize or flannel and the contents packed in felt to prevent them rattling. Inside were a transmitter and a receiver and an instruction manual. There was a combination power pack for either battery or mains operation, a box of spares containing sixty feet of aerial wire, a ten-foot earth wire, a transmitting key, a telephone headset, twelve fuses of assorted amps, four spare valves, two brass pins to convert the mains plug to a continental fitting, a screwdriver and a Bakelite container to hold the two delicately cut quartz crystals, one for day and one for night operations. Different ones were needed to tune to a particular wavelength to determine the transmitting frequency. Sometimes, for additional security, these crystals were carried in a separate tobacco tin. Some operators, they were told, referred to them as 'sugars' because they resembled sugar cubes.

The aerials needed to be invisible to passers-by. They were shown how to lay them out in the attic of a house, how to fasten them under the eaves around the outside of a building and how to disguise them from inquisitive observers. They were told that they would not have to disguise the sets in an emergency, so they only had to learn the basics.

They were also given practice at taking sets apart and reassembling them, identifying faults and resolving them. They were probably shown an alternative power source, should they be anywhere without electricity. The 'boffins' had come up with a pedal-powered dynamo. A wheel-less bicycle had a stand welded to its frame and the cyclist's pedalling turned the dynamo, which could be connected to the set.

Given the number of wireless operators that had been caught, lessons were given in security. It was drilled into them that they should not use the same house for transmitting. They had to move frequently. Ideally, they ought never to transmit from the same place twice and to vary the time and frequency of their transmissions.[14]

It is very likely that Didi had lessons on radio detection. Over the years of the war, the *Funkhorchdienst*, German teams of *radio-goniometres*, had built up expertise in locating buildings being used by the SOE's wireless operators for their transmissions. They used vehicles disguised as local delivery vans, bread vans and ambulances with wooden superstructures to reduce interference with their readings. The driver was often a 'thug' with a *sulphateuse*, the French slang for a machine gun, and the radio detection expert sat in the back with his radio detection and communications equipment, compasses, sheets of small-scale street maps, note pads and an early mobile telephone. Their equipment provided a compass bearing for the transmission, which was then plotted on the map. If there was only one van, they would drive somewhere else, take a second reading and plot another line on the map. Where the two tines intersected was a guide to the location of the transmitter. A third reading was necessary to give an accurate fix – basic trigonometry. The French term for these detection teams was *gonios*. The process took twenty minutes so it was essential wireless operators did not stay on air long and moved locations regularly.

In some areas the Germans were using planes with specialist direction-finding equipment on board. When detection teams worked together, once one picked up a transmission signal, they determined its bearing and telephoned the details to the coordinator who plotted it on their map. For even more accurate localised detection, a man might walk the streets with the equipment under his coat and wires threaded through his sleeves. When the three bearings were successfully plotted, it was a simple task for them to locate the intersection and send a message through to the hit squad. What they would do was to switch off the power to each street to confirm exactly where the transmission was coming from. Unscrewing the fuses one at a time from the box on the outside of each building helped them to identify exactly which apartment the wireless set was being operated from. A short telephone call later and the *Milice* or the Gestapo were then brought in with sledgehammers and guns for the search and arrest.

Returned agents and Resistance members reported seeing these detection vans in the streets. When they parked and nobody got out, it looked suspicious. A man walking around with a bulky overcoat fiddling with some equipment was also an indication they were taking direction findings. Some agents reported being given a 'minder', someone in the Resistance who would keep a look-out and let them know when the detection teams were in the area. There is no evidence Didi was given one.

During her time at Beaulieu, Buckmaster paid the group she was with a visit. In an article in the *Chamber's Journal*, published shortly after the war, he admitted that:

> The way of a radio operator is always hard: when he is being trained to work a Morse set in conditions of absolute secrecy, he requires almost more than human perseverance and concentration. The instructors at the school will say, 'So-and-so is not feeling well today; his speed is down to 31.' Men and women in training become moody and disgruntled: there was much bickering and bad-tempered gossip, for the strain was intense. In this school hidden away in the heart of the countryside, there were in the winter of 1943 some fifty or sixty students, who were being trained to be dropped by parachute in occupied countries, whence they would send home by Morse those messages, which were essential to the carrying out of underground warfare.
>
> In response to messages, aircraft, flying by night from secret bases in England, would take loads of containers slung like bombs, and

release them over small fields in the heart of France or Norway, where anxious patriots awaited the distant hum of the aircraft motors before flashing their torches at the western sky. But these parachute operations could not take place without communications, and radio was the essential link. These solemn students, men and women alike, in this country-house, would become the radio operators who would make these parachute operations possible. They had to learn how to install a set, to fix the aerial so that it attracted the minimum of attention, to remedy minor defects, to tap out their messages at speed, to identify, despite jamming, their distant home station. They had to become familiar with the touch on the key of their partner at the home station, and more important still, they had to acquire an individual technique by which they would themselves be infallibly recognised. They, more than any other officers who were to be sent into occupied countries, had to learn how to live unsuspected and unnoticed. The need for self-sufficiency was great; they had to be prepared to live alone without friends, for months at a time if necessary. The preparation was long and severe; it required much patience to go on tapping day after day without apparent progress. Disheartenment was very frequent and any form of mental anxiety was apt to retard progress in the most spectacular way.

Among the group of pupils in December 1943 was Eileen, her fair curls bent low over her set, patiently practising hour after hour, desperately anxious to pass the test, which would permit her to be sent to France, where her sister Jacqueline was already working. Eileen was young, and looked even younger than she was. But the determination to succeed was in her, and she showed all the signs of becoming a really first-class operator.

The day I spent down at the school was the occasion on which the instructor was lecturing on radio-detector vans. He explained that the Germans used harmless-looking delivery vans for the purpose of tracking radio transmitters. The principle was as simple as the apparatus was complex. If the equipment in a van picked up a transmission on a wavelength, which was not catalogued, the site of the transmitter was stalked by three vans, each moving in the direction in which the signals became stronger and stronger. By this means a 'fix' was obtained, which enabled the detectors to locate the transmitter within an area of twenty or thirty yards square. A police cordon was then thrown around the suspected area, and the flats or houses combed until the set was found and its operator arrested. Eileen's face was grim as she listened to this explanation, but her chin was thrust forward as the means for avoiding detection were examined and explained. She was determined to remember this complicated business. She felt that Jacqueline would be pleased if she could get through the examinations with credit. Besides, her life might depend upon her remembering. But she found the effort a great strain, and when the time came for her to leave the school and prepare for her departure, she showed by certain signs of emotion that she was not as confident as her ready smile would lead one to believe.[15]

According to her supervisor's report, Didi was not as successful as had been hoped.

She is not very intelligent or practical and is lacking in shrewdness and cunning. She has a bad memory, is inaccurate and scatterbrained. She seems keen, but her work was handicapped by lack of the power to concentrate.

In character she is very feminine and immature; she seems to lack all experience of the world and would probably be easily influenced by others.

She is lively and amusing and has considerable charm and social gifts. She talks a lot and is anxious to draw attention to herself but was generally liked by the other students.

It is doubtful whether this student is suitable for employment in any capacity on account of her lack of experience.

CODES. Taught Innocent Letter based on Playfair, with conventions.

Considerable practice required.[16]

Buckmaster was known for overruling some of these negative reports and sending in agents anyway. Maybe Didi got the required practice in the weeks before she was flown out. However, there were other courses students attended at Beaulieu before being sent into the field.

The chief instructor at The Drokes was Major Skilbeck. Nancy Wake, an Australian woman who attended the course, recalled giving him the shock of his life. She didn't know who he was, but wanted to ensure he knew that women were a force to be reckoned with. She sneaked into the drawing room, hid behind a sofa and took out her Colt pistol. Maybe he'd seen her go into the room as he didn't bother knocking and walked straight in. She heard him talking to the others and then, when she was sure he was in the room, she stood up and pulled the trigger – twice. He reacted as if he'd really been shot, but when he realised it was just a hoax, he just laughed. It turned out that he was supportive of women's rights and was very impressed by her sense of security and quick reactions. 'Be aggressive and alert', they had been taught. 'Surprise is essential' and 'double tap'.[17]

His preliminary lecture started by emphasising the need for tight security. His French, like that of almost all their instructors, was fluent. They were not to leave the estate unaccompanied, not to enter the village and not to use the telephone to make or receive calls. Codenames must be used at all times with him and all their instructors. Under no circumstances were they to use their real Christian names or surnames.

Then came an outline of what they were going to do over the three weeks, how they were going to do it and why. The main course involved agent technique, clandestine life, personal security, methods of communication and recruitment in the field. Other sessions would cover how to recognise the different French and German police and security forces, how to recognise their badges, how to act if under surveillance and how to maintain cover if arrested. The answer to a question as to whether there would be any practical sessions was yes.

They were told that they could help the war effort strategically, economically and politically. He then launched into a fascinating lesson on propaganda – applied psychology, really. As agents, they would be in a position to influence the morale of the people they mixed with, friend and foe. What they said and what they did could improve their morale or destroy it.

Later they were introduced to their propaganda instructor, a well-spoken, handsome, highly intelligent man with kind, sparkling eyes who made a big impression. His name was Kim Philby.

Germany's Fifth Column had been successfully infiltrated into many countries. Potentially, they were already in Britain and action needed to be taken to counteract them. He detailed how propaganda was already being used to influence the opinion of the people in Germany and its armed forces in occupied Europe. He explained how the BBC and other organisations were trying to raise the spirits of the subjugated people who opposed occupation. It was this latter group who Great Britain was helping. Particular groups of people were pointed out who they ought to target, the opinionists, local government officials, trade union officials, religious leaders and, interestingly, the most important group, he stressed, was women. It was women who helped keep the families together during the war. It was women who helped keep the children's spirits up and looked to the future. It was women who could influence their fathers, their sons, their husbands, their brothers, their uncles and their cousins. It was women who were helping the resistance groups in France, Denmark, Belgium, Holland, Norway, Poland, Czechoslovakia, Greece, Italy and the Balkans.

Black, grey and white propaganda was explained – black being completely false, white being completely true, grey being somewhere in the middle. Examples of black propaganda were BBC and newspaper reports exaggerating the number of German losses, over-emphasising the success of Allied bombing missions, stories of top German officials having hospital treatment for venereal disease or disclosures about secret hoards of stolen gold and paintings being found in their homes – all meant to disillusion their subordinates. They were asked to imagine other examples. Imaginary football matches between prisoners-of-war and their German guards in which the Allies won.

White propaganda included the football results, the weather forecast and concert reports. 'Propaganda may lead to passive Resistance; passive Resistance plus propaganda may lead to sabotage; passive Resistance and sabotage plus propaganda may lead to guerilla warfare'.

To prepare Didi for life in France, he also referred to French propaganda. The Vichy police put out the message that agents were coming from England under the orders of de Gaulle to cause trouble – and eventually death – amongst the peaceable French folk who would otherwise live in peace and relative tranquillity. Should they have any information about these 'insurgents', 'agents provocateurs' or 'terrorists', they would be rewarded for anything that might lead to their arrest.

They were shown copies of the *Courrier de l'Air*, four-page A5 leaflets that the RAF were dropping over France. They included a selection of carefully chosen news items and photographs that were supportive of the Allies and derogatory of the Germans, as well as weather forecasts, BBC French Service transmission times and the sports results.

There was advice on how to convince groups, in their own interest and in the interests of liberation, that there was action they should and ought to take. Everyone had to be encouraged to take part, young, old, male, female, rich and poor. Random acts of sabotage, recalcitrance and pernickety attention to dotting every 'i' and crossing every 't'. Office staff, shop workers, factory workers and railway employees could do their bit to bring down the *Boches'* war economy. Forms could be incorrectly filled in, vital sections omitted, references could be misspelt, index cards filed in the wrong place, quoting wrong telephone numbers, taking huge amounts of time before answering the phone, picking the phone up and then putting it down or not answering it at all, telling people to wait and going to the toilet or going outside for a cigarette before dealing with their enquiry. Pure and deliberate procrastination.

Drivers needed to be encouraged to drive slowly and take detours, consciously delaying delivery times, by several days preferably. Traffic jams had to be encouraged. Sharp stones could be carefully inserted in bicycle, motorcycle, car or lorry tyres. Boxes marked 'FRAGILE' could be accidentally dropped. Cartons or piles of tins could be stacked at precarious angles so they would collapse at the slightest knock. Wrong numbers could be chalked on the side of delivery wagons and wrong destination labels stuck on the side of crates and railway trucks. Railway guards could lock lavatory doors when *Boches* VIPs were on board. Business post could be delivered to the wrong address or accidentally spilt into the river. Light bulbs could be accidentally broken by electricians carrying out repairs, fuses and valves removed, connections loosened and circuits overloaded. Mechanics might under-tighten nuts. Plumbers might accidentally flatten lubricating pipes with their hammers or stuff rags into pipes causing a blockage. Welders might under-heat rivets. Architects and engineers could design minute flaws in their blueprints. Leaving the tap dripping on a freezing cold night in the factory or laboratory workshop was recommended. In particular, known *Boches* sympathisers or collaborators had to be reported to their superiors or to the Gestapo as being involved in guerilla activity for some of these subversive activities.

Later they were shown how to organise an opinion poll, how to spread information and, as they did not have time to learn how to print, were given examples of fliers and clandestine newspapers. In his mid-thirties and quite handsome, Philby was well-liked. But of course there was no possibility of romance.

Major Skilbeck introduced their weapons training by reminding them that the SOE's principle was that whoever fires first wins the day. Although Didi had had some weapons training at Winterfold and Thame Park, he insisted that they polished their technique. The best method he suggested was in front of a mirror. In one movement they had to turn, draw and fire. Again and again they were forced to do it. If the turn was too slow, the leg was in the wrong position, the arm was too high or too low, they had to do it again. They must have practised twenty or thirty times before they got it right. It then became natural.

They used Sten guns and pistols with live ammunition in an indoor firing range and also outside in the grounds. Sometimes, faced with about ten moving mannequins in the shape of German soldiers and civilians, they had to open fire and shoot the right target. Not only did it test their reflex speed, but also identification. When the gun jammed they were told bluntly that, if that happened, they would be dead for sure. Greasing weapons regularly was essential.

No doubt Didi had many early nights, exhausted with the day's work and intense physical exertions. However, sometimes she would be woken up by loud banging on the door at some ungodly hour in the morning. An officer would storm in shouting at them to get up and, without dressing, they were ordered downstairs for questioning. Two men wearing long black leather coats and wide brimmed black hats shouted and screamed at them, asking them questions about their identity and demanding they answer. They had to make sure their cover story was kept exactly to the letter.

As their interrogators were also their examiners, there was double the anguish as they wrote thorough comments on their performance, which were read out during their debriefs at the end of each course. As the interrogation intensified, it became more and more realistic. They used bright spotlights that they shone in their face. Sometimes they were handcuffed so they could do nothing as they were hit about the head, on the arms and had their legs kicked. Some reported being forced to strip in front of the others and stand there whilst they searched her mouth, vagina and backside. Imagine what Didi felt like if she had to endure this or was forced to watch the same thing being done to the others.

The tension must have been extreme. There would have been the smell, not just of the human bodily odours, but of fear. 'What were you doing at five o'clock? Why did you go out? Why were you at the railway station? Were you meeting a friend? What was his name? What were you wearing? Your accomplices have confessed. They know everything. You're lying. You're lying.' They were very realistic. Far too good perhaps, but deep inside the students knew that this was probably one of the best exercises they could get. It certainly helped Didi later that year.

In their debriefing session they were told of agents who had escaped imprisonment in France and got back to Britain. They had been able to provide details of the tortures being used. Being stripped naked, being hung up by the wrists or skewered on meat hooks, having your teeth and nails pulled out with pliers, having cigarettes stubbed out on your skin, being given electric shocks all over your body or nearly being drowned. It must have filled Didi with absolute horror. Most tortures made you semi-conscious after a time. It was said that if you could withstand the first quarter of an hour without 'talking', you probably would not talk at all. As well as giving them confidence at withstanding interrogation and torture, more importantly it would have motivated them to avoid capture.

It is not known if there were religious services during the course. Maybe Didi found opportunities to call in to the Blessed Virgin and Holy Child parish church in Beaulieu, but more likely, she received communion during visits from a Catholic chaplain.

On a few evenings after supper they were treated to a showing of Ministry of Information films. A cine-player and screen were set up and a bag of boiled sweets was circulated as they watched *Target for Tonight* and *Fighter Pilot*, both about RAF pilots engaged in secret operations. A much shorter one featured a commando raid on German shipping and factories in the Lofoten islands in Arctic Norway. Others were stirring talks encouraging good old British patriotism. Do your duty for King and Country sort of thing.

Some of the more interesting lessons were in the Great Hall of the Abbey. There was a monastery built in the thirteenth century, which, they were told, looked identical to its mother abbey in Normandy. Applied espionage was completely new to Didi and the others. They were taught how to ensure no-one had entered their room by pulling out one of their hairs, licking it and laying it across the outside door jamb. When they came back later, they could check to see if it was still there. They were also taught how to put a dead leaf in a door lock and dust wardrobe and drawer handles with talcum powder to see if they had been tampered with.

One skill of particular use, and a bit of fun to practice, was surveillance. They were given lots of theory, first as the pursuer to make sure they were not spotted and then as the quarry to ensure they were not being followed. The best use of shop and downstairs windows, doorways, side streets, subways and crowds was explained.

They spent some time learning how best to use telephone booths. First of all they would write a message on a piece of paper, put it in a newspaper remembering which page it was on, go into a booth, use the phone, leave the paper on the shelf and, when they rendezvoused with their contact, tell them the page number. When it was their turn to do the pick-up, they would hear the page number when they passed, go into the booth, make a fictitious call, get the message and leave. In fact, they did not need to tell them the page number, they just mouthed it. Hours practising French lip reading helped.

After the theory came the practice. On some of the early sorties they were taken out in a covered truck and dropped in Bournemouth or Southampton and took turns as hunter and prey. They had to find key buildings and be able to plot them on a map when they were debriefed. Keeping to the crowds was drummed into them. The objective was to get to a particular destination without the tail touching you on the sleeve. One student recalled being given a bit of a start, walking casually along the main shopping street, turning suddenly into a side street, entering the side door of a shop and leaving by the front entrance and then doing the same thing in pubs and in the train station. The bigger hotels like the Norfolk and Royal Bath had lifts so they would enter the foyer, take a lift, get out, go down the stairs and leave by another door.

They practised ruses like stopping to look at their wristwatch and then jumping onto a moving bus to give the impression they did not think they were being tailed. There was one piece of useful advice they were told that Sherlock Holmes recommended, which was not getting into the first waiting cab, not the second, but the third and to have made a mental note of the first two cabs' number plates and a description of the drivers. Why? So that you could look around every now and again to see if they were following. Other smart advice was to give the wrong address when you got in and then change it later on, not to where you wanted to go, but somewhere nearby like a church, a bar or a department store. Then get out and walk to your destination.

That way, if the cab driver was questioned, they would not know exactly where you went.

The debrief was not just an account of how well they did. Before that they had to give as detailed a description as they could of the person who they were tailing or who was tailing them, the route they took, what they did, who was contacted and when and what precautions were taken, if any, against the surveillance.

Didi and the other students would not have realized how much of what they were taught was acquired from the experiences of the Irish Republican Army and the guerrillas of the Spanish Civil War. They learned about absolute secrecy, the procedures of codes, passwords, disguises, only using safe houses, never using small guest houses, only staying in modest-sized hotels, never staying in the same house more than one night and using *cachettes* or *boîtes aux letters*. Eccentric methods suggested for the latter were to hollow out a turnip or a pumpkin, like at Halloween, put the message in and float it downstream to the next village. Tapping oil drums in Morse was suggested as was using smoke signals like American Indians. The ideal locations for leaving messages would be at bakers, butchers, chemists, tobacconists, the waiting rooms of doctors or dentists and if they could manage it, a nunnery.

The SOE's liaison officer used to visit. His clothes were the envy of them all, so well-cut they looked like they had to have been made by professional gentleman's tailor. His illustrated lectures were on the German Army and how to recognise the different ranks within in its hierarchy. 'Know your enemy' was his motto. The *Shutzpolizei* were the Germans' semi-military town police who did mundane jobs like controlling traffic and keeping law and order, and the *Sicherheitdienst*, sometimes known as *Sipo*, were the Security Police, which included Heinrich Himmler's *Schutzstaffel* – the SS.

He showed them uniform identification charts pinned up on the wall, which they had to study. Then he spread out dozens of photographs on their desks, which they had to put into sets, those showing the Gestapo, the Vichy police and the *Milice*. In a brief aside, he told them that when the French army surrendered, a semi-chivalrous body of gentlemen set up the *Milice* to restore military honour, but ended up collaborating with the Germans and attracted a range of underground criminals and thugs who, they were told, disgusted the Gestapo. One French man claimed that they were not just the scum of the earth, but the scum of that scum.

The Gestapo *dienstrock* was easy to identify by their black gabardine jackets with silver-buttoned jacket pockets, silver-piped collar with the runes and SS tabs, red armbands with the swastika on, tight-fitting black corduroy breeches, black tie, peaked caps with silver piping and two small silver badges – the outstretched eagle holding the swastika in its claws and the skull and cross-bones.

The *Milice* wore the distinctive black berets, a black jacket with silver buttons, a leather belt around their middle and various insignia on their lapels and breast pockets. Their trousers were baggier than the German uniform and were worn inside black polished riding boots.

What he called the *feldgendarmerie* might also wear a brass breastplate underneath their jackets. Their winter clothing included steel-grey ankle-length greatcoats, which, in the case of the officers, were made of leather. Probably to reduce their worries, he told them that many of the German officers in the Gestapo were more likely experienced in the criminal underworld than counter intelligence.

The local gendarmes were easily identified by their round, flat-topped, black peaked *kepi*, which had a white rim around the top. Like the *Milice* they wore a black gabardine jacket with silver buttons, insignia on their lapels, leather belt and loose black or dark blue trousers. Most had a pistol holster, but some carried a wooden, lead-filled cosh. Where their sympathies lay would be difficult to assess. Some had been helpful to the Resistance in losing important documents, being lax about their security between the police station and the prison and accepting bribes to allow prisoners to escape. The *Milice* were a different kettle of fish.

Following Germany's invasion of the Soviet Union in June 1941, Joseph Darnard, a Vichy politician, collaborated with the Germans by organising a right-wing military group called *Service d'Ordre Legionnaire*. This group, they were told, was instrumental in the *rafles*, the rounding up of anti-government individuals and what the Vichy government described as insurgents and terrorists – members of the Resistance. They had grown into the *Milice Française*, the Vichy government's secret police with an estimated 45,000 fanatical Nazi sympathisers. No wonder some called them the French Gestapo. Although many unemployed urban poor joined as the wages were good – 2,500 francs a month compared to the 1,300 of an industrial worker – there were also opportunities for pillage when Jews and other 'undesirables' were thrown out of their properties. Most seemed to be criminals, violent, sadistic thugs from the underworld who, rather than face imprisonment, volunteered to work for the Germans. They were generally in their late-twenties or early-thirties.

Didi's group was told the Germans referred to them as *V-Männer*, a nick name for *Vertrauensmänner*, the 'trusted ones'. The Resistance called them *Doriotistes* or *Malprat*, hooligans employed by the police who were impossible to identify unless you were in big cities as they tended to go around night clubs dressed in the latest fashion of white turtle-neck jumpers, tight black trousers and white leather shoes. The local *gendarmerie*, they were told, might well be friendly or at least neutral, but they would be less likely bluffed than the Germans.

There were some fascinating lectures on using what were termed 'secret' inks. Didi must have heard of 'invisible' ink and played with writing with lemon juice and blood when she was a child, but she would have been amazed and probably shocked to learn and actually see how you could also write with saliva, urine, semen, egg white, milk, fruit juice and solutions of everyday household items like sugar, baking powder, borax, starch and porridge oats. However, they were all discouraged as they could easily be read when the writing material was exposed to heat. Instead they were shown how, using dissolved headache powder, certain laxatives and chemicals found on the waxed wrapping paper around fruits, the writing only became legible when exposed to ammonia fumes, mercury vapour, fluorescent light, ultra-violet light and even certain sounds.

It was a bit like a conjuring trick. He brought out of his pocket one of the one-time pads and a torch, which, he told them, had an ultra-violet beam, which lit up hundreds of tiny letters on the silk. These were WOKs used in coding and decoding messages. To make them disappear, all that was needed was for an ordinary-looking pencil to be rubbed across the cloth. It wasn't ordinary though. It contained special chemicals that reacted with the invisible ink.

The favoured medium though was newspaper. Simple, really. All you had to do was carefully place small dots of the secret ink above or below selected letters or words that spelt out your message. Obviously, the method had to be agreed with your contacts.

Another lesson Didi had was using disguises. An extremely well-dressed gentleman reeking of money and expensive after-shave came especially for the day from Max Factor in London. Although Didi would have known something about make-up, this man was an artist. His point was that there may well be circumstances in which they needed to change their own or someone else's appearance in an emergency, as a matter of life and death. They were told how they had to become extremely observant – not just about themselves, but also with others. He drummed into them that they had to look natural and ordinary whilst they were doing unnatural and extraordinary things. 'He that has a secret to hide,' he told them, 'should not only hide it, but hide the fact that he has it to hide.'

Within half an hour they had to be able to completely change their appearance, and not just their clothes. Didi would have been able to darken her hair with powdered charcoal or ash from the fire, to lighten it with chamomile juice or to 'grey' it with a special whitener. By combing her hair back off her forehead, back-combing it or fluffing it up a little, she could assume a different persona. She could change the contours of her face by stuffing sponge pads into her cheeks and using ordinary lead pencil and water to emphasise her wrinkle lines or highlight or lessen spots. Shadows could be created with make-up, iodine could be used to discolour teeth and collodion to fill in cleft chins, dimples or even to create scars.

Just in case, they were also shown how to change a man's appearance by making him look unshaven and adding fake whiskers. Reducing breast size only required a strip of torn bed sheet strapped tightly around one's chest.

It was all very clever. Whilst they were practising their disguises, the instructors disguised themselves as well, so it was virtually impossible to tell who these new people were in the room. Very disconcerting. They were asked what aspects of a person never change. This led them to practice observing and then describing the shape of people's heads, their eyes, noses, ears, forehead, Adam's apple, even their hands and feet. Then they had to identify those physical features that did change. They could only come up with spots, suntan, bruises and perhaps a tattoo. The discussion led them to recognize that, should it be deemed necessary, they, or others, had to be able to alter their whole outward appearance, personality and mental attitude.

Idiosyncrasies had to be created or subdued. Light-skinned people had to appear tanned. Tall people had to learn to stoop. There was the suggestion that putting folded cardboard inside one of your shoes would help make you limp. Wearing shoes with and without steel tips was suggested instead of the wooden-soled clogs many people in France were wearing. Spotlessly clean people had to become grubby. Town clothes had to be replaced with country clothes. Even favourite cigarette brands, newspapers, restaurants, football teams, politics and religion had to be changed. Having several hats of different shapes and scarves of different colours that you could swap around at different times of the day was suggested. Hand writing had to be altered. Even one's accent, intonation and unconscious mannerisms like fidgeting, ring turning, finger tapping, hair twisting and head and skin scratching had to be changed if you were to adopt a completely new identity.

To help them improve their memory and observation skills they spent time on Pelmanism, spot the difference, and games where you had to study a person for a minute. The students went out and the instructor changed something in the room. The students came back in and they had to guess what it was that had been changed.

Preparation and adherence to your cover story had to be perfect. Things they were told might catch them out included questions like 'where did you get your laundry done?' or 'where did you get your hair done?'. There was one occasion when a student reported being taken for a map reading exercise and picnic in the New Forest in a large black Daimler. Very pleasant. On the return trip they were ushered into the car so that they sat in a different seat than on the way and told to ensure that under no circumstance were they to divulge the fact that they had swapped seats.

There was a report of one woman student being told to use a convincing cover story that she and a male student had spent the afternoon making love in the meadow by the river. One imagines that this was not Didi, given her strong religious views. Thinking that they would be given the third degree, they went over it again and again with each other in minute detail. When they were interrogated, her cover story broke down when she was asked whether the lovemaking was *'le style Indienne ou classique?'*.

It was drummed into them that the simplest thing to do when being interrogated was to stick as closely as possible to the truth. Anything complicated just made things ten times worse. Looking someone full in the face and telling them lies would not have come easy to Didi. She had been brought up to tell the truth, especially to people of importance. Lying was what con-men and criminals did. She wasn't naturally devious. The advice was to look at it as if you were an actor on stage, learning a role, convincing the audience who had paid good money to be entertained. They wanted to see a good play and good actors had to be convincing. Keeping up playing a role for a long time was a challenge. Not letting your guard down was of key importance, especially when faced with challenging circumstances. All this training was to enable the students to pass as ordinary French citizens once they were in France.

There were some particularly unpleasant incidents, which are etched indelibly in some female agents' memories. Throughout the course the women grew to trust and respect the instructors, impressed not only with their knowledge, but also their level of understanding of the intricacies of everyday life as a secret agent. What some of them did to them was shocking, yet, in retrospect, they probably recognised it was essential.

One student recalled chatting in the sitting room and listening to music on the wireless one evening when the house was invaded. Caught completely unawares, four men, faces blackened, wearing black shirts and pants, ran in screaming and shouting and jumped on them with the aim of tying them up. Although the women retaliated and used a variety of French expletives, they didn't get the chance to inflict many injuries. Whilst some put up a struggle, there was the element of knowing it was a set-up so they felt compelled to go along with it. Their brute force eventually overcame them. Sticking plaster was stuck over their mouths, cuffs were put on their wrists and they were bullied and beaten, dragged into the dining room and made to stand on chairs with their arms over their heads.

One by one they were taken into the kitchen and forcibly sat down on a chair. No sooner had they done that than it was pulled out from underneath them so they collapsed on the floor. Hauled back up again and sat down, spotlights were shone in their face. The tape was torn off and they were interrogated at length in French about that day's events by two thugs in black leather greatcoats and tin hats toting rifles with bayonets attached. All the time, the conversation was being recorded. Before long they realised that they were being tested to see whether they would change their story about where they had been sitting in the car.

They then played back what the previous student had said and forced them to listen carefully to the exact wording of their answers and identify any flaws in their statements. It became very clear that their interrogation had been recorded too, ready to use on the others. The whole event lasted a couple of hours, but it must have been very nerve-racking to have been so badly treated.

The debriefing identified that, should a similar occasion arise whilst they were in the field, they had to speak slowly. Never answer a question immediately. Think carefully before you say anything. Never display any affection towards your interrogator. Don't react. Don't retaliate verbally. Try to stay calm and indignant. Try to sublimate all emotions. Desensitise yourself. Don't believe any of their statements. They may be true, but they may well not be. Some returned prisoners had reported that the Germans seemed to know the codenames and real names of agents as well as details of their training courses and instructors' names. Whether this was bluff, double bluff or even triple bluff, ignore it. One imagines Didi listened intently during these sessions. It was vital, elemental human survival.

One useful suggestion – instruction, really – was to count whenever they were under duress. Count into the hundreds and thousands if necessary, especially if they give you an injection. All that would be in your mind under anaesthetic would be numbers.

Never say anything that could shed any light whatsoever onto your real mission. The person who you talk to may be a paid informer. There may be hidden microphones or cameras, even two-way mirrors. Even when you are released, be very suspicious. Almost certainly they would put a tail on you. It was then that they had to 'disappear' and change their appearance and make triply sure they did not lead them to any other members of their network.

Returned agents explained to them that 'intelligence' was one of the new military sciences. If Didi had not heard of psychological warfare, she began to get an inkling of part of it. Knowledge of the enemy's intelligence gathering was being updated by the day. Agents in the field were sending back invaluable wireless messages as well as bringing back to England written and verbal reports. They included details of escaped prisoners' experiences and contacts in sophisticated escape networks that were in place to ensure downed pilots, aircrew and Resistance members received as much help as possible to return to 'Blighty'. The SOE's intelligence officers used their debriefing sessions to glean enormously valuable information about the Gestapo's interrogation methods as well as the current situation behind enemy lines.

Didi would have been very reassured to hear this; also that huge sums of money were regularly supplied to the Resistance specifically to bribe the *Milice*, the Gestapo and prison guards into letting prisoners escape, as well as to pay for secret accommodation, food, medical supplies, to arrange transport and ensure the silence of potential helpers. She might have been reassured to be told that even if they were to be arrested, all would not be lost. The reputation of the Gestapo was built more on terror and ruthlessness than intelligence. Whilst they might well try to frighten prisoners into divulging their secrets; they were also looking for ways of 'turning' the agent, persuading them using any variety of methods, to work for them.

Before their visitors left, they added that their best bet was to keep up the impression that they were normal, honest, hard-working French citizens, going about their everyday business. They had to tell them that they would do their very best to answer their questions, but stress repeatedly that they had no real knowledge of what they were looking for. The bottom line was that, the longer they were interrogated, the more chance it would give their colleagues to get away. All this proved very useful to Didi when she was sent into the field.

In one highly illegal session, a man, introduced to them as a convicted Glaswegian burglar called Johnny, gave them the benefit of his experiences. Like another visiting mentor known as 'the Forger', he must have been specially released from prison to contribute his criminal expertise to the war effort. What he stressed at the very beginning was that they had to learn the cat burglar's skills so that they could teach the local people how to break into properties. Obviously they might have to, and in which case it was absolutely imperative they made every effort not to get caught. Those they sent in could plead, if they were caught, that they were a real burglar and not give away the true nature of the crime when tortured.

He took them outside and showed them how to open and start locked cars and trucks with a long strip of celluloid, a gear or brake cable from a bike or even a piano wire if you could find one. He started both the car and the truck within four and a half minutes without breaking any windows. After a few practice sessions they could as well! House-breaking also became surprisingly easy. In theory, Didi would have learned how to use brown paper and a tin of treacle to break open a window silently, how to climb up drain pipes and what items of clothing are best used for burglary. The way to stop a dog recognising your scent apparently is to defecate somewhere in the building or outside.

The theory was pretty safe. The practice wasn't. They were encouraged to try out these new skills on the officers' cars and trucks and on some of the other properties on the estate. Whilst it was meant to be a bit of fun, some of the resident trainees did not take kindly to being disturbed by burglars at three or four in the morning.

Opening safes was a bit tricky. To do so they were taken to a nearby pit in the woods. A large 'tin opener' could be used on the older models if you had the strength, but gelignite was the key. Putting some in the lock or by the hinges usually did the trick. If the safe wobbled when you pushed it, then it was recommended you turn it around and get in from the back. If all else failed and it was essential you break it open, use more gelignite. He also showed them other useful skills like how to unpick handcuffs, how to make false keys and how best to poison a guard dog.

What would have interested Didi was what she could expect when she was back in France. Whilst she had been out of the country, the occupying German administrators had ordered the Vichy government to implement various new rules and regulations. She would probably have known about the *Ausweis*, the official pass that allowed people to travel between the occupied and the Free Zone. It was stamped onto the back of identity papers. In 1944 it helped people evade suspicion during the night curfews if they had a journey to make. Didi would have

Left: 1. Didi in 1937.
Above: 2. Eileen Nearne or 'Didi' as she liked to be known (the first on the left) with some friends.

Right: 3. Didi's sister Jacqueline, 1937.
Below: 4. Didi (on the left) at Boulogne-Sur-Mer in 1938.

Above left: 5. Didi's father, John Nearne.
Above centre: : 6. Her brother, Frederick Nearne, who left France for England when war broke out in 1939.
Above right: 7. Her brother, Francis Nearne, who was recruited by Jacqueline in May 1943 to work as a courier and Lysandered back to England five months later.
Left: 8. Didi (on the right) with her mother and her sister at St Egreve (Isere) France, 1942.
Below left: 9. Didi (on the left) with her sister Jacqueline (on the right) in 1942 before leaving for England.

Above: 10. Didi in London.
Right: 11. Didi in her FANY
uniform.

12. Didi in London.

13. Jacqueline in her FANY uniform.

14. Jacqueline again.

15. Didi in Nice, 1941.

16. Didi (on the right) in her FANY uniform.

Top: 17. Didi's medals – including the MBE and the French *Croix de Guerre* with palms.
Above: 18. Jacqueline's medals – she also has the Belgium *Croix du Merite* with silver palms.
Left: 19. Didi after the war.

20. With Jacqueline, her sister (on the left) in front of one of Didi's paintings, 1970.

21. Didi's Camden town retirement in June, 1986.

22. Didi October, 1962.

23. Didi, left, and Odette (Sansom/Churchill) Hallowes, at the 1993 unveiling of a plaque commemorating those who died at Ravensbrück concentration camp. They were two of the few survivors.

24. Didi with Odile in 2009 at Teignmouth.

25. Didi in later years.

26. The blue plaque that Odile had put up on her aunt's home at 2 Lisburne Crescent, Torquay.

been provided with one before she left by X-Section, the SOE's forgery department.

Didi had left France in April 1942. If she had delayed her departure much later she would have been arrested and interned as an enemy alien. The Germans started their takeover of what had been the unoccupied zone on 11 November, two days after the Americans invaded Algeria and Morocco in North Africa. Italian troops were sent into parts of south-east France; Nice, Toulon, Monaco and Corsica. Although this had made life for the Resistance much more difficult, it actually meant that there were increasing numbers joining up.

They were told that there would not be much fuel. There was no coal. Why? Almost all French coal was exported. The only cars they'd see on the road, apart from German military personnel, would be doctors on medical missions and community and business leaders. Farmers made do with *gazogéne*, methane obtained by heating charcoal. Everyone else, including the priests, cycled everywhere and at home people burned wood. In the south they burned olive branches. Didi had had to collect firewood when she lived in Grenoble.

She was told what to wear, what not to wear, to renew her tobacco, bread and other *cartes d'alimentation* – ration cards – on the first of every month and what not to ask for in *magasins*. The *jours sans* were the 'days without', when spirits were not available in the cafés. Asking for café noir or café crème was a dead give-away as there was hardly any milk in France – it was all exported. Should she find a restaurant that did have some, she was never to put the milk in first. Everyone in France would know you're British if you did that. She had to ask for ersatz café and '*limonade*' not 'Vermouth cassis'. The only drinks she was recommended asking for that were worth drinking were *Grenache, Banyuls* and *Muscat*.

She would have been shown agents' ration cards with the letter A stamped on them. If she had asked what the A meant, she would have been told 'adult' and that it was important that new agents knew what the different letters stamped on them meant. E was for children under three, presumably *enfants*. J1 was for children between three and six. J2 was for those between six and thirteen. J3 was for thirteen to twenty-one-year-olds. A was for those between twenty-one and seventy. T was for those in the latter group who did heavy manual work. C was for those in agriculture. V was for those over seventy. The J3 group got better rations. Those in urban areas got more than those in the countryside as Vichy thought that they grew their own food. Children got better milk rations. Pregnant women, nursing mothers and anyone who was sick got more as did those working in *Boche* industries like Todt.

One particularly useful session was where a returned woman agent visited The Drokes to give them the benefit of her recent experiences. The first thing she did was to empty her bag out onto the table and tell them how they had to be able to use the correct French for all the items. She did the same with her purse, stressing that the most important were what appeared to be family photographs. These, she explained, were part of her cover story. There must have been about twenty coupons and ration cards. She recalled an identity card with details of her parents, a medical card and a work permit. She also told them there'd be petrol ration coupons and that women were not issued with tobacco coupons. It was imperative they paid their bicycle tax on time and learned what the blank coupons at the back of the ration book could be used for. Listening to *Topo Culinaire* at 06.00 hours on Saturdays would enlighten them, as would reading the latest food regulations column in the newspaper.

There was also advice about travelling on the train. Although it was the quickest means of transport, it had its disadvantages. The carriages were often crowded, the corridors jammed with people without a seat who stood by windows or sat on their luggage.

There was often a chaos of exhausted travellers. Some slept on the floor amid their valises and parcels with the smell of dirt, dust, the musky coverings on the seats and the mix of human sweat, pipe and cigarette tobacco and the wafts of mostly cheap, but occasionally expensive perfume. There were icy draughts in winter and there was debilitating heat in summer. You didn't need to fill in forms, though, as you did in a hotel. Some in the Resistance virtually lived on the trains. They caught a few hours' sleep between stops and managed to bluff their way through ticket inspections and guard checks. Getting the slow train rather than the express was recommended as they had fewer checks. They had to be prepared for cold nights as trains weren't heated. The other advice they were given was to get off the train a stop or two before the main destination and steal a bicycle. Larger stations had more *contrôles*, often with armed gendarmes or, worse, the Gestapo.

A successful method recommended for putting off the advances of an unwelcome *Boche* soldier was to tell them you had syphilis or bite your cheek, cough up blood and tell them you had tuberculosis. They questioned her about women's things, like where they could get tissue paper for their periods, what the attitudes were towards relationships and free love, how to get hold of condoms if they needed them and how to go about procuring an abortion.

After answering all these questions frankly, she showed them the best places to hide documents. It was best to unpick the hem of your coat or jacket and insert them in the lining and then carefully sew them up again. Underneath shoulder pads was a good location. She'd heard of prisoners sending messages out in the hem of their dirty lingerie. If they were lucky enough to be lifted out and brought back to England, she had no hesitation in saying the best things to bring back would be Chanel No. 5, *Moët et Chandon* and expensive French dresses.

Before they left she stressed that being in the field was a very lonely life. It wasn't glamorous. They'd miss their families. They'd not have friends to confide in, but, if they could cope, the sense of reward for helping liberating France would be enough. To raise their spirits, she told them as many of the current jokes in France as she could remember, the most popular songs, and the names of the latest cult figures on the radio, on stage and in films.

They were also given preparation lessons that were called 'schemes'. These were days out, initially in nearby Southampton or Bournemouth, but later they might be sent to any town or city in the country. They were given a detailed description of people they had to rendezvous with and the locations. They were instructed to always leave an hour between each rendezvous and avoid using cafés or cinemas. Whatever the weather – rain, sleet, snow, freezing temperatures or red-hot sunshine – they had to keep walking. This reduced the chances of them being spotted and gave them a chance to see if they were being tailed.

To help with the scheme they were shown the local Ordnance Survey map from which they had to learn the routes they would take. They were given a password they had to use and the one they had to expect in return. There was an amusing element to passwords. They had to pause somewhere in the sentence. If they responded with a pause in their sentence, they were on their side. If, and only if these passwords had been correctly used, were they to deliver the message and make their way by train back to Beaulieu Road station, where they had to ring a given number to arrange their pick-up. They had to memorise and repeat back to the instructor all this information – the description of the person they were going to meet, the routes they'd used to get to the rendezvous, each other's passwords, the message they had to give, where they had to make their way to afterwards and the telephone number to ring. After all this they were told there would be someone trailing them, pretending to be a German counter-intelligence officer, whom they must elude.

It was suggested to the women that if they did spot a man tailing them, a good idea would be to find a department store and make for the lingerie department. The tail would find it embarrassing to hang around as you searched the hangers for an attractive bra. The other thing that was stressed was looking natural and ordinary when you're doing unnatural and extraordinary things.

The next scheme was rather more complicated and demanded swotting up on the relevant Ordnance Survey map. They were given a detailed cover story, which had to be learned off by heart and then tested on by their conducting officer. They would then be given a list of tasks that needed to be undertaken before returning to Beaulieu. They might be asked to make contact with someone in an office or factory, use passwords, break into a building and steal documents, or find suitable 'safe' houses that an organiser, courier and wireless operator could rent, of which they must be able to describe the rooms, the landlord or landlady and how much the rooms would cost. They also had to find suitable *boîtes aux lettres*.

Although no information on Didi's schemes has come to light, one imagines it was similar to Yvonne Baseden's, another of the SOE's wireless operators. She was sent to a town in the north of England, where she had never been before. She had to find digs and operate her set without being caught by the police who were on the look-out for her, and without being located by the SOE's own detection finders, which were called 'D-Effers'.[18]

There was often a second interrogation session, at about 04.30 when the body's resistance and vitality are at their weakest. Students were violently awoken by a tape being stuck over their mouth, and their hands handcuffed behind their back. A Luger was held at their head before a bag or hood was put over it. All the time two men were screaming at them in German. It would have been really terrifying. Although they may have tried to resist, at that time in the morning they were too weak and, in a state of shock, uncoordinated. They were violently turned out of bed and, not given the chance to put clothes on, were trussed up half naked and forced downstairs. Lights were switched on. When the hood was pulled off their head, they would have seen the 'intruders' in dirty, field grey German uniforms. Their faces were in shadow beneath their caps. Their interrogation was very realistic and they were forced to watch the other students being mistreated.

All attempts to reason with them failed. They were forced to stand on a chair with their hands up. They would not let any of them go to the lavatory. Strong electric lamps were shone in their faces and the heat, the nervous tension, excitement, sweat and fear must have produced an acrid, musky smell.

Their questioning was fierce. They were desperate to break their cover story. Again and again very hostile methods were used, including slaps around the legs and backside and beatings with a cane. Then someone else took over being gentle and polite. Then came more caning. Thankfully they did not try to burn their cigarettes out on the exposed flesh. After about fifteen minutes they were pulled down and left on the floor. It was then the turn of the others.

The intense feeling of humiliation, unwarranted personal intrusion and physical abuse by people they had trusted was juggled with an acknowledgement that it was all a set-up. Were the men doing them a favour or were they taking advantage of their power? The reality of the whole experience was that it was a lesson. A painful one indeed, but they were told that it might happen. And it could be much worse. They had to be prepared for any eventuality. What would they do if it happened? How long would they be able to withstand being beaten? Or real torture?

Would they ever be prepared to change their cover story? What might they be prepared to reveal? How much money would it take? What if they were offered their freedom? Or someone else's? Would they be able to withstand someone being tortured and killed in front of them? Could they tolerate being sexually abused in front of others? These questions were unanswerable then.

There was one question at the end which was meant to throw them. When they finally sat back before being debriefed, one of their superiors asked in English: 'Pass them the ashtray.' If they did, they'd fail. Jones claimed that Didi was able to resist the pressure of her interrogators and, despite witnessing other students breaking, she stood her ground. She realised that she was not like them. Being extremely determined and secretive by nature, she gained strength from these traits. 'You have to be a bit tougher you see, a bit hard on yourself. You have to live in the shadow.'[19]

When the interrogation was over and they were 'released', they were told to keep the whole thing quiet. 'Official Secrets Act,' 'For King and Country,' 'In the interest of security,' 'A valuable learning exercise' and 'Doing the thing that you most fear is the death of fear,' were comments often used. The first fifteen minutes were the worst. If you managed to stay conscious and not reveal anything, you had a good chance of tolerating further pain. Exerting pain and torturing others was in itself exhausting. Sometime it would stop. Be patient. Endure it.

Captain Jimmy Wilson, Didi's survival instructor, was a large, well-built and, as they were to discover, most knowledgeable man in his early-forties. He had a sun-burnt face beneath of shock of sun-bleached fair hair. Despite his obvious experience and skill, he often made comments about how it was wrong that there were women being trained for dangerous work. It was a waste of time and effort in his opinion. He told them they ought to be at home looking after children instead of gallivanting off to the continent. If Didi had had children, being a devout Catholic, she would most certainly have been looking after them, but, as she didn't, this training seemed the best way that she could help with the war effort.

Jimmy taught them field-craft, how to survive on the land. They were to be, in his words, 'Diana's foresters, Gentlewomen of the night, minions of the moon.' They had both morning and evening sessions, which started as walks around the estate. He taught them how to recognise which plants, leaves, fruit, roots and fungi were edible.

Maybe he was asked about French fungi. He stressed that they needed to be 100 per cent certain in their identification and be particularly careful as a number of European species would kill you very painfully, some in minutes, some in hours and some in days. One, he said, was the perfect murder weapon. Put it in someone's omelette and they'd die a few days later; a post mortem would never be able to determine the cause of death.

They ate worms, snails and most kinds of insects, the bark off trees, shoots, roots and leaves. Not in any great quantity, though. Of everything he'd ever eaten, in his experience he thought that moles and bluebottles tasted the worst.

When he started talking about how to catch fish, some of the students who had undergone paramilitary training in Arisaig may have avoided telling him that they had shot Scottish salmon with their Sten guns. Here there were salmon to be caught, but it was mostly trout. His method was using hand grenades. The skill was finding the right part of the river at the right time of day without letting them see your shadow on the water. The shock stunned them, so, depending on how far into the river you'd thrown the grenade, it was simply a matter of finding a long enough stick to poke them towards the bank, taking your shoes and socks off and paddling for them, or going skinny dipping. He was not keen on them doing that.

He showed them how to catch ducks with and without dogs. It was harder without, but basically it worked best if you had a net, string and a narrow stream with ducks on. Pheasants were easier. They were stupid enough to fall for the trap of eating a handful of grain you'd placed underneath a carefully balanced tin, which had to be large enough to trap the bird when you pulled the string holding the stick away. Killing birds was easy, once you got the hang of it. Hold them by their feet and give them a couple of hard chops with the side of your hand on the back of their necks. Plucking them is a waste of time if you're hungry. They were shown how to gut, skin, fillet and cut them into cookable chunks in minutes.

Baking them plastered with clay over a wood fire and ripping them apart with your bare hands was recommended, much juicier than roasting them skewered on a stick. However, boiling them in a pan over the fire for a few hours with roots and berries produced a far better flavour and was a lot more satisfying after the exertion of the hunt. The only problem with that was how hungry you were. Hiding the evidence of their poaching – the feathers, the bones, the carcass, the fire and the disturbed ground – was a useful lesson. The only things they couldn't hide were the screams of the birds. Catching rabbits was easy after ducks.

Poaching skills also included learning how to move silently and stealthily towards their prey, animal or human, to give them the advantage. He emphasised human. They practised sneaking up on each other in daylight and in the dark with varying degrees of success. Jumping on their prey to permanently immobilise them probably proved great fun for the women. Trying to squeeze them into submission produced squeals and giggles of nervous laughter. Jimmy was furious. 'War is a serious business' he kept on telling them.

Other things he taught them in field-craft were marking trees in a wood so as to be able to find their way out, making a bed from bracken or fern, and basic First Aid. In particular they were taught how to fasten splints, tie a ligature around a limb to reduce blood flow and how to treat wounds, especially gun-shot wounds. What Didi's field-craft report was like is not known.

Jimmy taught them another poacher's skill, what he called 'night-craft'. His advised that night outfit be black overalls, black boots, a black balaclava and black silk or woollen gloves. Preferably cotton as you got a better grip. The black for their faces they got from burnt twigs from the fire. Cork was an alternative, but he didn't drink. His objective was for them to acquire the ability to move about silently at night and to recognise the sounds of blackness.

Walking without breaking twigs or causing leaves to rustle took some practice. So did his 'bear crawl', where they moved about on their hands and knees. The 'snake crawl' was flat on the ground, inching forwards using elbows, fingers and toes and not worrying about getting dirty. There wasn't just wet soil, but slugs, snails, all those creepy-crawly things you associate with forest floors as well as animal droppings. It was not the time to be squeamish. Their objective was not to disturb the wood pigeons, the rooks or the jays, which caw loudly if roused. They mustn't scare sheep. Isolated ones might amble away if disturbed, but a flock would stop and stare at the intrusion – a dead give-away. They had to be even more careful about ducks and geese. Not only do they honk loud enough to be heard miles away, they also tend to march towards you – again giving your location away.

Whilst Didi and her group were well looked after at The Drokes, it would not have been not long before they realised that there were other agents being trained in different parts of the estate. Out in the park, Didi would have seen men in battledress on exercises, heard the sound of shots being fired, explosives going off as well as shouts and laughter. There was a miniature railway in one part of the grounds, which she may have been given the chance to ride on. That is if the track hadn't been blown up by aspiring saboteurs.

Part of their field craft lessons included being shown a sketch of the phases of the moon and being told there were only one or two days a month when there was no moon. No light. Recognising those nights was part of their field craft. Equally, the nights on either side of the full moon were the brightest for clandestine activities. The police report that there is a significant increase in crime about the time of the full moon and superintendents of lunatic asylums often used to beat up the inmates before the full moon to subdue their eccentric behaviour.

They were told that when your bedroom light is switched on and wakes you up, it takes several minutes before your eyes completely adjust to artificial light. It's less if you wake up and it's already daylight. But, if you go from the light into the darkness it takes about thirty minutes before your eyes gradually adjust. Staring at something in the dark can play tricks with your eyes. Clouds can become mountains, treetops hills, bushes animals, nearby thistles or clumps of grass distant trees. They were told to try to keep their mouths open as it helps you to hear better and that sound varies according to altitude, temperature, the terrain and even the vegetation.

The lesson was followed by solitary night exercises. The heightened sense of awareness meant that they would become suspicious of everything. A bush or tree in the dark might be a person. It was extremely disconcerting to be taken out on one's own, full moon or none.

Part of their orientation exercises involved being picked up, taken out in the car and driven miles into the depths of the New Forest. They were kept in the dark about this mission. Like other car journeys Didi had been on, her conducting officer used all sorts of roundabout detours to try to confuse them. As it was dark, they would not be sure, where they were going. Some of the journey was along forestry tracks so they thought it might be to one of the other houses. Eventually the car stopped, somewhere in the middle of nowhere and in the middle of the night. They were told to get out, given a haversack and told to find their way back to The Drokes without being apprehended.

More sociable night-time schemes put into practice the sessions they had on landing grounds. A pilot from one of the Special Duties Squadrons provided them with insight into the air side of 'the business'. His aim was to ensure that they would be able to select the best landing grounds. Ideally, each potential site needed to be coded. The choice for what he called a *parachutage* or a 'pick-up' needed to be sent to London, either brought back to England in the organiser's briefcase during a pick-up or transmitted by an S-phone operator on the ground up to a radio operator in the overflying plane. Coordination was a vital key in this game.

He showed them a collection of photographs and silhouettes showing all the different planes that he and his colleagues were flying over France – and Belgium, Holland, Denmark, Norway, Germany, Czechoslovakia, Austria and Poland. They had to be able to recognise which one was which. One, two or four engines was one helpful criterion.

The Lysander and the Hudson would be flown over to deposit agents on the ground and pick up returning agents, downed pilots, crews and 'VIPs'. The Lysander, sometimes called 'The Flying Carrot' or 'Lizzy', could carry two passengers and luggage comfortably. Three would be a tight squeeze. One might have to sit on another's knee. He told them that he could land a Lysander on a stretch of open grassland and stop within 35 yards. Anything longer would be better – a sports field would be good, as long as it was in a remote village. His ideal strip would be closer to 50 yards so the wheels would not get caught in any tree tops or hedges.

After stressing how important it was that there should be no telegraph wires nearby, no ditches or boggy patches, he went on to tell them of a very hairy experience he'd had. On his last trip he'd landed his Lysander in a field in central France, turned ready for take-off, dropped two agents and got out for a smoke. When his three new passengers and their vital documents were safely squeezed in, he climbed back into the cockpit, but, as he began to accelerate, the plane took a nose dive. Its wheels were stuck in the mud. He couldn't go forwards. He couldn't go backwards. He was well and truly bogged. Luckily the 'Reception Committee', members of the French Resistance, were still at hand. The passengers had to get out and everyone pushed and shoved, but to no avail. The longer they waited, the lighter it got and the greater the chance that the Gestapo cars might have arrived. There was no way they could get oxen or horses to haul it out using ropes so he took the executive decision to abort the mission. The plane had to be burned.

He had to destroy his plane to stop it from getting into enemy hands. A couple of matches into the fuel tank did the trick. But there was no time to stand and watch. He was whisked off by the Resistance, walking and running across fields and through woods so that he could be hidden in an isolated old barn. He had to burn all his kit, including his beloved flying jacket, dress up in local clothes kindly brought to him by one of the locals and become French. He was kept moving from safe house to safe house for a month. The wireless operator had reported his misadventure and aborted mission, but it wasn't until the next moon period that two Lysanders were flown out to pick him and the original passengers up. He'd been back in England just over a week and was now sent on these training sessions. A sobering story with a moral for the students: walk the field to check for boggy patches. On occasions, the police stuck posts into the ground of potential landing grounds, but he reported villagers removing them after curfew and replacing them after the plane had left.

The Hudson, being a much bigger plane, could carry up to twelve passengers. It needed a landing strip of at least 1,000 yards and, being much heavier than the Lysander, it was essential it had better drained, firm ground. The other planes, mostly Whitleys, Stirlings and Halifaxes, but occasionally Albermarles and Avro Ansons, would drop containers. These held a vast assortment of essential supplies sent to help the various resistance groups in occupied Europe.

He showed them some of the containers that were being dropped so they knew what to expect and told them they carried all sorts of guns, rifles, machine guns, grenades, plastic explosives, fuses, time pencils, limpet bombs, tyre bursters and ammunition. Other things included wireless sets, typewriters, printing presses, paper, ink, tape, string, glass cutters, wire cutters and medical supplies. Even crampons, skis, sunglasses and sun protection cream could be provided.

One kind, called a 'cell', looked like a large metal drum with a flat lid secured by quick release catches. Empty, it weighed about a stone. However, two hinged handles on the top made its transportation easier and there were attachments for a parachute harness. They would be used for carrying small arms and/or small arms ammunition, suitably packaged to avoid exploding on impact.

The container looked a bit like the copper tanks you have in your airing cupboard, but about eight-foot long, one-foot-six-inches wide and hinged along the middle. The bulkhead at one end was the parachute compartment; a flattened 'percussion pad' or 'crumple zone' at the other end showed very clearly how much energy it had absorbed on impact. There was a suspension lug on the top to assist its lifting when laden and attachments on the side for the parachute fastenings, four handles as well as a slot for a small spade, which could be used to dig a hole in which to bury it once its contents had been emptied. When they released the openings, you could see there was enough space for rifles, machine guns and a host of other supplies.

The other containers were box-shaped. One was a canvas-covered wire pannier about two feet by two feet by two feet. A folded parachute sat in a brown pack on the top with its static line attached on the top and four strong strops positioned vertically and horizontally. They were shown how to unfasten the chute and open them. They would carry bulkier items protected by what was called Koran fibre, shock-absorbent material made out of what looked like coconut-hair. The other was basically a cardboard box, used for packing clothes, gloves, socks etc. Before they put them back they were shown how to fold it flat so it could be buried.

Once back inside they were given a mission. A team of four was provided with an OS map and told to choose a potential landing site and a parachute dropping ground within a five-mile radius of the house. A six-figure grid reference and its latitude and longitude were needed. They were then taken in the back of the truck to each site in turn. It was made abundantly clear that they had to actually visit the prospective drop zone and see it for themselves. Were there any uneven features not marked on the map like ditches or ponds? Were there isolated trees or bushes? Were there any sunken farm tracks or ditches? Was it being grazed by animals and importantly, when in France, was the landowner supportive of its intended use? Were there any dry watercourses running across it that might be boggy after rain? Were there facilities nearby to store the canisters and their contents? Ideally, isolated farms, old farm buildings and wells should be used, but ponds and lakes were useful, as long as they were accessible.

Once they had walked the length of the field to ensure good drainage, there was another exercise. Regardless of whether they went out to meet a parachutist or to pick up containers, they had to get rid of the evidence. A parachute needed burying. So did the containers, but it was suggested that, if they chose a DZ close to water, they could put the chutes into the container with some earth and submerge them. If there was no water feature nearby they had to dig with a small spade attached to the container, especially for this job. The hole had to be deep enough to bury a folded parachute or container, leaving no evidence on the surface.

Although it could take up to half an hour, it was recommended as good practice if they were ever dropped blind with no reception committee. Returned agents recommended getting rid of the parachute silk as it was in great demand in France – for sheets, shirts and lingerie. Unravelled, the threads of the parachute cords could be made into socks and gloves. However, if anyone was caught with such silk, they'd be arrested as being involved with the Resistance.

There was then a lesson on how to set up a lighting system on the selected DZ to indicate to the incoming pilot not only the location, but also the wind direction, the windward end of the field, its width and its code letter. They were shown some low-powered, battery-operated lights, which could be buried in bucket-shaped holes so that the light was visible only from above. They needed to be covered over by day and switched on, individually, only when the engine-noise of the approaching plane could be heard. Some resistance groups had been sent these, but if they hadn't, they had to use torches. The ones he showed them had a specially adapted plastic dome on the top to diffuse the light. Should they be desperate, bonfires would do, but, they were warned, they would be unreliable in damp or wet weather.

The cleared landing strip, where possible, had to be about 1,500 yards long and up to 300 yards wide. It had to have a good hard surface and be as flat as possible. The RAF didn't mind a bit of bumpiness, he told them. They would prefer unploughed fields, but there had to be no sort of ditch and no telegraph poles or tall trees at either end of the runway. They didn't mind water at either or both ends, as long as there was enough field to land and take off from. Close to a track would be helpful and as far away from any built-up area would be an advantage. Finding as many of those criteria as they could would suit the RAF down to the ground, he said, waiting for a laugh.

There needed to be at least three lamps or torches, A, B and C. If it was to be an *atterrisage*, a landing, they were arranged in a letter 'L'. If it was a *parachutage*, it was a letter 'T'. The main signal lamp, A, was the first torch in the 'flarepath', placed near to where the reception committee stood to the left of the lamp. The holder of lamp A, normally the leader of the reception committee, flashed his group's agreed Morse code letter to the pilot. If the pilot did not recognize it, he was instructed to abort the drop. If it was correct, he would flash his code letter, which the *chef de parachutage* would have been provided with. If it was incorrect, he'd issue the instruction to disappear quickly into the night.

Presuming everything went according to plan, the person with lamp A would then shine his torch down the line to ensure the others had cottoned on and shine their torches towards the plane. A little tongue in cheek, he commented that the wisest *chefs de parachutage* would place two members of their committee up wind with luminous prismatic compasses to take bearings should any drops be too long.

If it was an *atterrissage*, the pilot would touch down to the right of lamp A. Lamp B would show him how much runway he had available before he turned across the strip between lamp B and C and taxied back to lamp A. Then he'd turn the aircraft and stop to the right of the reception committee, ready to take-off into the wind. All lamps had to stay where they were until the plane had stopped. The arriving passengers would get out except one who would hand the luggage out and put the departing passengers' luggage in. Once they were out and the new passengers in, the pilot would be ready to leave. If everything went according to plan, the whole operation should take less than five minutes, enough time for the pilot to have a wee and smoke a pipe.

Additional advice included how to detach the parachute from the container and how to bury it. As each container weighed up to 200lbs, they'd need two men to carry it. Ideally, the reception committee should be between twelve and fifteen people, mostly men, but women could also be enlisted to help out. Four people were needed on the lights, four or sometimes eight were posted as sentries and the rest posted as observers on the extreme perimeter of the landing ground to check for unwanted visitors. For extra security, where a truck or horse and cart was to be used, it was to be kept in a safe place about a half a mile away until the containers and packages were dropped. After collection, great care had to be taken to remove any undesirable tracks or tell-tale signs in the field. It was common for the Germans to send reconnaissance planes over the countryside when they got reports of possible drops. These did not take off until after dawn so there would be time to restore the DZ to its natural state.

After the pilot had left to be driven to RAF Tangmere, they were then introduced to 'Rebecca', 'Eureka' and 'Sugar', the 'back-street boys' latest 'hush-hush' means of allowing a friendly aircraft to drop supplies to a beleaguered group on the ground with pinpoint accuracy.

'Eureka' was a hand-held radar device, which sent out a signal that the navigator of an incoming aircraft could use to pinpoint their position from a distance they were told of about twenty miles. It was basically a heavy black box the size of a biscuit tin with knobs and dials on the top and numerous valves inside.

'Rebecca' was on-board equipment that picked up Eureka's signal. It consisted of three small aerials attached to sides or bottom of the cockpit, which were connected to a receiver panel and control unit, which the wireless operator used to inform the navigator of Eureka's exact location.

'Sugar' was the name used for the S-Phone, a portable phone with which a member of the Resistance could communicate with a radio operator on board the plane. Instead of broadcasting in all directions, it broadcast vertically, allowing them to have a conversation and send any verbal messages to one another when they were in range.

After the evening meal, they were driven off to check out the most suitable DZ to practice what they had just been told, supplied with torches, a Thermos of coffee and a sandwich tin. The conducting officers then went through the procedure so that they'd know what to expect when they heard the plane. One of them was given 'Sugar' to practice on. To gauge the wind direction they used the age-old finger sucking method, holding it up in the air to feel which side was cold. They were given torches and told to take up the 'T' position.

The person given 'Eureka' would switch it on and the rest would listen to the dark noises and wait. Eventually they would hear the drone of an aircraft approaching from the east. They rushed to their places. Even though it was a moonlit night they couldn't make it out until it had crossed Southampton Water. It was a Whitley, flying very low and with no lights. 'Sugar' could now be used. When the code letter was flashed from the ground and the pilot responded, the plane veered towards the south, then turned and dropped to approach them into the wind. They all had a go at chatting with the radio operator as the plane approached. And then, just before it thundered overhead, they would be able to spot the circular 'Joe hole'. Out popped a container, closely followed by the second. Within seconds their parachutes opened.

As the plane roared into a large curve south towards the Channel coast, the Whitley tipped its wings and headed east. They probably didn't watch it disappear, making sure they were out of the way of the containers as they thumped into the field. They ran across, released the parachute strings and bundled it up. There was no point burying it as they'd been taught. What was important was trying to remove the evidence of the two impact craters in the field. Then they had to lug them to the side of the field. It was hard work. Luckily there were handles on the sides, but dragging it all the way across the field was exhausting. When the latch was slid open, inside were three damp, heavy sacks tied up with string. It was wet sand. They hauled them out, replacing them with the crumpled up parachute.

Once they emptied the sacks and scattered the sand across the forest floor, they carefully covered the evidence with dry humus, dead leaves and pine needles. It was then easy carrying the two empty containers back to the truck.

Sometimes, after only a few hours' sleep, they were up for PT lessons on the tennis court. Seven o'clock was the usual time for PT. After breakfast, there was a lesson on 'agent management'; not their own, but guidance into selecting suitable people to help them in the field. One student recalled them being led by a tall, bewhiskered gentleman, probably in his early-forties, who spoke impeccable French. He had just come back from the Paris area and had valuable, up-to-the minute advice that would be very relevant.

It included the history of the Resistance. Many French people had been shocked at the speed of their defeat. Few saw any way they could continue a war that had been so comprehensively lost. The Germans had divided the country into six separate zones and ensured restricted movement and communications between them. Their massive military presence in the north subdued any opposition, especially when their troops were often seen out sightseeing, organising food distribution and distributing soup. They still had a legitimate government, albeit in Vichy in the south, and many believed Pétain, a First World War hero, was playing *un double jeu*, stringing the Nazis along until the right moment. As a result, resistance was minimal and ineffective. Turning one's back on a victory parade or giving incorrect directions were the most significant acts of resistance until telephone lines started to be cut and a clandestine tract, *Conseils á l'occupé* started to be surreptitiously pushed through people's letterboxes in June 1940. It contained thirty three ways of expressing personal resistance. Pouring sugar into the petrol tank of the enemy's vehicles or throwing three-headed nails on the road were two. Although there had been small-scale opposition within the military, the brutal massacre of the Senegalese troops of the 1st colonial regiment at Lyon for not recognising the armistice put paid to further opposition. Many disillusioned troops had gone AWOL, disappearing into the countryside, taking their uniforms, weapons and ammunition with them.

By the end of 1940 he estimated that there were only about a thousand active in the Resistance. Some were *réfractaires*, men who avoided conscription. However, as it became more organised and, as people got to know about it, the Resistance grew. The three main categories were propaganda, intelligence gathering and escape networks. The *Musée de l'Homme* distributed Resistance tracts and a magazine called *Resistance* around Paris. However, it met its demise when its leaders were arrested and murdered. Other groups emerged around prominent military figures, academics, intellectuals, active communist party members and even priests. He listed the major groups as it was going to be important that they were aware of them. The major groups in the northern zone were: *Défense de la France, Ceux de la Résistance, Ceux de la Patrie, Défense de la Patrie, Ceuxé de la Libération, L'Homme libre, Libération-Nord, Organisation civile et militaire* and *Le Front National*. In the southern zone were: *Combat, Libération-Sud, Francs-Tireurs et Partisan, France d'abord, Le Coq Enchainé, Témoignage Chrétien, Le Movement Charte* and *Libérer et Fédérer*. Their motivations were many and varied. *Francs-Tireurs* was Socialist.

He presumed they knew about General Charles de Gaulle, the leader of the Free French who was living in London. His speech on the BBC on 18 June 1940 had let the French know that there was another option. Many thousands had escaped France to join him. The *Francais de Londres* formed the *Republique Francaise*, financed and supplied by the British. Churchill's objective was to unify all these disparate resistance groups with de Gaulle as their leader. The RAF had been dropping agents and supplies to support their activities in France since 1941, but it was largely an intelligence gathering and collation operation until the Germans took over the 'Free Zone' in November 1942.

Recruiting people is always risky, more so in wartime. There was always the risk of taking on collaborators so it was essential they tried to identify their motives. Some would be prepared to risk their lives out of Germanophobia, pure hatred of the enemy, out of revenge for themselves or for someone close. They may want to experience the adventure and excitement of doing something dangerous and secret. Maybe they had religious or political reasons or were extremely patriotic. Some saw resistance as defending France's republican tradition of democracy and civil rights. Others were opposed to the growing authoritarianism of the Vichy régime. Some saw the Resistance as a possible means of overcoming the difficulties of food and fuel shortages, should they succeed. Others might join for financial reasons, to pay their rent or to be provided with food and lodging in a 'safe house'. Some might do it in return for items they could not find in the shops like food, medicine or tobacco. Others may feel empathy for those who were prepared to risk their own lives to save their country, especially when they saw women actively engaged in

Resistance work. Others felt that the treatment of migrants, Jews, socialists, communists and Freemasons was wrong. Whilst these were all perfectly good reasons, those who had several of these reasons were considered to be the better choices. However, if they were desperate, they could consider taking on board those who might be able to be bribed or blackmailed. He hinted, with sparkling eyes in the direction of the women, that some people could easily be recruited if sexually compromised.

Over time, the Germans had recognised the increased threat from the various *réseaux* and established specialist units to minimise their impact. *Réseau* is the French word for a net or, in the case of Resistance fighters, a network or circuit. The Germans aimed to gather information, infiltrate, capture and interrogate both *resistants* and *resistantes* in order to gain better knowledge of their operations. At the same time they created a smear campaign utilising all manner of propaganda. In the collaborationist press there were daily reports of sabotage by traitors, reactionaries, communists and terrorists and other disreputable elements in the population. In the streets were large posters condemning their activities; similar exhortations to right-thinking, decent Frenchmen to deplore such riff-raff could be heard on the wireless. Financial rewards were offered for information leading to the arrest of suspected Resistance members.

To counteract their efforts to undermine support for the Resistance, winning over someone with power and influence would be invaluable. Opinionists in the local community could much more easily influence their compatriots than 'outsiders'. Anyone with a title had to be particularly wooed. A *Duc* or *Duchesse* would be a real catch. The German traditional respect for authority acknowledged anyone with a 'de' in their family name. They'd have a large demesne and lots of properties to rent. Wealthy landowners with decreasing influence, but equally useful, would be a *Marquis, Comte, Vicomte, Baron, Seigneur, Sire* or *Chevalier*. If they weren't successful in winning any of them over, they needed equally inconspicuous locals like taxi drivers, station porters, teachers, postmen, priests, lawyers, opticians, dentists and doctors. They had ideal cover occupations and would make excellent couriers and liaison officers. Of course, there were probably any number of factory workers, railway workers, bargees, office workers and general and agricultural labourers who'd be the backbone of any Resistance organisation.

It was imperative, he suggested, that there be no dealings with anyone connected with other *réseaux*. From his recent experiences, he described how some couriers and radio operators worked on several *réseaux*, which made them extremely vulnerable to betrayal.

The ideal arrangement was based on the Russian communist cell system, where small individual groups worked within a larger one. Each cell had its own organiser. Didi would have noted how male-dominated it was. It was he alone who was responsible for recruiting another group, and only he should know the identity of its organiser. The organiser of the whole *réseaux*, another man, should appoint his own sub-agents and let them pick their own subordinates. For security purposes, only their details had to be sent up the chain for his approval, not their names. The whole idea was that the unit was made up of watertight compartments. If one cell was what he called *brûlé*, burnt or broken, the ship would not sink.

Although one wanted the network to expand, allowing each member to recruit their own small group, on occasions it had led to security leaks and networks being broken. The concept he wanted them to use was of a factory unit – a production line – where each cell was responsible for a particular area of expertise. The overall policy was dictated, following the SOE Committee meetings in Baker Street, to the organisers of the networks, down through the system to the man in the street. The section Didi would be working with was the French Section run by Buckmaster.

He told them about the difference between the *réseaux* and the *Maquis*. In the early years of the war, resistance to German occupation was small-scale and predominantly urban-based. With support from the Allies, it became better organised and supplied. The *Maquis* in its traditional usage, was the typical low, bushy vegetation that covered much of the high ground in the southern Mediterranean.

From February 1943, the Germans introduced the *Service du Travail Obligitaire*, compulsory work service. All French men had to register their births. Most of those between nineteen and thirty-two were sent to work on the *Atlantik Wall*, a coastal defence network that stretched all the way south from the Arctic Circle in Norway, through the Pays Bas to Les Landes. Some went to factories in Germany and others went to the Russian front as so many German men were engaged in military duties. As an enticement, for every three volunteers, one prisoner-of-war would be returned.

The first group to go were criminals from prison, domestic servants, casual labourers and the unemployed. The uptake wasn't as great as Germany expected so they made it compulsory. The second group included skilled labourers, people in the retail trades, those in luxury industries like fur, leather and jewellery, bank clerks, and large numbers of postal workers were sent to work in the Deutsche post office. The *Miliciens* rounded up the *'oisifs'* , the lazy types they didn't want on the streets and sent them. At one stage it was estimated that about 20,000 men a week were being picked up on the streets of Paris. A million were said to have been sent by April.

To avoid conscription, many wanted jobs in the *affectés spéciaux*, reserved occupations like firemen, ambulance drivers, gendarmes, even charcoal burners or in the *Milice*. Those who evaded the *rafles*, police round-ups, were described initially by Vichy as *defaillants* or *insoumis*. Eventually they became known as *refractaires*. Many migrated to relatives or friends in the countryside. If they were lucky they found work or joined the Resistance. The Maquisards became an honorary title for them.

The reality of French Resistance was that it was largely made up of political, racial and economic migrants, many of whom had arrived in the 1930s. They included German anti-Nazis, Italian anti-Fascists, Spanish Republicans, Catalans, Poles, Jews fleeing the violent anti-Semitism of Central, Eastern and Western Europe and assorted members of the International Brigade.

Their difficulty was not just differentiating between *Maquis* and *réseaux*. Within these groupings there were sub-groups, often fiercely independent. There were right-wing conservative Catholics, liberals, anti-fascists, communists, trade unionists, anarchists and even Jewish, Spanish and Polish resistance groups. He spelt it out. These groups had to be able to work together to successfully defeat the Third Reich. In reality it was a civil war between those who supported and worked with the Germans and those who opposed occupation.

He also clarified the difference between the French section of the SOE and the RF. The former were largely British-run and British-funded. The *Republique Francaise* was largely French-run and British-funded. When he was asked whether the Americans were funding any of the *réseaux* he hesitated and said he couldn't be sure.

Any collaboration between the F Section and RF was forbidden unless authorised from above. The delicate political situation did not need to be explained. There was growing support amongst the British for de Gaulle as the only real alternative to Petain's Vichy government. The majority of the French agents Didi spoke with on these courses would probably have been motivated by his speeches to do something to help, not to go along with the ideas of an eighty-five year old collaborator.

Although they would probably find that many in the *Maquis* and *réseaux* would refuse payment, there had to be a pay structure as in industry. Under normal circumstances, the money to pay members would arrive with the agents. On occasions it would be in the dropped containers. Sometimes it ran to several hundred-thousand forged French francs. They were told that there may be gold sovereigns, which could be used to bribe prison guards to allow prisoners to escape, to pay boat owners for helping people get out of the country or guides for taking people over the border. It could be used at the discretion of the organiser. In certain circumstances payment could be in kind, like food or medicines.

Bonuses had to be paid to those who undertook special missions like sabotage or assassination. *Cloisonnement*, compartmentalisation, was essential. There had to be different responsibilities in each section and information shared on a 'need-to-know' basis. Should someone be interrogated, they wouldn't be able to reveal the secrets of the whole network. Separate sections needed creating to include security, propaganda, sabotage, reception, accommodation, internal communications, external communications, transport, storage and the distribution of goods and equipment.

Security had to keep their eyes and ears open for enemy activity in the area and were responsible for obtaining relevant passes and papers. Some of these were documents forged in France like one's identity cards, ration books and coupons. Others would be supplied by English forgers.

Propaganda involved passing on reports to relevant people, disseminating leaflets, putting up posters, even graffiti. Whilst the RAF dropped millions of propaganda leaflets, they also supplied fake material like labels to stick on goods wagons that sent trucks to the wrong destinations. Some containers would contain printing press, paper, ink, stamps etc.

Sabotage, small or large-scale, had to be undertaken on the direction of the organiser in collaboration with the goods and equipment section. There would be plenty of *plastique* supplied, and weapons and ammunition. There was also the instruction that double agents, collaborators and informers should be assassinated.

Reception met and saw off agents, picked up supplies, arranged with landowners the DZs and landing strips, made sure torches and spare batteries were available and provided a plausible cover story to explain people's night-time activity after the 21.00 hours curfew. The most plausible cover stories would necessitate a forged gamekeeper's or doctor's travel permit.

Accommodation had to find and secure suitable safe houses for organisers, couriers, wireless operators and, where necessary, VIPs like downed RAF and USAAF pilots and crew. It was essential that there were a wide range, from rooms in a château to town houses and apartments in the urban areas to *maisons*, *gîtes* and even barns and caves in the rural areas. These had to be rented and any taxes paid on time.

Internal communication had to deal with the messages necessary throughout the network. It included the movement of couriers, accommodation addresses, live and dead *boîtes aux lettres*. External communication involved the wireless operators sending messages back to England, receiving transmissions and, on occasions, contacting other networks.

Transport was to be predominantly by bicycle. With petrol rationed, cars, *moto-velours* and trucks could be used, but only sparingly. *Gazogenes*, charcoal-driven trucks, would often be used in rural areas. Horses, carts, oxen, donkeys and mules might also be called upon as draught animals when transporting containers.

Storage involved hiding the contents of the containers, in particular the weapons and ammunition in preparation for what they were told was 'Zero Day'. This was the codename for the day when the Allies planned to invade. As they were informed later, it was changed to 'D-Day'. Attics, cellars, farm buildings, caves and wells had to be found.

Distribution had to liaise with Storage to ensure supplies were sent to the right people at the right time. This, they were told, was going to be especially important in the run-up to and the days immediately following D-Day.

In some cases, training had to be provided by the agent, whether in the use of weapons, *plastique*, tactics or wireless set work. If it was deemed necessary, arrangements could be made to lift people out for specialist training in England. It was not lost on the students that almost everything they had learned from the SOE syllabus might have to be taught to others. Although Didi would have been told about the role of the organiser, as the course progressed, it became clear that women were expected to take on subordinate roles.

The role of the courier was to carry messages verbally or by hand. They could walk, cycle, take a bus, catch a train, even drive a car, truck or motorbike and, if they felt confident, they could ask others to give them a lift if needed.

The courier might have to find suitable accommodation for a headquarters as well as safe houses for incoming organisers, wireless operators and couriers. The ideal HQ would be a bar or an office, which had a genuine business being undertaken already. It had to have more than two exits, preferably with good escape routes, not into a walled garden or fenced yard. In remote areas, isolated farm buildings, lumber camps, quarries or mountain ski huts could be used. It was imperative that rents, taxes and any telephone, gas, electricity and water bills were paid in the same way as the owner. They had to find out. If they were slow making payments, pay slowly.

Everything would need to be kept exceptionally tidy. It was then much easier to see if there had been any disturbance. Use a strand of their hair over drawers, doors and windows and talcum powder on surfaces and dead leaves in locks. It would save lives. One imagines that Didi's room would have been deliberately 'broken into' on occasions and things taken, just to test her observational skills. The emphasis on tidiness was repeated almost daily so that it was drummed into all of them.

Other useful ideas he encouraged them to adopt included a system of visual and aural codes. A good one was to agree with your rendezvous that, if you kept your hands in your pockets, you were being followed. Others could be leaving doors, windows or shutters open if it was safe, closed if dangerous. Leaving the doormat askew likewise, open or closed curtains, hanging a hat on a hook in the porch or moving a flowerpot or birdcage to the middle or other side of the window ledge could inform visitors from a distance. Any incriminating material, codes, message transcriptions, notes etc. had to be placed where they could be rapidly destroyed in an emergency. Strategically setting a small amount of explosives next to items impossible to get rid of was recommended.

Conventional means of communication were discouraged. There were inherent problems involved in using telephone and telegrams. The sender had to show their identity card at the Post Office, which kept a record of your name and address. Duplicate records were put on file. Whilst public telephone calls could be used for local calls, making calls from telephones in bars, restaurants, hotels and even from people's homes was discouraged. If you did, then you had to be extremely careful to be as brief as possible. The operators may well be in the pay of the *Milice* or Gestapo.

Ideally, there ought to be as little contact between the organiser and their courier as possible. Potentially, he or she could know too much about the network, which could be disastrous if they were caught. It could put individuals, cells or even the whole network in jeopardy. Having a watertight cover story was essential; not just your own identity, but also having a reason for every visit you might undertake.

Messages had to be learned off by heart. If it was too long or too difficult to memorise, the best method would be to write it on rolling paper and use it afterwards to make a cigarette. Unroll it when you needed it and 'smoke' it when you were finished with it. Other material included edible rice paper and soft fabric that could be found in coats and jackets. But this involved unpicking the seams, inserting the message and then sewing them up again. You had to repeat the operation to extract the message when you met up with your 'rendezvous'. The 'tear off codes', used by the wireless operators, could be hidden in the seams of your clothing and then burnt or swallowed when used.

When they asked where on the body they could possibly hide messages, they were told that, as a means of concealment, this was discouraged. The German security forces were not novices. They would examine every orifice, with little sensitivity to one's dignity and often without gloves or ointment. They might even extract a filling or remove skin if they suspected it might hide a message. The *Abwehr*, the counter-espionage section of the German armed forces, were extremely proficient at methodically searching every item of clothing, even scraping the dirt from under your fingernails and testing it to see if the soil was English.

Should they ever be arrested and taken to the police station for interrogation, they had to react according to their cover story. There were two choices. Answer questions straight away with confidence and sensible answers or deliberate and act as if you weren't the brightest card in the pack. Accept that the officers were only doing their duty and comply with their every request without giving anything away. Showing justified indignation, nervousness and even indifference was acceptable. So was anxiety when they were close to – or actually found – something incriminating like forged currency or something acquired on the *marché noir*, the black market. Anger and resentment should be modified. It always led to worse treatment. Passive resistance was best, but the key was to be as inconspicuous as possible. The final piece of advice was never to relax in their precautions or fool themselves into thinking the enemy would be asleep. They would be watching them all the time so they had to watch their step.

The night before the end of the course, a party was organised with plenty of alcohol and high jinks. Agents recall having a gramophone with some 78s of the Ink Spots to which they danced most of the night. One game played involved the students being blindfolded, given a rolled-up newspaper and told to go around on all fours whacking one another. Those who removed the blindfold were more accurate.

Following four or five weeks at Beaulieu, Vera Atkins arrived shortly after breakfast in the Wolsey and, after a short chat with her about how they had got on, Didi and the others packed their valises. They were advised to wear their FANY uniform whilst in London as it would give them a lot more respect from people. Having packed, they were bundled into the car and taken back to London for a few days' break.

Once back in her digs at Darenth Road, Didi may well have met Francis. Suffering from nervous exhaustion after his experiences in France, he had failed his paramilitary course in Scotland and, before joining the army, was being 'looked after' by the SOE at the Berkeston Gardens Hotel. Whether she met Frederick, who was already in the army, is unknown. One wonders whether, if she did meet Francis, she was able to maintain the lie about how she had spent the last few months or her imminent return to France. Saying it was working with the military may have been enough to keep him quiet. He probably would have understood if she told him she had been told to say nothing. In wartime England, there were posters with the message, 'Mum's the word!' Whilst he may have been able to tell her about his experiences in France and his time in England, he would not have been able to tell her much about Jacqueline. She had been dropped in France the previous January.

How Didi spent her time in early 1944 is unknown. Maybe she had made some friends on the various courses and arranged to go out with them to restaurants, the theatre or to watch a film. One imagines she met up with Savy and spent time studying the sketches and aerial photographs of their DZ and their immediate plans on landing. There is evidence she met up with Mac, her supervisor at Thame Park, for some final training:

> When Didi disappeared so I thought, 'Oh, she'll be sent somewhere,' so when I found her actually as an agent in training, I nearly dropped out, but I looked as if I'd never seen her before and said, 'What's your name?' Mind you, I would have done that anyway because they didn't always train under their own names; some of them did, but others didn't, I don't know why. One didn't see it as serious. So, there she was, and we had our lesson, and we prepared her piece and after it was over, and it was all found out, and Didi pretended (she was good at pretending) that she had left something behind and she came back, and the first thing she said was 'Mac, you mustn't tell anyone that you saw me here,' and I said 'Didi, and you mustn't tell anybody where I came from,' so, but we kept sort of in touch, you know, after that.[20]

In an interview Didi gave after the war, she said that her reason for becoming a spy was that, 'I had patriotic feelings and I knew

I could do that kind of work since I was by nature a solitary person, and that was essential to be able to adapt to that kind of life.'[21]

Before Didi left for France she would have been taken to have a chat with Colonel Buckmaster, probably in Orchard Court. Jones mentioned Didi telling her that Buckmaster said, 'No reaction' when testing her cover story. 'There was no reaction when I lied. They thought I would be alright because I lied so well. Also I could be a bit hard and secret. I could be lonely. I could be independent.'[22]

Buckmaster wanted her to understand that what she was undertaking was work, unrelenting hardship, not one of your ordinary nine-to-five jobs. This would be special work contributing to the Allies' war effort. There would be no paid holidays, no weekends or Bank Holidays off, no home leave and, in all likelihood, no letters from home. The odds on their returning to 'Blighty' were fifty-fifty. She had to decide, but, he reminded her, the reward was victory – France's liberation.

However, because of the nature of her mission, Didi's presence in France would be, and he emphasised it, '*insaisissable*' – unacknowledged. If she got caught, she would be suspected of being – and in all probability treated as – a spy, and there would be nothing he could do about it. Nobody would know who she was and the Geneva Convention would not save her. If she wanted to withdraw, she had to tell him there and then.

As Didi must have expressed her willingness to help, he opened one of his desk drawers, took out a buff-coloured envelope with a diagonal red stripe across it and marked TOP SECRET. He pushed it across the desk towards her. Inside were several sheets of typed paper. One of them detailed her new identity, where she was born and on what date, her star sign, where she had lived, what schools she had been to, what Lycée she went to, what her 'baccalaureate' was in, her parents', brothers', sisters' and grandparents' names, where they were born and how old they were, the names of her aunties, uncles and cousins, what jobs they had done, what jobs she had done, what job she was in now, where she had been on holiday, which hotels she had stayed in as well as the names of all the streets and buildings in the places she had lived.

As far as possible her cover story was close to the truth, but, unfortunately, it was not included in her personal file. All we know is that she had a false identity card under the name of Marie Louise Tournier, but was also known as Jacqueline du Terte. There were no mission papers in her personal file, other than that she was to act as Jean Savy's wireless operator. Although her codename was Rose, a note in her personal file identified her wireless identity as Petticoat 82. There was a memo in her file identifying her post box as a red-tiled cottage with a car port at the end of a dirt road off the main road in Mouy, a small village on the railway line about sixty kilometres north of Paris. It belonged to Monsieur Maurice Ployet, a theatrical director.

Meeting Vera again might well have been a relief, knowing that there were plans for her to be imminently returned to France. Sometimes Vera met agents in the Trocadero, a popular restaurant near Baker Street. Perhaps it was in Orchard Court.

At this meeting, Didi was given some very serious instructions. It was imperative that she wrote a will. Not having a solicitor, Vera would have arranged for her to meet one who had been appointed by the SOE. Before that she had to write a list of all her personal possessions as well as stating who they had to go to. Not owning a property or renting a flat must have reduced the amount of red tape. One imagines Didi nominated Francis, her elder brother, as her executor as the SOE had his contact details. However, it is extremely unlikely he was informed that she was returning to France.

Vera gave departing agents useful advice – to write out five postcards and letters addressed to their next of kin with short, nondescript messages saying they were all right, not to worry and that they would see them soon. As they would be incommunicado for some time, Vera explained that they would be sent every few months to stop anyone from worrying too much. The contact address for family and friends whilst they were away was '*Room 98, Horseguards, London SW1*'. Any correspondence would be collected and then brought to them by personal courier using the services of the Special Duties Squadrons.

There had clearly been quite an effort to assuage their worries about leaving family and friends behind. Vera also asked them if there was anyone they wanted her to send birthday or Christmas presents to. Should they want to be told of any domestic event like births, engagements, weddings or funerals, she would arrange to send an agreed *message personnel* via the BBC's French Service.

She told them what clothes to wear, what was chic and passé, what personal belongings to carry around, how to do her hair, what perfume to use and, if any of them needed reminding, how to hold their knife and fork French style – well, classy Paris restaurant style. She also gave them lessons on social etiquette, how to greet the reception committee, the owners of the safe houses or concierges, information about curfew times, travelling arrangements and working. Looking the wrong way when crossing the road or when waiting for the *autobus* was a dead give-away. She also advised them not to use brand-new large-denomination notes to pay small bills in bars or restaurants. It would draw unwanted attention. All the currency sent to the Resistance would be used notes – and professionally forged.

When Leo Marks was asked by a psychologist what agents were most frightened of, he told them that above all else they were scared of Beryle Murray-David, a lady dentist who had a practice on Wimpole Street in London. They were always driven there by car and accompanied inside to ensure they kept their appointment. As well as drilling out fillings, she had to change the impressions of their teeth before they left, just in case the Germans had records of them. She also used continental style Platarcke to hollow out a tooth to create a cavity in which the 'L'-pill could be stored.

A few days before the departure, there would also have been a visit to the hairdressers to ensure her hair was washed in French shampoo and cut in an appropriate French style. Whether the Germans had learned to recognise the smell of Lifebuoy or Wright's Coal Tar soap is undocumented.

There was also a trip by car up the A1 to 'The Thatched Barn', the SOE's clothing department. Here Didi would have been taken to the room where all the French clothes, shoes and other personal possessions were stored. She would have been provided with appropriate attire for her trip so that she looked the part, fitted with the character created in her cover story. It would have included appropriate French toiletries and probably a bottle of *eau de Cologne* or perfume. There would have been a used French valise, umbrella, hat, shawl and gloves.

Sometimes a trip to Savile Row was necessary, but not to buy a new outfit. In a basement under the Police station, the SOE had a dedicated Jewish tailor and a team of tailors and seamstresses who would do any necessary alterations. Gleeson reported that this team made first-rate copies of genuine French suits, dresses, bodices and knickers. 'He used to go to synagogues all over London looking for refugees wearing the genuine articles, which he bought or borrowed. He collected all the labels and name tags he found and inserted them in the agent's clothing. A Nottingham boot and shoe manufacturer produced French boots and shoes, most of which contained secret compartments in the hole or shoe.'[23]

6

WORKING FOR THE
RESISTANCE IN FRANCE:
3 MARCH 1944–24 JULY 1944

In Savy's personal file was Buckmaster's report, which commented on his previous work in France and mentioned the new mission he was undertaking. It stated that he had:

> ...Contributed very materially to the operational efficiency of F Section. M. MILLET is now proceeding on a difficult and dangerous mission in which my Section is jointly interested with the representative of the French National Assembly in LONDON, and I consider that the results of the said mission – if satisfactory – will be of equal benefit to British and French interests, and more particularly to the rapprochement for which both countries are working.
>
> M. MILLET had declined financial assistance from us when giving us over a period of many months his expert advice, and we desire herewith to mark our appreciation of his most valuable advice and counsel.[1]

According to Hugh Verity, Savy's return flight was initially planned for 16 November 1943, but Flight Lieutenant Hankey, the Lysander pilot, considered the landing zone chosen by the reception committee to be unusable. When an agent in the field chose what they thought was a suitable drop zone, detailed map coordinates and sketches of the field and surrounding area had to be taken back by hand in one of the pick-ups. The Air Liaison Officer would order a fly-over of the site and aerial photographs would be taken. It was these that Hankey examined, and he asked for another landing ground to be found.

A new landing ground was located, codenamed Faucon, near Ménétréol-sous-Vatan, two kilometres southwest of Villeneuve in the Indre department. When the new flight was scheduled for 10 February 1944, Didi and Savy would have been shown the sketches, maps and aerial photographs to study. When Liane Jones, the historian, started researching the SOE agents for her book, *A Quiet Courage,* she interviewed Didi, who, she said, had not told her story before because her time in German captivity had left her badly traumatised. Didi spoke vividly and forcefully as her memories were precious to her. Didi told her, 'I had met my chief in the office and we were going out together on the night of the new moon. He said, "Are you quite sure you want to go?" and I said, "Yes, I do." So we left and went to Tempsford, where the planes were.'[2]

Other agents who were taken to France by Lysander recalled being driven down to RAF Tangmere. Being closer to the continent, it reduced travelling time and saved fuel. Maybe the weather conditions were bad on the south coast that night.

After Buckmaster's final briefing, Vera probably drove them on a winding route up the A1. It was essential agents did not know the exact location of the airfield so they would be unable to divulge it should they be captured. Locals recalled seeing blacked out cars driving through Everton, the small village near the airfield, on the nights of the full moon, but they were unaware of the identities of the passengers being taken to the airfield. They were not meant to know. All they knew was that planes took off at night and returned in the morning. They thought they were going on bombing missions.

The road leading to the airfield's main gate had checkpoints at either end and armed guards would not let anyone continue without a pass. All the local telephone boxes were chained up to prevent any outgoing calls. Once past the guards on duty at the main gate, the driver took them around the concrete eastern perimeter track to Gibraltar Farm. The Air Liaison Officer in charge, known to his colleagues as 'Pink gin Charlie', would have welcomed them when they went into the barn, referring to them only by their codenames. Didi's was Alice and Savy's was Alcide.

Their passwords, messages and other information were checked to see that they had learnt them off by heart. Savy's suit would have been checked to see if there was a buckle at the back of the waistcoat. As continental suits did not have buckles, it had to be cut off and the straps sewn together. No British tags were to be on them, no used bus or train tickets, cigarette packets or matchboxes, no initialled handkerchiefs. Shoes had not to be new so as to arouse suspicion. Hats were checked to see if there were any markings on the leather band inside. Any identifying mark was removed by rubbing it very hard with Milton's sterilizing fluid. New gloves had their buttons wrenched off and shirts had holes rubbed in. Trouser turn-ups and the soles of their shoes were checked, sometimes with a magnifying glass, to ensure there was no incriminating evidence, like strands of Virginia tobacco, that would indicate they had come from Britain.

All loose change had to be handed over, a contribution to the RAF's Benevolent Fund. Hard rations were given out, a flashlight, first-aid equipment, radio parts, secret maps and papers. The cashier would issue them with their foreign documents, enough foreign currency to run a resistance operation and a collection of loose change for use on arrival. The serial numbers were never consecutive and notes had often been trampled on to give them a slightly tattered look. Didi would have had her Colt revolver and bullets. Other useful gifts were a hip flask full of rum and an 'L' pill , should they decide to use it.

'L' pills contained lethal potassium cyanide crystals in a biteable, thin rubber coating. They were often hidden in a specially hollowed out cavity in a wisdom tooth, the top inside part of a jacket, in hollowed-out wine bottle corks, tubes of lipstick or a specially engraved signet ring. Once chewed, 'L' pills would kill a person in fifteen seconds. If you swallowed it, it would take longer and there were many reports of the Germans resuscitating those who had by rushing them to hospital and pumping out their stomachs. Some SOE agents reported being told that the Catholic Church had given them a special dispensation to use the pill 'in extremis'.

Other 'medications' included 'A' pills for airsickness; blue 'B' pills containing Benzedrine sulphate for use as a stimulant (the amphetamine Mecrodrin was also issued); 'E' pills, a quick-working anaesthetic that would knock a person out in 30 seconds, and 'K' pills, which would induce sleep for up to 24 hours. Some were given 'M & B 693' (May and Baker's sulfapyridine) pills, which were used before penicillin to counter wound infections and reduce the risk of pneumonia and gangrene. There were also 'Q' and 'U' poison pills and halibut liver oil capsules. One deadly poison the SOE issued left no trace except those of endemic syphilis.

There is no evidence Didi took the 'L' pill. Given her Catholic upbringing, the idea of committing suicide would have been an anathema to her. However, needing to stay awake to transmit messages might have meant she took the 'B' pills.[3, 4, 5]

To make agents look more authentic, they might have been issued with a recent French newspaper, Gauloises cigarettes or perhaps a photograph of a 'relative' to make their cover story more realistic. Sometimes a dab or splash of appropriately sourced perfume or after-shave was used. If any last-minute adjustment of clothing was necessary, or an improvement to their disguise, it was done then. The final thing was being given a good luck gift. This might be cuff-links, a cigarette case, powder compact or a piece of jewellery – a reminder from Buckmaster and Atkins that Baker Street was thinking of them. When they ran out of money, they were told it could be pawned or sold on the black market.

Some of these smaller items were used to conceal codes, messages and microscopic photographs. Hiding places included fountain pens, pencils, wallets, chess pieces, bath salts, shaving sticks, toothpaste, talcum powder, lipsticks, manicure sets, sponges, penknives, shoe heels and soles, shoulder padding, collar studs, coat buttons and cigarette lighters.

What Didi would not have been told was that, wearing civilian clothing on operational duties, it would be very unlikely that she would receive favourable treatment if the Gestapo caught her and that, in all likelihood, she would fall under Hitler's directive of *Nacht und Nebel* in which captured enemy personnel would disappear without a trace in the clouds and fog of war.

Sue Ryder, one of the FANY conducting officers who accompanied the SOE agents to the airfield, commented that:

> Though the pre-mission hours were naturally very tense, there was also a wonderful sense of humour and cheerfulness among the Bods. I can't remember any false bravado; on the contrary, it was real wit that came through. No written word can recapture the warmth of the atmosphere throughout the station. Whenever the atmosphere was especially tense or a feeling of dread pervaded, someone in the small group would rally the spirits of the others. They had, too, an extraordinary humility and a religious faith, which was exemplified in the way they prepared themselves for their missions, such as making their confessions to a priest who would come to the ops station especially for this purpose.[6]

One imagine Didi had made her confession before leaving. The weather that night was dire, so bad that Captain Milsted, a 161 squadron pilot, had to abort the flight. Freddie Clark mentioned that 50 per cent of the Squadron's missions were cancelled that night so it is doubtful Didi and Savy took off. One wonders whether they were relieved or disappointed on hearing the news. In circumstances like this, agents were put up in Gaynes Hall, near Perry, a large and secluded country house a few miles west of St Neots and about half an hour's drive from Tempsford. It was a three-storey, yellow brick mansion set in 23 acres of parkland, with 13 bedrooms, nine bathrooms, a ballroom, sitting room and lounge, dining room and library.

It had been requisitioned shortly after the war started and, until the Americans joined the Allied cause, was used for packing the containers being flown out of Tempsford. When the USAAF 'Carpetbaggers' began helping the Special Duties Squadrons, the packing operation was transferred to Holmewood Hall, another country estate near Peterborough.

Gaynes Hall, STS 61, was one of the SOE's 'Holding Stations'. Agents were accommodated there prior to their flight, or when the flight had to be postponed. According to Michael Foot, to make their stay there 'as delectable as possible, a large number of FANYs, girls in their late teens when recruited, with quick brains and quiet tongues, performed an essential service for SOE'.[7] They also entertained them at mealtimes with light conversations. They would offer to dance, play a game of billiards with them or a few hands of bridge, help them with a crossword, a game of chess, draughts or to do a jigsaw. Some FANYs took them for rides on their horses or drove them out for a meal in Cambridge and took them punting on the Cam. They took them to nearby pubs, bought their drinks and ensured they did not talk to any of the locals. When the ground was covered in snow they took them sledging. No expense was spared in trying to ensure the last hours the agents spent in Britain were as pleasant as possible.

The following day another flight was planned, this time piloted by Captain Whitaker. However, the bad weather continued and the flight had to be aborted. As this was the last chance to fly during the February moon period, their departure was postponed until March. That meant Didi and Jean would have been driven back to London and expected to wait. Again, where they stayed and what they did is unknown.

The next attempt, Operation Gitane, took place on 2/3 March, but to a new DZ. After going through the same checking-in procedures at Gibraltar Barn, sometime after dusk, Didi and Savy were escorted to a waiting Lysander. Didi recalled '… how dark it was and we saw the pilot, but it was very much in the shadow'. Usually waiting by the plane was the station's padre in his black cloak, cassock and surplice, offering departing agents God's blessing. Maybe he had become immune to the commonly used farewell phrase of departing 'Joes' – 'Merde'.

Although it was still wintry, Flight Lieutenant Murray 'Andy' Anderson of 161 Squadron took off.[8, 9] Clark's book sheds no light on the drop, only saying 161 Squadron went on seven sorties that night and 138 Squadron on seventeen. Waiting nervously in a snow-covered field two kilometres from Les Lagnys, six kilometres north-west of Saint Valentin and twenty-five kilometres north-east of Châteauroux in the Indre department, were George Lovinfosse and Maurice Durieux. Lovinfosse had been running the GREYHOUND network, an SOE escape line run from a country house near Châteauroux. The field he had planned to use was too deeply covered with snow so he had to set up a flare path in a nearby one. As well as setting the torches up himself, he also had the arduous task of helping Durieux who had had one leg amputated following a bad landing during a parachute jump.

Didi recalled it being a bitterly cold and cloudy night. 'I was with the head of my circuit and he suddenly said, "Look, there are the lights of the reception committee."'[10] She even remembered the emotion she felt when she saw the red lights, but was probably not told by Flight Lieutenant Anderson that they were in the wrong field. However, when Lovinfosse flashed the correct identification code from one nearby, given the urgency of the mission, Anderson decided to land. Despite a few bumps the Lysander came to a stop.

When she landed, everything happened so quickly. Once she got out of the cockpit and climbed down the ladder, she was welcomed by a voice with a pure Parisian accent saying, 'OK? We have to act quickly to avoid being caught.' One of them said, 'Oh, a young girl. Go back. Go back. It's extremely dangerous. You must go back.'[11] Her response was that she had no intention of doing so.

Lovinfosse handed Savy their luggage before he got out, helped Lovinfosse get Durieux on board, bade them farewell and closed the cockpit. Then, after they both thanked Anderson and watched him take off into the night, with their revolvers ready, just in case, they crossed the fields to a waiting horse and cart. Didi recalled falling asleep to the clacking sound of the horse's hooves.[12]

23-year-old Didi, with two identities – Mademoiselle Marie Louise Tournier and Jacqueline du Terte – and 35-year-old Savy made their way along snow-covered farm tracks to a stable belonging to one of Lovinfosse's members of the MI6-sponsored MITHRIDATE network.[13] Her mission was to work as a wireless operator in Sceaux, one of the south-western suburbs of Paris. Savy's mission, Operation Mitchell, was an extension of Antelme's, to establish the WIZARD network, locate financial support for the resistance from amongst the business community in and around Paris, to arrange supplies for resistance groups and to organise the arrival of the Jedburgh teams. These were three-man teams of French, British, American or Canadian officers with specific missions to liaise and support Resistance networks prior to and after D-Day.

After a very brief rest, she was woken up at five o'clock so that two local men could escort her safely to the station. The safe house they had arranged for her was in Orleans, about ninety kilometres away. Savy went independently to rendezvous, so he hoped, with Antelme and some of his former contacts in Paris.

Once getting out of the station at Orleans, Didi came face to face with her first German soldiers in almost two years. Jones reported her saying, 'It was full of Germans and I turned to look at them. The people with me said, "Don't do that! Oh my God, never do a thing like that."'[14]

She survived her first trauma and was quickly taken to the safe house, where she spent the night. The following day, she bravely made her own way by train to Paris to rendezvous, as instructed, with 'Louise' beside the snow-covered statue of King Henri IV on the Pont Neuf bridge. Whether 'Louise' was a locally recruited French courier or someone sent in by the SOE is unknown. People walked past, wrapped up warmly against the cold and, trying not to draw any attention to herself, Didi looked carefully at them all, trying to identify her contact.

Eventually a young woman her own age approached her. This was Louise. Once the correct passwords were exchanged, Didi was taken to Louise's apartment on Boulevard St Michel, where she lived with her mother and sister. This was Didi's *boîte aux lettres*, where she could leave or collect messages for Savy's network. However, she could not stay there. She needed her own apartment.

Didi found the conditions in Paris in the spring of 1944 chaotic. The city was crowded and accommodation was very difficult to find. The Germans had penetrated a number of

Resistance networks, and surviving members and SOE agents were competing for new safe houses. The Gestapo were regularly checking on empty houses and apartments. Posing as an innocent young girl from the south of France, she had come to the capital looking for work. She also needed somewhere to hide her wireless set and make her 'skeds', wireless transmissions, ideally somewhere with complaisant neighbours or none at all.

During this time, the wireless operator at Thame Park assigned the task of transcribing and decoding Didi's transmissions must have been anxiously waiting for her first transmission, as would Marks.

Her first impressions of the France she had returned to were not positive. 'People were suspicious. Houses were few and far between so it took something like a month to find a single house from which to transmit.'[15] Eventually, after spending nights in small hotels and eating at small restaurants, she found a room for herself in Porte Champerret, 5 kilometres north-west of the centre in the 17th arrondissement, and a deserted house for her 'skeds' at 116 Rue de Bagneux, Bourg-la-Reine, a suburb about ten kilometres south. It belonged to a Monsieur and Mademoiselle Dubois who were out of the country, so one imagines, she paid no rent. How much money she had available was not documented, but agents were never at a loss for cash.

However, getting her wireless set across the city to the new house proved extremely stressful. Whilst looking a lot younger than twenty-three would have made her less likely to be identified as someone in the Resistance, being single brought some unwanted attention. Having managed to get herself onto the train for Bourg-la-Reine with her heavy suitcase, she found herself a compartment and sat down, only to find that it filled up with young German privates. She told Liane Jones that:

There was this German soldier who kept looking at me and smiling, so I smiled back. Then I was looking through the window and he said, 'Cigarette, Mademoiselle?' and I said, 'No, thank you, I don't smoke,' and my hands, you see, were stained with nicotine. You could make mistakes like that.

He was looking at me and he said 'What is in your suitcase?' So I said, 'Oh – c'est un phonographe, savez, de la musique,' and he said, 'Oh, oui' and he was looking at me and I thought Oh la, la, I must get out quickly, but I thought I'd better not get out at the next station. I waited – I could see them looking at me in the window.[16]

As one of them would not stop looking at her, she knew he was suspicious and realised she had to get off the train at the next available opportunity. When the train stopped at the next station, she quickly got up and pretended she had reached her stop and stepped onto the platform with her heavy suitcase. As she walked past the carriage window, she could see him whispering to the other officers about her. She knew she had been right to get off as they would certainly have asked to see inside the case. 'It would have been dreadful as they would have seen the transmitter.' Shaken by her encounter, she had to walk the rest of the way.[17]

Once safely in the empty house, she was faced with another anxiety – would she be able to get through to Thame Park? She recalled the interference she had whilst in Scotland, but she erected her aerial and prepared her set. When she turned it on, inserted her crystal and tuned to the right frequency, she experienced such relief to hear the signal come in loud and clear.

Three weeks after her arrival, on 26 March 1944, Didi sent her first message beginning, 'Met Louise, my contact.' Having hidden her set in the box room, she caught the train back into the city and went to Louise's apartment to listen to the radio. In recognition, the SOE arranged that the BBC French Department included the following coded message in the *messages personnels* after that evening's 21.00 hours news: 'Happy to know that the duck has had a good trip.'[18]

Didi's life now began taking on the rhythm of her 'skeds'. She had to go 'on air' twice a day, sending the messages she had encoded on the first sked and receiving them on the second. On occasions she took the train from her apartment in Porte Camperret and the house in Bourg-la-Reine, but on others she walked to avoid any German controls. She had to rendezvous with Savy almost every day to receive his information and pass on the decoded messages she had received.

When Savy first got to Paris he discovered that Antelme had been arrested on landing and was in prison. Knowing it was best to avoid his old office and Antelme's friends, just in case he had talked under interrogation, he had to liaise with his other contacts to continue his mission. This involved collecting important military and economic information, which Didi had to encode and send back to London.

Through Savy, Didi made contact with 36-year-old Major Réne Dumont-Guillemet. Born into a bourgeois Parisian family, he led an extravagant life before the war, working in a film production unit and spending weekends on the French Riviera. When Sydney Jones, his friend, started resistance work in Marseille, he first helped by loaning him money, then joined in sabotage missions and built up a network in Paris.

However, when Jones returned to England, Dumont-Guillemet took over the running of the INVENTOR network. On Jones' suggestion, the SOE decided Dumont-Guillemet needed training so a Lysander flight was arranged to bring him to England on 16/17 October 1943. After paramilitary, parachute and clandestine training, on 5/6 February 1944 he was flown from RAF Tempsford and dropped blind at Les Tronchay, near Laons, about twenty-five kilometres from Clèvillier in Eure-et-Loir.[19, 20]

Codenamed Armand, one of his first jobs was to reorganise the remnants of the FARMER and MUSICIAN networks to create a new SPIRITUALIST network, which operated in the Paris and Lille area and was estimated to have about 1,500 stalwarts and a further 5,000 members if he could provide them with arms. Having met Savy, he gave Didi the task of making arrangements for the dropping of containers of weapons, ammunition and supplies in fields outside Paris. These then needed to be trucked to his members in the north-east of France.

Some of Didi's messages involved her informing London that Savy had persuaded French financiers to lend him money. To guarantee that the loan would be repaid by a British bank after the hoped-for liberation, they were asked to come up with any short phrase they could think of. He gave it to Didi who transmitted it to London, where the SOE arranged for it to be included in the BBC's *messages personnels*. This would confirm to the donor that they were dealing with a genuine SOE agent and not with some German stooge. Once they heard their phrase, they would then hand over the money to Savy.[21]

In Liane Jones *A Quiet Courage* she pointed out that:

Since autumn 1943, Paris had been almost a no-go area for F Section. The PHONO radio game had duped Baker Street into thinking there was still an organisation in the city and only now was the truth beginning to dawn. Meanwhile, there were many Resistance groups springing up of their own accord, but they were fragmented and most of them were barely equipped. Outside the city, in the industrial suburbs, communist *Francs-Tireurs et Partisans (FTP)* groups were thriving – they had long been receiving arms from Allied drops and had developed good organisation and support structures – but in Paris itself the various groups of *resistants* were divided, sometimes by politics, sometimes simply by lack of communication.

Arnaud began a campaign of vetting and recruitment among Paris *resistants*. Many different groups joined SPIRITUALIST, swearing absolute loyalty to the Allied armies as they did so and promising to put the interests of the invasion above any political or personal ones.[22]

With plans for the invasion being at an advanced stage, the SOE arranged for another wireless operator to be sent to help Didi. 20-year-old Jean Gerard Maury, codename Arnaud, arrived on 5 April, but it is not clear whether he was landed by Lysander or was parachuted in. Known as Maurice Faurie, his radio call sign was Minstrel.[23]

When Dumont-Guillemet succeeded in making contact with a network in Lille, he arranged for stores of parachuted equipment to be trucked down from 'safe depots' near Paris. This revived network then planned sabotage of the enemy's communications and was able to provide Savy with vital information about the location of one of the Luftwaffe's V-1 flying bomb storage depots in Seine-et-Loire.

An estimated 2,000 bombs, ready for shipment to launch sites on the north coast, were hidden in 32,000 square feet of limestone caves under the Liverny plateau at Saint Leu d'Esserent, near Criel in Picardy, which had formerly been used for growing mushrooms. The facility included anti-aircraft batteries, concrete bunkers, blockhouses and railway sidings in the limestone quarry.[24] This was highly sensitive military information, which was too important to be transmitted by wireless so Didi had to arrange Savy's return to Britain in order for him to hand it over personally.

Unbeknownst to Didi, after fifteen months in the field, Jacqueline's life had been one of constant train travel. London eventually became so concerned about her health that they arranged for her to be picked up by Flight Lieutenant Robert

Taylor in a 161 Squadron Lysander on 9/10 April 1944. Chalked on the side of the plane were the words: 'JACQUELINE MUST COME.' After four days' wait in the open air close to Galèteries farm buildings, Jacqueline, Josette Southgate, Maurice's wife, and a Mr Régis would have been very relieved when the plane landed in a field two kilometres south-south-west of Villers-les-Ormes, north-west of Châteauroux. Once Philippe de Vomecourt, Lise de Baissac and Captain Charles Corbin disembarked, they got in with their luggage and were flown back to England. Buckmaster told how, a few days later, Maurice Southgate and Jacqueline's photographs figured on the local notice boards as: 'Wanted. Reward offered for the capture dead or alive of individual known as Jacqueline or Josette.'[25, 26, 27]

Savy's departure was a triple-Lysander pick-up organised for the night of 9/10 May. 161 Squadron Leader Leonard Ratcliff, Lieutenant Hysing-Dahl and Flight Lieutenant Bob Large took off from Tangmere and landed their planes in a field, codename Planète, 2.5 kilometres west-south-west of Luzillé, thirty-five kilometres east-south-east of Tours. The six passengers who got out included Denis Rake, a wireless operator. Those who got in and were flown back to Britain with Savy included Richard Heslop, codenamed Xavier, Colette Mizrahi, Colonel Belleuse and four others.[28]

With her organiser gone, Didi was then ordered to attach herself to Dumont-Guillemet's SPIRITUALIST network. Part of his mission included re-establishing contact with the remaining members of the FARMER network in Lille, whose leader, Michael Trotobas, had been killed by the Germans on 27 November 1943. It also included sabotage attacks on the Bosch-Lavalette engine plant, aluminium, rubber and munitions factories, and disrupting railway communications.

Dumont-Guillemet made contact with a group that was preparing an attack on Fresnes prison. This was where most of the captured

SOE agents and French Resistance were being held. It may well have been Didi who had to encode the messages that fifty keys had already made and tested. However, when the SOE was informed that the group's leader had been arrested, the response passed back to Dumont-Guillemet was that the plan had to be abandoned.

She might well have reported his plan to kidnap two Germans, Herr Bochler, an engineer who was working on V-1 rocket sites, and Jacquet, one of the rocket scientists. The plan was aborted when it was discovered that Bochler had a bodyguard and the SOE did not agree to Jacquet's capture.

One imagines that, having to encode Dumont-Guillemet's messages, she was aware that he was also trying to locate and liquidate the double-agents who had infiltrated and brought down Francis Suttill's PROSPER network that had led to hundreds of arrests.[29, 30, 31]

Within weeks of Savy's debrief informing the SOE of the V-1 storage dump, a United States Army Air Force strike was launched on 5 May. Didi may well have reported that it was not successful as 70 per cent of all the flying bombs sent into England during June came from this site. Bomber Command's Lancaster Squadrons then made attacks using 'tallboy' bombs on 11, 12 and 18 July, seriously hampering its operation and destroying 85 per cent on the town.[32]

Given the urgency of the situation and the importance of the information she was receiving, Didi continued to send messages to London about German troop movements, railway sabotage, general military intelligence, arranging arms drops for the MUSICIAN and FARMER networks who were attacking railways carrying German troops to the front line in Normandy, and the reception of the Jedburgh teams. She admitted that, 'When I put my hand on the signal keys, there came a feeling of patriotism. I was pleased I was doing something. It was perhaps a little emotional.'[33]

There were occasions in the evenings when she went back to Louise's apartment to pick up messages and listen to the BBC news and *messages personnels*. In this atmosphere of secrecy and shared trust, it was important for Didi to have some human contact. Just seeing the lights on behind the white curtains gave her reassurance that there were others working with her. However, in her debrief once back in England after the war, she admitted that, having to avoid meeting people who could have been German agents or collaborators, life for her in France was often lonely:

> I used to go out a lot and have my meals in restaurants alone. Sometimes I would meet my contact Louise, but all we would do was to pass a note. It was very solitary.
>
> I wasn't nervous. In my mind I was never going to be arrested. But of course I was careful. There were Gestapo in plain clothes everywhere. I always looked at my reflection in the shop windows to see if I were being followed. One day I went into the *Métro* and on the train I saw a man. He was very nervous and he was reading a newspaper, but at the same time he was looking at me, my shoes, my clothes. This made me suspicious so I got off the train suddenly, about two stations before the one I wanted, and then looked to see if I was being followed. But there was no one there.[34]

Buckmaster also acknowledged that Didi's life in Paris was a solitary one:

> From time to time she had to meet her Organising Officers, the people from whom she received special instructions. These meetings had to take place in streets, trams, trains; a message would be passed and possibly no word spoken, so great was the danger of being observed and discovered. Living in houses

from which she had to move constantly, she continued to send and receive messages in code. She knew that discovery meant interrogation by the Gestapo, with possibly torture, the concentration camp, or death.

Her state was made no easier by her inability during her service in France to get in touch with any of her family. How were her father and mother? Her brother? What had happened to her only sister, engaged on such hazardous work? Eileen went for lonely walks, thinking, worrying, passing cafés, where the invader lounged at ease. Paris can be lovely in June, but for Eileen the loveliness was encased in nightmare. [35]

One can imagine how uplifted Didi must have been when she learned that the Allies had successfully landed on 6 June. Despite the exuberance of knowing that the liberation of France was imminent, there was still a job to do. Resistance groups across France sprang into action with the aim of delaying German reinforcements reaching Normandy. Attacks were made on telegraph lines, railway lines, trains, bridges, tunnels and telephone exchanges. Trees were felled across the roads to delay traffic and all sorts of bombs placed on the roads to blow up tanks and troop carriers. These attacks intensified the German's attacks on the Resistance and their efforts to locate the transmissions of the wireless operators.

Over the time Didi spent on her mission, she sent 105 messages back to HQ. In an interview with Liane Jones after the war, Didi admitted that she was aware of the Gestapo's detection teams. She reported hearing police car sirens when she had finished transmitting, and detecting interference on her transceiver indicating they were trying to jam her, so she frequently moved between transmitting places, but eventually the Gestapo caught up with her.[36]

Two days after Savy had left and about five months after her return to France, disaster struck.

7

ARREST, INTERROGATION, TORTURE & ESCAPE: 25 JULY 1944–25 MAY 1945

Having transmitted from the same house for three months, it was becoming increasingly likely her transmissions were being picked up. Her contacts found her another house in Le Vésinet, a pleasant residential suburb, about twenty kilometres west of Paris. Arnaud was already transmitting from there, but had told her he experienced occasional interference.

When her Chief ordered her to move, she went to the apartment on Boulevard St-Michel and found a message that needed transmitting urgently. In a quandary whether she could go to Bourg-la-Reine and transmit one last time from there or whether to pick up her set and take it to Le Vésinet, she decided, due to the urgency of the situation, on the former. Rather than go by train, she walked and, arriving in the early evening, encoded the message whilst waiting for the hour of her night-time sked. As it approached, there was a power cut. She had to wait. The electricity was not restored until the following morning so, unwilling to wait until the evening, she decided to transmit during the day. She set up her set, erected the aerial and began to tap away on the Morse key. What this message was is unknown. Jones claims that all radio messages were destroyed after the war.

She had finished by 11 o'clock when suddenly she was disturbed by loud noises coming from outside. There was shouting and banging on the door of the adjoining property. She could tell it was the Gestapo. This was the moment Didi had been dreading. They had found her. According to a note in her file by M. S. Milar, seventeen members of the Gestapo and the *Milice* arrived in seven cars and surrounded the house.[1] There is a discrepancy over the date. Didi said it was Tuesday 25 July. A note in her personal file stated it was 22 July and Buckmaster gave 26 June. One imagines Arnaud, the other wireless operator, passed on the information to HQ who then informed Jacqueline and Francis, and indeed one imagines the worry they must have experienced on hearing the news.

She reported after the war that she wondered whether she would ever be able to escape, but she knew there would be little chance of surviving alive, even if she used her revolver. She had just enough time to pick up all her papers, run into the kitchen, burn them and hide the ashes under the oven. She dismantled her set and the aerial and hid it in the box room. There was no mention of her hiding her revolver and no reference to an 'L' pill. Didi did not want to die. Her only alternative was to bluff her way out of it.[2,3]

When they started banging on her door, she went down to open it. A Gestapo officer stood there pointing his gun at her. He told her it was a house search. She asked him what was going on when he walked in. He had a cursory look around and then returned to the door. She thought he was going to leave, but he called for back-up. They came from next door and began a thorough search of the house.

She hoped against hope that the officer would not go into the box room. Three more officers burst into the house, armed with guns. It was not long before they found her set, her one-time pad and the revolver. Pointing the machine gun at her, one of them told her, 'You have finished your war, be happy.' Immediately, they demanded her code key. In response, she told them: 'Huh. How many sailors, how many captains...' When they asked her questions about the code she was using, she told them lies. They weren't fooled. One of them rushed at her and slapped her around the head as hard as he could, calling her a liar, a spy, a dirty bitch. Another told her that they had ways of making people talk when they didn't want to.[4]

Once they had handcuffed her, she was dragged downstairs and bundled into one of the waiting cars. One imagines her sitting there, wearing only a light summer frock, heart thumping and mind spinning with a welter of thoughts about how she was going to survive.

She was driven back into Paris, across the Seine and through the grand buildings of the 8th arrondissement. The car stopped on the Champs Elysées to pick up a man wearing the long black leather coat and the hat of a senior Gestapo officer. She had to defend herself from him trying to beat her as they drove on to their headquarters nearby on Rue des Saussaies. All the time Didi was preparing to 'lie like a tiger'.

Once inside, she was taken to the interrogation room. A short, sallow man began the questioning by asking her what nationality she was, to which she answered, 'French.' When asked her name she said, 'Jacqueline du Tetre.' When asked who the gun belonged to that they had found in the house, she told him it had been left by a gardener who used to work there. When told she was a British agent, she denied it. When told she was a spy, sending information to England and ordering weapons for the Resistance, she denied it. When asked about her work, she claimed she was an innocent shop assistant who had no idea that the messages she was sending for her boss were being sent to England. She thought they were his commercial affairs and did not understand what they meant. She just did her work and got paid. When queried about whether she had any other friends working with her, she made up some addresses of people.

Having lived in France for twenty-one years, Didi naturally behaved like a French girl, even though she only looked seventeen. Jones described her as having 'a direct, innocent look; her manner of talking was intense and unsophisticated and these things began to work on the interrogating officer; as she persisted in saying she was French, he started to have doubts'.[5]

When asked how she had begun this work she told him that she was a governess from the south of France who had come to Paris looking for work. As she could not find anything immediately, she used to sit in cafés reading the jobs pages in the newspapers. After some time without work, she was getting desperate. On noticing a man who kept looking at her whilst she sat in a café, she got up to go, but he came over and asked her if she wanted a drink. She thought she ought to refuse, but she was so short of money, she thought it would be nice to talk to somebody.

She went on to say that, when he commented that she looked concerned, she admitted that she was, that she had little money and was desperate to get a job, he said he could help. He told her he was a businessman, but added that she must never tell anybody about his work. He did not like people talking about the work he did, but she would find out one day. He told her not to talk, gave her a surprisingly large amount of money and told her he would not be there the next day, but a friend of his would. Through him she would meet other people.

Women today would very likely not have talked to such a man, nor accepted money from a complete stranger, thinking he might have sexual motives. But this was the story Didi told her interrogators. When asked what this businessman looked like, she described him as wearing glasses, having a moustache – anything to create an imaginary character. She later admitted, 'All sorts of things I pulled out of my head. And the more I was lying, the more I wanted to and the more it was easy coming to me. In the training course they were quite right – they could judge. They said I was a good liar and I would come out of it and I did.'[6]

Jones commented that this lying eventually saved Didi's life as it diverted attention away from her and may well have saved others. For her it was a personal victory. She had been caught, but she was not going to give up. By lying, she distracted her interrogators; 'She was carrying the Resistance war with her even into the prisons.'[7]

She was congratulated on her operating skills. She was told that they had been monitoring her transmissions for some time having detected her set by using their direction finding equipment. When asked where she had learnt how to operate a wireless set, she told them that she had to learn Morse code and use a set when she worked in the Post Office. They did not fully believe her and presented her with the one-time-pad they had found in the house. When asked to explain it, she said she had been given most of the messages already encoded. On threatening her, she gave them a false key and claimed that she had used it on some messages. When they demanded she used it on a message they gave her, she struggled to complete it. 'I said, I don't understand. It's not working. I can't understand this. When I said that he turned on me – that was their way – and said "Liar! Spy!" and came to hit me on the face. So I turned around and he hit me here, quite strongly. And he said, "We have ways of making people who don't want to talk, talk. Come with us."'[8]

Still handcuffed, they escorted her from the interrogation room, down to corridor to one of the torture rooms. In order to extract information from reluctant prisoners, the Gestapo used the *baignoire*. 'To refresh, my clouded memory,' Didi recalled. This was a bath of cold water, often contaminated from the previous victim's body fluids. One of the interrogators stripped down to his underwear to avoid soaking his clothes. Her head was pushed underwater and held until her lungs almost burst. Not getting enough oxygen brings sharp pains in the chest, sickness, disorientation and panic. On being pulled out by her hair, the questioning started again. If she refused to talk, the repeated the process until she did. According to Didi, she claimed she couldn't talk as they were choking her.

'You suffocate under the water, but you stick to your story. I remembered what we had been taught, never be afraid, never let them dominate you.' When they pulled her out of the water, her hair and upper body dripping wet, she threatened to complain to the *mairie* [Mayor] of the district about what they had done. They then asked her if she had had a nice bath to which she replied 'Excellent.' She admitted being rude and complaining about how they were treating her.[9]

Jones reported Didi telling her that another Gestapo officer arrived to take over the questioning. She described him as being very tall, wearing a highly decorated uniform and looking very impressive. He asked her if she understood German. She said she didn't. He asked her if she was French, to which she answered, *'Mais, oui.'* He then wanted to know if she knew that British agents were being parachuted into France. Showing surprise, she said, 'What do you mean, British agents parachuted into France? But where?' He told her they were being dropped at night, in the countryside and asked her if she knew about the Resistance. 'But who would tell me a thing like that. It's fantastic!' He then revealed that the man she was working for was a British agent. 'A British agent! But look – ah, I understand now; I understand.'[10] She was then asked if she would be prepared to work for them, transmitting messages back to London. As an incentive, she was told that she would be well treated.

Didi was convinced that they really thought she was French and that a British agent had been attempting to recruit girls like her. When she was told she had been used, she told them that it was her chief who ought to be being questioned, not her.

She was then asked when and where she was next due to rendezvous with her chief. To gain time, she told them that she was going to meet him in a café opposite Gare St Lazare at 7 o'clock. It was a completely false story, but she thought there might be an opportunity for her to escape through the women's toilets. After they called for a car to drive her there, she was told that if she tried to warn him, they would both be shot. The café would be surrounded and neither of them would be able to get away. She believed them and went on trying to convince them that she was confused and did not fully understand what was going on.

A team of Gestapo officers then drove her to the station and made her sit, still in her wet clothes, at a table the far end of the café. Not having any money for a drink, she brazenly asked to be given some, arguing that it would look strange if she had none. She was given enough and just sat there, damp and nervous in her summer dress, knowing no-one would turn up, whilst the men sat at the other end – waiting.

Unsure about how events might unfold and how long she might have to wait, an air raid warning was sounded. It was 7.15 p.m. As the confusion might give her a chance to escape, she told them she was desperate to go to the toilet. They allowed her to go, but one of the officers followed her to the door. The ladies' toilet was on one side, the men's on the other and there were quite a lot of people around. She went into a cubicle and noticed an open window. However, it was far too small for her to climb through. She stayed in the toilet as long as she dared, trying desperately to think of a way out of her predicament. Having no alternative, she went back out and told the Gestapo that her chief must have been caught in the *Métro*. The one who gave her the money then angrily asked for his change.

They then took her back to Rue de Saussaies and put her in a cell guarded by a young *Milice* with a gun. According to Jones, when Didi asked him if he was French, he said, 'Keep quiet or I'll gun you down. Don't be strong-headed with me. You gave false addresses for your employers, didn't you?' 'I gave the addresses they gave me. But of course they were false. If they were agents, they would give false addresses, wouldn't they?'[11]

Later she was transferred to a room on the upper floor of the building, where there were two captured RAF officers and locked in. It is probable they had the room taped to see if she spoke English. Noticing a high window on the outside wall, she motioned to the men to give her a leg up. She might be able to escape onto the roof. They told her it was no use, they had already tried it. There was nothing to hold onto on the outside wall and nowhere to go, but to jump several storeys. With no alternative, she was forced to sit there and wait to discover what was going to happen next.

There was no more interrogation. When they came for her the next time, it was with a pen and paper on which they demanded she write down her statement. Repeating exactly what she had told them, she had no qualms about signing it and handing it over, tried not to show how excited she was at managing to get away with it. She was convinced they hated the British and feared them even more.

Didi believed she had been tortured because she had maintained she was French. Yvonne Baseden, another British SOE agent captured on 26 June 1944, was taken to the same Gestapo HQ where she too kept to her cover story. She recalled being placed in a basement cell, which had no light with a tiny, blacked out window. The bed consisted of two boards completely covered with blood and she only had one blanket. She was left in this cell for three days and three nights with no food, no water and no toilet facilities. Only twice did she get any visitors during her incarceration, who asked if she was prepared to talk. On the morning of the fourth day she was taken back to the interrogation room to answer questions. One of her interrogators attempted to intimidate her by drawing his revolver and firing a couple of shots into the floor directly between her feet, but she made no mention of being tortured.[12]

Odette Sansom fared worse than Didi and Yvonne. She had been landed by a *felucca*, a Spanish fishing boat, on the Mediterranean coast in early November 1942 and worked as a courier for the SPINDLE network in the Jura mountains of south-east France. Within hours of her meeting Peter Churchill, another British SOE agent who had just been parachuted in to help, they were both arrested on 16 April 1944. In Jerrald Tickell's biography of Odette, he states she was taken to a cell, where they:

> Began leisurely to unbutton her blouse. She said, 'I resent your hands on me or on my clothes. If you tell me what to do and release your hands on me, I will do it.' 'As you wish, unbutton your blouse.' Having already been burnt by a hot poker on her spine, she was then told to take off her stockings and her toenails were extracted. 'To be tortured by this clean, soap-smelling, scented Nordic was one thing. To be touched by his hands was another.' Before her fingernails were removed, a higher ranking officer stopped the interrogation, but she was warned. 'If you speak about what has happened to a living soul, you will be brought here again and worse things will happen to you.' Though she had kept silent, she was filled with sickness and fear for she had heard of some of the other things that the Gestapo could do to women's bodies.[13]

Odette said she endured fourteen interrogations, during which she refused to give any information about her friends. She could have told them what they wanted to know: where their radio operator was and where another British agent who had arrived some time before them had been to, but she refused. 'I'm not brave or courageous, I just make up my own mind about certain things, and when this started, this treatment of me, I thought, "There must be a breaking point." Even if in your own mind you don't want to break, physically you're bound to break after a certain time. But I thought, "If I can survive the next minute without breaking, this is another minute of life, and I can feel that way instead of thinking of what's going to happen in half an hour's time, when having torn out my toenails they're going to start on my fingers."'[14]

The Gestapo did not take up Didi's offer of visiting the addresses she had given them. Instead they transferred her to the grey, fortress-like Fresnes Prison, a few miles south of the capital, near what is now Orly airport. She was put in a cell with two French girls. Who they were or why they were in prison was not revealed.

In a 1950 interview with James Gleeson, Didi told him that she had created the impression that she had been imprudent and was unaware of the political implications of her involvement with the Resistance. She claimed she was 'a bit of a scatterbrain and a tomboy ... helping the Resistance for fun and excitement.'[15]

In Foot's *SOE in France*, he noted that Didi 'put on her act of being a sweet little thing who knew nothing she ought not' and that, consequently, she 'brought off a dexterous bluff, and persuaded the Gestapo she was only a foolish little shop girl who had taken up resistance work because it was exciting'.[16]

Pattinson commented that this gendered strategy was only open to women. Didi had been informed by her training instructors that she was a good liar and found that, during interrogations, she could improvise plausible explanations and remain calm: 'All sorts of things I pulled from my head. And the more I was lying, the more I wanted to and the more it was easy coming to me.' Her conscious strategy was 'to act confusion and misunderstanding'.[17]

Maisie McLintock told Pattinson that Didi was very clever:

It explained a lot when she survived the Germans and that concentration camp using the same method as she had done when she was a FANY. Wide-eyed innocence ... One of the first things she said when she was telling me about her experience, she was taken to the Avenue Foch in Paris, that was where she got her preliminary going over, and she said, 'You see, Mac, I did what you said, I played the daft lassie with them.' ... She was still getting through life somehow, looking innocent and not quite sure why she was there. [18]

She spent almost three weeks in Fresnes prison. She later recalled the last words her interrogators spoke to her before they decided to send her to Germany. 'We are giving you the benefit of the doubt, but we are sending you to a concentration camp. You'll have a good laugh there. Yes, it won't be like here. It will be your punishment for having worked against us.'[19]

On the morning of 15 August 1944, Didi, still known to the Germans as Jacqueline du Terte, was trucked to one of the railway stations and pushed into a cattle truck with a batch of women suspected of being British agents and a number of French girls who had been working for the Resistance. One imagines she was still wearing the same cotton dress and underwear as she was when she was caught. At 4 p.m. the train stopped at Alsace Lorraine, where they had to change trains. The 'passengers' were led out, under armed guard. According to Jones:

Didi understandably longed to escape. Since she had been captured, she had thought continually about the possible ways of doing it, and now, as she looked out of the stationary train and saw open fields, fringed with woodland, she realised that this was a chance that might not come again. The distance across the field was dangerous, but if she could reach the trees beyond she might be able to escape.[20]

Turning to the woman nearest her, she told her of her plan. Warned that she would be shot as soon as she started running, she ignored this, feeling a compulsion that her only means of survival was to escape. She knew her field-craft training at Beaulieu would have stood her in good stead if she had to live off the land. When her group of women, ignoring the suggestion, descended from the carriage, she broke away and started running across the field. Instead of a barrage of bullets, there was a loud scream behind her. It was a German soldier telling her to stop or he would shoot. She had no chance of avoiding being shot down so she stopped, her instinct for survival getting the better of her. Standing still in the field, she waited until she was seized and marched back to the line of women, all the time being shouted at by German soldiers.

Once the new train arrived, she was pushed into a proper carriage, but there was hardly room to sit down. All the time she thought about what possible opportunities might arise for her to escape. Shortly after the train started rattling its way into Germany, a German officer walked along the corridor telling the passengers that someone had tried to escape when they stopped. If this person tried again, they and all the other women would be shot. With the eyes of the other women glaring at her, Didi knew she could not be responsible for their deaths.

At one point, Red Cross representatives boarded the train and started distributing food parcels. Didi stared incredulously as a nurse handed the woman next to her a parcel, inside which was a nurse's uniform and a pass. Having divested her old clothes, the woman put the uniform on, followed the nurses and managed to walk off the train, showing her pass to the guard.

Imagine how Didi must have felt. Sometime later she was particularly pleased to discover that, in all the commotion whilst she had tried to escape, two women used it as an excuse to get away themselves. By the time their absence was noted, they had disappeared.

Didi spent a week in an overcrowded train with little food, drink or sleep on the journey to Ravensbrück, fifty miles (80 km) north of Berlin. This was one of several Nazi concentration camps, built in a beauty spot, noted for its lakes and secluded villas for wealthy city-dwellers. Its site was on marshy ground, often infested with malarial mosquitoes. There were enclaves outside the camp for working parties doing factory or heavy agricultural work in the community, as well as a *Jugendlager*, or youth camp, where those too ill or unfit for work were accommodated. Squadron leader Beryl Escott, the WAAF historian, gave a long account of Ravensbrück, which is worth including to give you an idea of the conditions Didi and many of the female agents had to endure:

The main camp surrounded by high walls was built for about 6,000 prisoners. Inside were wooden huts for living quarters containing three tiers of bunks, a few brick buildings for kitchens, showers and a concrete cell block. Cinder paths divided the huts in front of which blossomed flowers in profusion. But there, all semblance of cleanliness and proper conditions stopped. The place was in fact known to the French as L'Enfer des Femmes, the Women's Hell.

Nearly all the prisoners were civilians, both young and old, from conquered countries either as slave labour or on suspicion of involvement with the Resistance, all being imprisoned without trial, though this did not prevent them being cruelly tortured during questioning in the camp's political department. During the war years over 50,000 women, at the lowest estimate, died in this camp from dirt, disease, overcrowding, squalor, starvation, overwork and ill-treatment, apart from those who were shot or gassed or sent to die elsewhere.

When Cécile Lefort was admitted in 1943, she spent her first days in the quarantine hut, where new arrivals were kept for three weeks to ensure they brought no new infection to the camp. After being checked in, though weary from the long train journey, she had to stand several hours before being admitted to the bathhouse, where she was told to strip and her former clothes were taken away. Here she waited naked in the cold for a further few hours under the tiny hole in the ceiling, where the shower worked, and that was only for a few minutes. With a sliver of soap and a pocket handkerchief of a towel she had to clean herself. Again a long wait and then a shock. Two men came in, one to look at her teeth and one to give her a cursory medical examination, which revealed that something was wrong.

Then she was issued with prison clothing, thin and inadequate for the advancing winter, and dispatched to the quarantine hut. There, no one was to be allowed outside, though all were awakened well before dawn for bitter acorn coffee. They were crowded at the window watching while the other women lined up five deep in front of their huts, in the freezing cold and rain, the living and the dead together, and stood for the hour-long 'Appells', where they were counted and appointed their work for the day. Some were detailed for gardening, some for sewing or knitting, some for corpse, rubbish or coal collecting, some for road mending, cleaning latrines, tree-felling or potato picking, women being used instead of horses to drag the heavy carts. Work went in shifts of 10 or 11 hours each, day and night, lights out coming at about 9 p.m. Food, mainly vegetable soup and half a loaf of bread a day, was not sufficient for such heavy work. This was the life that awaited them when quarantine was finished.[21]

Foot informed the readers of his *SOE in France* that:

> Those who have not experienced these modern hells can form no properly vivid conception of their beastliness; and the right to try to picture it on paper belongs best to the sufferers who survived. It is worth remarking that the camps had a considerable role to play in the Nazi economy, and that their prisoners were expected not merely to exist, but to work, and work hard, on a diet of acorn coffee, turnip soup, and a little dried bread. It was expected, in fact it was intended, that they would all be worked to death.[22]

Didi's debrief after the war contained few details of her fifteen days at Ravensbrück, but she told Jones about her arrival at night. After a roll-call, they were sent into the shower hut to wash. Their accommodation was in long huts with bunk beds. The next morning, when they went out for the morning roll-call, she saw the tall chimney by the main entrance and heard people whisper that is was the crematorium. There was then the 'Rêvier', long sessions of medical inspections, examinations and the issuing of prison clothes. She was put in a hut with other French women, but there were others for Swedes, Poles, Russians and even German women who had been convicted of criminal offences. Conditions were filthy and the food was poor, which led to a general deterioration of health.

Her first task was hard labour in the vegetable plots in the camp. Within weeks everyone was walking around in a daze. The brutality of the punishments, beaten with whips for not working hard enough or arguing with guards, had both a physical and psychological effect. She recalled seeing a woman stretched naked on the freezing ground for some offence she had committed and another being put in an underground bunker with no food for stealing a potato.

> Conditions were very bad. We had clear soup, it was like water, with a piece of dry bread. For soap we had a piece of stone. And we were dazed, like drugged. It was bitter cold and we had to work and as I was walking up and down the camp I met Violette Szabo and another girl, called Denise [Bloch]. 'Oh!' she said. 'You too!'[23]

Didi told Violette that she was passing herself off as a French woman. When Violette asked her what the Gestapo had done to her during her interrogation, she was horrified when Didi told her about the *'baignoire'*. She told Didi that neither she, Denise nor Lilian Rolfe, another captured SOE agent, had been tortured, and advised Didi to change her story. 'You should have said you were English. English girls are better treated than the French.' but I said, 'No, I'm sticking to my story.'[24]

Denise looked unwell and weak, whereas Violette appeared in good spirits, convinced they would be rescued eventually. Although Didi admired her courage, she was wary of being seen with the British women. Keeping to her cover story that she was Jacqueline du Tetre was important to her as all her fellow French prisoners knew her as Jacqueline and it was her way of ensuring the Germans remained ignorant of her involvement with the SOE.

One of the Frenchwomen she told Jones she befriended in Ravensbrück was Geneviève Matthieu, who had the bunk above hers. Didi kept up friendship with Geneviève after the war, describing her as having a strong personality and being very stubborn. She was always looking for little ways to thwart the camp rules without being caught, collecting forbidden things like pencils and scraps of material, and where Didi was a natural loner, she was a mixer and entertainer. Younger than most of the women around them, they talked together a lot, but like everyone else Geneviève knew Didi only as Jacqueline. [25]

Born into a wealthy family, Geneviève grew up in Paris. Her father, a World War One veteran, encouraged her, after learning how to ride a bike, to drive a car and fly a plane. Hearing de Gaulle's speech on 18 June 1940, Geneviève decided to keep the flames burning and helped her cousin, who had escaped from prison, to enter the 'Free Zone' and join the Resistance. Eventually, she worked as a courier in Pierre Fourcard's BRUTUS network, cycling up to 100 kilometres a day carrying messages to Lyon, stealing stamps when she was working in the Red Cross and in the *mairie* of the 17th arrondissement, making false documents and providing safe houses for escapees.

After being denounced by someone in her network, she was arrested in the summer of 1944. Like Didi, she was taken to the Gestapo HQ and 'miraculously' escaped execution to be charged with 'aiding the enemy' and was imprisoned in Fresnes. On 15 August she was transported in cattle trucks with Didi to Ravensbrück, arriving six days later. That summer, fifteen female SOE agents were being held in German concentration camps at Ravensbrück, Dachau, Buchenwald and Belsen. Only two survived.

Whilst in the camp with Didi, she suffered from typhoid, but managed to embroider on her dress, under the red triangle denoting she was a political deportee, her number: 57,552.

Often we marched naked in front of the officers who were inspecting our teeth and hands. Initially, we were asked who wanted to go to a brothel. Fortunately, two resistant prostitutes had dedicated themselves. Before she had time to attend the hangings, which were common in the camp, Geneviève was sent with several work units to work in a German armament factory. As political deportees, we knew we were in danger of death. So, as we were alive, the resistance continued: our biggest job was sabotage![26, 27, 28, 29]

In October, Didi, Geneviève, Violette, Denise and Lilian were among a group of women sent by train to another work camp in Torgau, about 130 kilometres south of Berlin. She stayed there for two months digging roads, farming vegetables and working in machine factories.

By this time, the Third Reich was in retreat. The Allies had advanced as far as the Rhine. The Russian Red Army was advancing from the east and the Americans were approaching from the south. With the *Wehrmacht* back inside its national boundaries, German cities were being hit nightly by Allied 'carpet bombing'. Unable to import requisitioned goods from previously occupied countries, the Third Reich relied heavily on foreign labour and the efforts of prisoners in their concentration camps, forcing them to work till they dropped.

Didi provided some details about Torgau in her debrief, but her friends' names were redacted from the transcript. 'I met [blanked out] at Torgau, where we all worked in the fields. I knew that [blanked out] wanted to escape, but after that I left the camp and arrived at Abteroda in October. [blanked out] and [blanked out] stayed in the camp and I worked in the factory.'[30]

She told Jones that she spoke with Violette Szabo about wanting to escape from Torgau and learned that she, Lilian and Denise wanted to. Violette told her that she had a plan. Being less well guarded than Ravensbrück, there was a possibility, if they could get hold of a key, they could get through a door in the outside wall and out into open fields. The door was close to the wash-room and behind a barricade.

Ten days later, Violette told Didi she had got hold of the key. How was not explained. However, before they could take advantage of it, someone informed the guards. To protect herself,

Violette had to throw the key in the gutter. That put an end to their escape attempt as the British women were then sent back to Ravensbrück and Didi was transferred to Abteroda, a sub-camp of Buchwald concentration camp, where prisoners were forced to work in an aircraft parts factory. According to Didi:

> At Abteroda the Commandant SS from Torgau came and we heard that he was looking for two English girls who had escaped from Torgau and there were rumours that it was [blanked out] and [blanked out]. They were always with a girl called [blanked out]. I did not want to work in the factory so they shaved my head and told me that if I did not work in 20 minutes I would be shot. I then decided to work.
>
> I worked 12 hours a day in a factory drilling holes in aviation parts. I tried to make myself break a bit every day. And my technique was good, up to a point. When I was caught, I was deprived of soup and my head was shaved.[31]

She told Jones how the guards threatened to lock her in a tower if she continued to disrupt production and ordered the other women to stop talking to her. There was no alternative. Didi continued to work, but did so as slowly as she dared possible. Although her rebelliousness had improved her morale, it brought her to the attention of the camp commandant. During the questioning Didi was told that some of the women thought she was English. Replying in English with a French accent, she argued that she had never said she was English, only that she spoke English. Having spoken rudely to the woman cheered her up. She also knew that the commandant was unnerved by her.

Whilst in these camps, Buckmaster commented:

> Eileen did her best to adopt the technique of the hunted animal and to merge into her background. At length she tricked the

camp guards and got herself included in a working party in a factory. But she had no intention whatever of helping the enemy war machine. She made up her mind to do all the sabotage that her instruments and gauges would allow. Day after day she succeeded in falsifying precision instruments and graphs, and the aero-engine parts she turned out were all rejected by the inspection department. To her delight, it was a long time before they traced the faults to her. As a punishment her long golden hair was shaved, and once more she went through the torments of the icy plunge. She was allowed to return to the factory, and although she now had only limited opportunities for sabotage, she contrived with one wild swoop to wreck a vital machine. She was careless of consequences, and would not yield to force.

The camp authorities decided that she must be punished again, and more severely. Meanwhile Eileen had disappeared among the thousands of French prisoners. By the time she had been found again, trace of her misdemeanour had been lost.

While in this camp she caught diphtheria through drinking filthy water.[32]

Jones described how the winter of 1944 saw Didi in poor health:

...chest pains ... she felt increasingly weak and tired. She and the other women worked crushingly long hours, often under bombardment from Allied planes. One day as they were working in the factory, an air raid began and they all had to leave their machines and take cover. Didi was so exhausted that despite the noise of the planes and the bombs falling, and the panic around her, she fell asleep. Geneviève was with her; she watched Didi sleeping and when the raid was over, wakened her. Didi was confused and didn't know where she was: for a moment she had forgotten all about the concentration camp and captivity.

'Where am I?' she asked Geneviève. 'Am I in England?'

For Geneviève it was one of the worst moments of all her time in the camps. Didi had no idea where she was and her face, though bewildered, was momentarily unhaunted. Geneviève had to watch understanding come back into it as she told Didi, as gently as possible, that no, she was not in England nor at home in France, but in a German concentration camp.

Didi was beginning to feel her strength ebb away. And in mid-winter they were on the move again, back to Ravensbrück, and then to another working camp at Markkleeberg, near Leipzig.[33]

She arrived on 1 December in Markkleeberg, an all-women sub camp of Ravensbrück, seven kilometres from Leipzig. There, she and her group were forced to work on the roads for twelve hours a day for months, trying to survive on a thin bowl of soup a day and a few scraps of bread. Dysentery was rife, but Didi hung on. She told Jones that it was, 'The will to live. Will power. That's the most important. You should never let yourself go. It seemed that the end would never come, but I have always believed in destiny and I had a hope. If you are a person who is drowning you put all your efforts into trying to swim.'[34]

She recalled that on 9 April the SS camp Commandant told the prisoners that they were going to be moved 80 kilometres away. Instead of being put on a train, they were forced to do a night march. Even though it was April, the temperature was below freezing. By this time, Didi must have learned that the Americans were not far from Leipzig so she decided to take the opportunity to escape, knowing that she would otherwise face death. About 11 o'clock at night, when they were passing through a forest, she managed to jump out of the line of prisoners and hide behind a tree. Then, running from one tree to another, she made her way deeper into the forest, listening to see if she was being followed.

Suddenly, she heard some rustling noises nearby. Using the field-craft training she received at Beaulieu, she waited in silence, listening and watching. As her eyes got used to the dark and her ears to the night noises, she could tell that there were two figures making their way through the trees. Listening carefully, she determined they weren't German guards. Further away she could hear the noise of footsteps as the line of women continued their march and the occasional flashes of the guards' torches but there was no search party. As they got closer, she made out that the two figures were French women about the same age as her who had also escaped from the line.

Without startling them, she joined them, recognising them as Renée and Yvette. They waited in silence as the procession passed and together they made their way through the forest and across fields in the general direction of Leipzig. Before dawn, they approached the outskirts of Markkleeburg and found a deserted house that had been destroyed by a bomb. There was a hole in the wall, a few feet above the ground. Renée climbed up and worked her way inside. Yvette was so small Didi had to help her up and Renée pulled from above until eventually she got through. Then Didi squeezed through.

They slept until dawn and when they saw the hole in the morning, Didi recalled being surprised to find it was hardly big enough to let a dog through. They spent the rest of the day there, but, faint with hunger, they had to go out to find food. Finding a farm with a chicken coop, Didi decided to steal one. However, when a guard dog started barking they gave up on the idea as they knew the farmer would come out.

Deciding to walk to Leipzig, where they hoped they would find the American troops, they started walking along a road, but, when they turned a corner, they spotted a German patrol. Rather than turn and try and hide, Renée volunteered to talk their way out of it as she spoke German. As expected, they were stopped and asked for their papers. Renée explained that they had none as they were *travailleurs libres*, volunteer French workers on their way to a new working party. They were believed and allowed to continue.

Every time they heard the sound of a vehicle approaching, they hid in the bushes at the side of the road. Still starving, they were becoming increasingly desperate. With no money to buy food, they had no alternative but to beg, borrow or steal. Maybe Didi found them some edible plants to stave off hunger. Finding a church, they decided the sleep in the graveyard. Early the following morning, too cold to sleep any longer and desperately hungry, they decided to walk into Leipzig. As Didi was a Catholic, she felt the best thing to do, rather than approach the residents, was to ask a priest. He would not refuse a request for help from a Catholic needing shelter. In France, priests regularly provided refuge for fugitives and members of the Resistance. It was worth a try.

It worked. Shocked at the sight of three dishevelled, emaciated women and aware that there were German soldiers out in the streets, he provided them with much needed shelter. He ushered them upstairs into the belfry of the church and told them to wait there in silence and he would bring them food and drink.

Didi told Jones that the three days she spent in the church were like a dream. She slipped in and out of consciousness, waking once to see a German woman doctor examining her and at other times to see the priest looking after them.

One morning they were woken from their sleep by the sounds of gunfire. Going downstairs they looked into the street to see white flags flying on many of the buildings. The Americans had arrived. It was 15 April 1945. Wanting to go out and greet them, the priest dissuaded them, saying they might be shot. Eventually American soldiers burst into the church, aimed their guns at the priest and the women, ordering them to lie down on the floor and demanded to know if there were any soldiers in the building.

Didi told them that she was English and that she and the other two had escaped from a camp and that the priest had looked after them. Ordering them to get up, they questioned the priest and decided to send Renée and Yvette to a French camp and take Didi with them. Embracing each other, the women separated. Didi had escaped.[35]

In her debrief she detailed how she asked to be taken to a Red Cross camp. However, they refused and insisted on putting her up in a house for one night. The next morning she was taken to an American camp, where the captain interrogated her with a lot of captured SS in the room. When he had heard her story, he presented her to the SS and told them that, as they had treated her so badly, they would have to pay for it. The SS denied any knowledge of her. The next day she was transferred to another camp with English prisoners and there Didi was interrogated by someone in the American Intelligence Service.

When she was asked for her identity number, she told them she had no number. They asked for her papers and Didi told them her story how she was arrested in Paris and that the Gestapo had confiscated all her identity papers. She told them she was a wireless operator and that she knew 'Colonel Max Baxter'. Whether she had forgotten his name or was deliberately avoiding having to name the head of F Section is unknown. They were not convinced and told her she would have to go through many more camps before she was passed by the British authorities. Throughout all this time she was forced to share accommodation with the Nazis and was treated as one of them.

At the last camp she was interrogated again and she told them exactly how she was landed in France and arrested by the Gestapo. They expressed great surprise at a plane being able to get there in the night. They were very curious and asked her a lot of questions about the organisation she claimed she worked for, the schools she had attended etc. As she did not want to give too much away, they told her they thought she was a German agent and would send a message to the British to confirm what she claimed. In the meantime, she had to stay in the camp with the Nazi girls. When she asked if she could be separated from them and they refused, she was treated in exactly the same way as the Nazis.

Although they apologised, they claimed that there were so many German agents they had to be careful. They said that even if they did receive a message saying that she was English, it would not prove anything as she might still be a German agent.[36]

The 5th Corps of the First US Army reported finding her on 15 April 1945 and after interrogating her, in a report issued a fortnight later and marked 'SECRET', they commented that:

> Subject creates a very unbalanced impression. She is often unable to answer the simplest questions, as though she were impersonating someone else. Her account of what happened to her after landing near Orleans is held to be invented. It is recommended that subject be put at the disposal of the British Authorities for further investigation and disposition. [37]

Didi was kept in the camp for a month, during which time she made a report to the Americans about the Nazi girls, saying that they used to ask the Americans for cigarettes and get them to come into their rooms. The next morning one of the Nazi girls had her head shaved. This was a common punishment for what were called 'horizontal collaborators'. After this they put her with a French girl. Then one day they presented her to an English major, who must have been sent to meet her once the British had verified her credentials. She described him as 'extremely nice and sympathetic'. He took her to Weimar, a city about 250 kilometres south-west of Berlin, where she was very well treated and provided with her first comfortable night's sleep in almost a year. She explained her story to the Major in detail and he arranged her flight to Brussels, where she was again very well treated. After repeating her story to an English captain, she was put on a flight to England, arriving on 25 May 1945.[38]

8

LIFE BACK IN ENGLAND:
26 MAY 1945–2 SEPTEMBER 2010

A reception committee of a very different kind was waiting to meet the plane carrying Didi. Buckmaster and Atkins hardly recognised the thin, emaciated, short-haired woman who disembarked as the smart, charming girl who had left two years earlier. One imagines she would have been asked all sorts of questions about her experiences as they drove her down to London to meet Jacqueline. Although she walked jauntily over the threshold of 97 Darenth Road, after embracing her elder sister, she collapsed in floods of tears.

Once she was fit enough, she was taken to be debriefed. Transcripts of her account of her mission are included in her personal file. Over the next few months she is reported to have suffered from nervous exhaustion, but found time to talk about her experiences to a reporter from the *News Chronicle*. Their heavily censored article appeared on 9 June 1945:

Some personal stories of the war may pass into history – and this may be one of them. It is the story of Miss Monique V, a 24-year-old English girl, as she told it to me in a London coffee shop yesterday. I cannot tell you her real name. It is still on the security list. This is her record. In Paris she joined the French underground. Her job was transmitting secret intelligence to H.Q. On a night in August 1944,she was at work preparing a message when, through a window, she saw Gestapo men approaching. She had just time to burn the message before they clapped hands on her shoulders.

They took her away and interrogated her. They plunged her into an ice-cold bath, in which she nearly choked to death. But not a word of her comrades or her work did she betray. A few days later she was one of a batch of suspected English and French girls packed into a closed rail truck. For a week they travelled like this, with little food, drink or sleep, until they arrived at the notorious Ravensbrueck camp in North West Germany. There, she was put to work in a factory. She began sabotage work, but was detected, and the SS guards shaved her head and threatened her with death.

Then they transferred her to a camp near Leipzig and attached her to a party of English girls working on the roads.

Guarded by SS men and women with formidable whips, they toiled 13 hours each day. 'The SS women were worse than the men,' Miss Monique said. The day came when, eight months after her capture, she made her escape through the wood to Leipzig. A few days later the Americans entered the city.[1]

There are few details of her life back in London. One of the tasks Vera Atkins took on after the war was to find out what happened to the sixteen captured female gents from F Section who did not come back. Another was to ensure that those who did were integrated back into society. It appears Didi had expressed an interest in 'beauty culture' as on 19 October 1945, Vera wrote the following letter to Mr E. M. Haslam Esq. of 76 Grosvenor Street:

Dear Mr Haslam,

Referring to today's telephone conversation, I have pleasure in introducing to you Miss Eileen Nearne who is anxious to learn facial massage and beauty treatment.

Miss Eileen Nearne worked in the F.A.N.Y.s since she fled to this country from France in April 1942. She went to the field for us in March 1944 and only returned to this country in early June of this year as she was unfortunately caught and spent ten months in various German camps.

She is, as I told you, completely untrained, but she is extremely reliable and thorough in any job on which she is keen.

You have encouraged me to recommend to you persons above the age of 25 and I have therefore taken this opportunity of introducing Miss Jacqueline Nearne, her older sister. She also worked for us in the field from January 1943 until her safe return to this country in March 1944. She has recently been engaged on a film telling the story of our work and would now be available for other employment. You may care to consider her for one of the more responsible posts of which you spoke.

Thank you very much indeed for the kind reception which you have promised these girls.[2]

Another letter was sent to Mrs Cooper at Helena Rubenstein, 48 Berkley Square, London, which stated that:

Miss Eileen Nearne has worked in this department since she fled to this country from France in April 1942. She volunteered for special work in France and was captured by the Germans.

In view of her extremely valuable war service and the hardship which she has suffered at the hands of the Germans, we are anxious to see her re-established in a suitable peace-time occupation. She is extremely keen to train in beauty culture and I have no doubt will work very hard on making a success of it if she is given an opening.

In the circumstances I am taking the liberty of writing to you this personal note in order that you may give her application most sympathetic consideration.[3]

Whether she was offered and took employment has not come to light. According to Liane Jones, for months after coming back, Didi was in a state of physical and emotional collapse so it may have been difficult for her to keep a job.

However, she must have been uplifted when she learned on 16 January 1946 that, in appreciation of the work she had done in France, Charles de Gaulle, President of the Provisional government of the French Republic, awarded her the *Croix de Guerre avec Palme Bronze*. The accompanying statement reported that:

She was transmitting (normally from SCEAUX) from 26.3.44 until her arrest on 22.7.44. She sent in total 105 messages. She had been arrested whilst transmitting. After many enquiries about WIZARD alias MILLET and others, it appeared that she had had time to destroy her compromising papers. She was taken to the German H.Q., Rue des Saussaies, then to Germany, from where we received today, 12 May 1945, a report that she was in the hands of the Allies. Her friends [blanked out], helped her a lot.

With the same great competence as her sister Jacqueline, who worked exceptionally, Eileen did serious and conscientious work in very difficult conditions. We are delighted to learn she is safe and sound. She has truly deserved this merit. [4]

It was not until 19 February 1946 that she learned that the British Government had also decided to give her an award. Her citation stated that:

This agent was landed in France by Lysander in early February 1944 as W/T operator to a circuit in the Paris region. For five and a half months she maintained constant communication with London from this most dangerous area, and, by her cool efficiency, perseverance and willingness to undergo any risk in order to carry out her work, made possible the successful organisation of her group and the delivery of large quantities of arms and equipment.

She was arrested by the Gestapo towards the end of July 1944 while transmitting, and was subsequently deported to Germany.

For her steady courage and unfailing devotion to duty it is recommended that Miss Nearne be appointed a Member of the Order of the British Empire.[5]

What it failed to mention was that her efficiency and courage also made possible the successful bombing of the St Leu d'Esserent missile store.

Didi was looked after by Jacqueline, who starred in a 1944 RAF film, *Now It Can Be Told*, a semi-documentary showing how the SOE trained agents to be sent with arms and other supplies to the resistance groups fighting against Hitler in occupied Europe. Jacqueline starred with Captain Harry Rée DSO, OBE, *Croix De Guerre, Médaille de la Résistance*. It showed the work of two fictional characters, Felix and Cat, an organiser and wireless operator in France. Three years later it went on general release as *School For Danger* and was released by the Imperial War Museum in 2007 as a DVD.

In the 1950s Jacqueline went to work for the Protocol Department in the United Nations in New York before returning to England. Neither sister married. After their experiences, it would have been particularly difficult to settle down with a husband and bring up a family.

Didi suffered from what would now be called 'post-traumatic stress disorder'. Her experiences of torture, the appalling conditions she endured in concentration camps, the atrocities she witnessed and then being disbelieved by the Americans and treated as if she was one of the enemy, all took their toll. Research by the *Daily Mail* revealed that it had left her with a variety of medical problems. A doctor's report on Didi's state of health dated 12 December, 1945 stated: 'This former agent has been under my care for some months. She is suffering from psychological symptoms, which undoubtedly have been brought on by her service in the field. I would assess Miss Nearne's disability at 50 per cent.'

Didi was demobilised on 1 August 1946 which meant her SOE pay finished at the end of July. That year, a secret pensions tribunal declared her 100 per cent disabled as a result of 'exhaustion neurosis' and granted her the maximum allowable pension at the time, £175 a year, the equivalent today of £4,500. A year later, without explanation, this was cut to £140.

Whilst she had been in France, Didi received an annual salary from the SOE, paid into a nominated bank account and made available to her on her return, or to a named relative if she did not. One imagines that it was the same as Noor Inayat Khan, who received £350 a year. In comparison, one of the male agents received £420 a year and 6d. a day as danger money. Another received ten shillings a day in the UK, but £2 a day in France. The SOE encouraged agents not to discuss their remuneration as each case was slightly different.[6]

According to a psychiatric report in 1948, she was suffering headaches, depression, sleeplessness, palpitations and a sense of unreality. The psychiatrist reported her showing some 'uncharacteristically schizoid representations' brought about by her traumatic experiences during the war. In the words of a *Daily Mail* reporter, 'a psychiatrist found she suffered premonitions and that she believed she had the gift of second sight'.[7]

Yvonne Baseden, another SOE agent who was imprisoned at Ravensbrück, said that mutual friends told her that she ought not to try to contact Didi. 'She's better left as she wants to be left.' Mac, Maisie McLintock, said that she suffered terribly and was very stoic about it. Eventually, she broke down completely.

A note in Didi's file at the FANY Headquarters dated 1948 indicated that she had moved from Darenth Road to 24 St Kilda's Road, Stamford Hill, N16. Whether Jacqueline was looking after her there is unknown. When she went back to France to recuperate later that year, the pension was reduced again to only £87 and 10 shillings and in 1950 it was stopped completely. One imagines she would have paid tax on the income she received whilst in France. Her mother died in 1950 and, after spending some years in a mental home, she returned to England in 1954, where she lived with Jacqueline in London. On contacting the Pensions Office to ask for her pension to be resumed, she was refused, even though she gave them the name of her doctor.[8]

When Didi began to recover physically, she was still too weak to work. She took to painting, producing violent, terrible pictures, which expressed the horror of her captivity and life in the camps. She tried to find work as a wireless operator, but, according to Odile, eventually found a job as a nurse at Branch Hill Old People's Home in Hampstead and from this received her Camden Town pension in 1986. One of the photographs in the family collection shows her receiving an award when she retired.

Odile recalls one of her earliest memories of meeting her aunt:

I remember when I was about four or five years old, being taken by my parents to visit Didi. I remember coming out of the tube station, turning right and going up a slope (perhaps it was when she was living in Stamford Hill, I don't know). At the top of the slope, I remember the house being on the left-hand side, and her flat being on the third floor. Anyway, in my mind's eye, I can still see her opening the window, moving her arms about in a very agitated way and sending us away. I was so very disappointed, because we'd come all the way from Hornchurch, and I really wanted to see her. It must have been in 1959, so she must still have been unwell.

In fact, her friend Jenny told me that in 1962 when she was living next door to Didi, she used to hear her scream in the night, so she was still having nightmares. It's terrible how those war experiences affected her – for she was unwell for a long time. But then she slowly recovered.[9]

Odile recalled Didi telling her about her paintings and how they were going to be on exhibition in an art gallery – she was very excited about it. After her father died in 1970, Didi invited Odile, then a teenager, to her flat in 6 Hampstead Hill Gardens, where she specially prepared a meal. Afterwards they went for a walk on Hampstead Heath. Occasionally, she met Didi and Jacqueline in Harrods, and sometimes in pubs, but she really got to know her aunt well from 1987 onwards, after she had had her twins. She came to Hornchurch to see them and then in 1988 they met up in Hyde Park, when she told her that she wanted to sell her house in Belgravia.

War researchers reported that their letters of enquiry to Didi went unanswered. The only historian who managed to strike up a relationship with her was Liane Jones. When she met her for the first time, she recalled Didi wearing bright pink trousers, pink sandals and a yellow top, and ordering a large sherry.' She had not told her story before she talked to me, because her time in captivity in Germany left her badly traumatised. But she spoke forcefully and vividly. Her memories were precious to her. She told me once: "These things live with you." And with Didi they did indeed.'[10] Jones's *A Quiet Courage*, tells the stories of Odette

Sansom (later Churchill and then Hallowes), Yvonne Baseden (later Cormeau), Lise de Baissac and Didi.

Didi joined the Special Forces Club in 1982. This was a London club for ex-SOE members and others involved in Britain's secret military organisations. Adrian Stones, the club chairman, in his eulogy of Didi, said that letters to the Secretary confirm that she had fond memories of her visits. They also reveal that she resigned once in 1992. The Secretary told a reporter that they would be surprised to learn the reason. Ordinarily it means that someone took objection to being pursued relentlessly for outstanding subscription payments. In Eileen's case she wrote to the Club to say that: 'I do enjoy the Club, but when I come to London I do take my guard dog with me, as a matter of fact everywhere I go, and your rules forbid dogs in the lounge.' Eileen was persuaded to change her mind and in 2006 she sent the Club a donation. She resigned finally in 2007. 'I believe Eileen's modest heroism was an inspiration to those around her in 1944. That heroism has remained an inspiration down the years. Her photograph hangs in a very special place in the Club. It will stay there.'[11]

Occasionally Didi met her wartime friends, including Vera Atkins and Flight Lieutenant Murray 'Andy' Anderson, the pilot who flew her out on that cold March night in 1944. She also kept in touch with French friends she met during the months she spent in captivity in France and Germany, particularly Geneviève Matthieu. Over the years, she visited them regularly for reunions at the Club de la France Libre in Paris, and almost always went to an SOE Bastille Day dinner.

After the war, Francis returned to Grenoble to rejoin his family and he died in 1965. Frederick stayed in England and found work as a continental operator. He married and lived in Hornchurch, but, before he died in St Columbo's Hospital, Hampstead in 1970, he had been living with Didi at 6 Hampstead Hill Gardens.

When Jacqueline died on 15 August, 1982 Didi was devastated. She remained in Jacqueline's flat in Belgravia until 1989 when she decided to sell it. She told Odile that it was expensive, for there were always repairs that needed doing to the outside of the house and redecorations on the inside. She realised that she did not want to live in London any more, but wanted to find a place by the sea, which she loved. This took her first to Broadstairs in Kent, then to Lyme Regis and finally to the south-west seaside resort of Torquay, which she loved for its continental feel. She was then 70 years old.[12]

She rented a small flat, 2 Lisburne Crescent, a few minutes' walk from the seafront, where she lived with a stray ginger cat she had found. Whether she knew her landlord, Michael Andrusiak's history is unknown. As he was Jewish, he had been forcibly moved from his village in Poland in 1940 and taken by train to one of the Nazi-run concentration camps. Unlike Didi, he never saw his family again. He reported that in the first few years she spent in Torquay, she would only communicate with him and his wife. They were the only people she trusted, and she would never let anyone into her flat without him being there. He thought it was because they were both aware of the traumatic, but different nature of their wartime experiences, although, he admitted, Didi's were far worse. Neither of them discussed their past in any detail, but they had a mutual respect for each other's privacy.[13]

On 10 June 1993, Didi attended a memorial service at Ravensbrück, organised and led by Gervase Cowell of the Special Forces Club, with representatives of the Foreign and Commonwealth Office, The British Embassy in Berlin and the Ravensbrück Museum. A commemorative plaque was unveiled by Didi, Odette Hallowes and Yvonne Baseden. Also present were Vera Atkins, Francis Cammaerts DSO and Brian Stonehouse, two of the SOE's officers in France, Leo Marks and representatives from the FANY, WAAF, Lillian Rolfe's sister, Violette Szabo's daughter, Judge John de Cunha, a prosecutor at the Nuremburg trials, and several former members of the French Resistance.

In her later years, Didi supported several charities, including The Princess Royal's Volunteer Corps, the Army Benevolent Fund, Our Lady Help of Christians and St Denis Roman Catholic Church and Animals in Distress. Denis Reid, the former Torbay mayor and founding member of Animals in Distress, said: 'She was indomitable. She went everywhere for us. She even went in pubs to collect, which she wasn't supposed to do. She couldn't have done more for us. She worked tirelessly.'[14]

In 1997 she agreed to be interviewed about her wartime activities for BBC 2's *Timewatch*. To protect her identity, she wore a wig, was introduced by her codename, 'Rose' and spoke only in French. In fact, she was given the last word in the film: 'When I returned after the war, I, along with lots of others, missed that kind of life. Everything seemed so ordinary.'[15]

In the 1990s Odile visited Didi in Torquay with her husband and twins:

In the beginning she made me promise not to tell anyone who she was, for she said that, if I did, she would do an Agatha Christie disappearance, and she would never see me again. I never told anyone as that was Didi's wish.

The first few years she arranged for us to wait outside the garden when we picked her up, then we used to go on lovely trips organised by her. In fact, her friend Jenny told me that she really enjoyed organising these excursions. They went all over the place, visiting castles at Dartmouth, Tiverton and Exeter, and going to Tintagel, which she loved. Even if there were many steps, she was never tired. She told me that the next time we should go further up and stay in a hotel. We used to go walking on Berry Head, and she walked for miles. Then in the evening we used to stop at

Berry Head Hotel and have a meal. Yes, she loved walking by the sea, also all around Thatcher's Rock and Babbacombe. We visited St Michael's Mount in Cornwall, and had to get a boat on the way back because the tide had come in. She said it reminded her of another monastery off the Normandy coast. I have wonderful memories of visiting Falmouth, Polperro and especially the little fishing port of Mevagissey with her.

Over the years she relaxed, and sometimes we used to just sit on the bench in her garden and chat. She loved going to the Living Coasts to see the seals being fed, for she loved all animals. It was a very sad time when she lost her ginger cat. She should have put him in a basket when she took him to the vet. We went with her to Newton Abbot to look for him and asked the vet. She was getting quite excited when she thought they'd found him, but unfortunately it was a much older tabby cat. One time we went to Lyme Regis and she showed me the little fisherman's cottage that she had rented before settling down in Torquay. We even went up a hill to see a RAF acrobatic show with the blue, red and white colours coming out at the back of the planes. I remember that I really enjoyed that, and so did Didi. I remember one time we even wanted to go and see the Isle of Wight, but my husband was tired of driving and refused to take us. We were both disappointed. Sometimes we used to take her to do her charity collecting at Brixham – she called it her work!

I never thought she would have talked about her experiences like she did with Liane Jones and for Secret Memories – I'm so glad she did. You see my father had always told me not to ask her about the war, because she had been badly traumatised and tortured. He told me that she would never speak about it. But that was in the 1960's (for my father died in 1970). So that time in 2000, when I'd been through Normandy before going to see her, and told her about the beaches I'd seen and the cemetery, I was almost on the brink of asking her, but I remembered my father's words, and then saw that sad look in her eyes. I'm very sensitive, and could feel her saying to herself 'Now she's going to ask me'. I got the impression that it would have been too sad for her – that she didn't want to talk about it. The next day though she took us to Slapton sands and showed us the Memorial there, so she must have thought about it during the night. I honestly think it would have been too emotional with me. You know it is one thing telling a stranger and another talking to one who is close to you. When I asked her about Jacqueline's death, you could see that it was so terribly sad, for she bowed down her head and almost cried. For all the memories came flooding back (she loved her sister so much). Imagine if I'd asked her about those terrible experiences she'd had in those concentration camps. I really think it was meant to be, even if she gave me the opportunity to ask her. For I remember her once telling me: 'Express yourself, I want to see how you think.' Of course if I'd have known that she had talked to Liane Jones and done that 'Secret Memories' episode, I would have asked her.

She was an incredible person, and I cherish the wonderful times we had together, where I got to know her as she really was, not as the secret agent. She was warm-hearted, kind and considerate, a truly beautiful person. She was extremely religious and this shone through in her interior self. Her eyes were full of compassion and wisdom. Bernard, she's the one who gave me faith – she helped me so much in my religious beliefs and still is helping me, for she's still around. I can truly say that she was an inspiration to me, just like a mother.[16]

On 2 September 2010, when neighbours became concerned that they had not seen Didi for some time, a search was made of her flat. Her body was found and the doctor called to the scene determined she had died following a heart attack She was 89 years old.

As Didi had lived as a virtual recluse, her neighbours only knew her as 'Eileen the cat woman'. They knew nothing to distinguish her from the many pensioners who chose to retire in Torquay. In the meantime, Torquay council officials made arrangements to have her body cremated and claim the expense from the value of her estate, as there was apparently no-one with funds to pay for a proper funeral.

As they did not know of any next-of-kin, council workers searched her flat hoping to find details of her family. Instead they found a treasure trove of wartime memorabilia. This was no ordinary pensioner. She had her MBE and *Croix de Guerre* medals for bravery. There was some discontinued French currency dating back to World War Two and piles of correspondence related to her time in France. Enquiries with her neighbours revealed that they knew nothing about her being decorated for her bravery behind enemy lines in occupied France.

One of the reporters on the *Herald Express*, the local paper, must have learned of the discovery and, on searching the internet, found out that Didi was one of the female agents during World War Two. Articles appeared in the national press over the next few days and, once her obituary was published, researchers used the Freedom of Information Act to persuade the National Archives in Kew, formerly the Public Records Office, to release the file that the SOE had created whilst she was under their control. With so many historians and reporters making enquiries, the file was made available as a PDF document, which could be downloaded from the front page of the National Archives website.

Concerns about Micky, her ginger cat and only companion, were abated when a former neighbour revealed she had carried it in in her arms to the vet in Chelston, only for it to jump down and run off, never to be seen again.

Adrian Sanders, Liberal Democrat MP for Torbay, put forward a motion in the House of Commons with eighteen signatories recommending that the government acknowledge Eileen in some way. It stated:

> That this House records its appreciation and thanks for the life and contribution of Miss Eileen Nearne who was one of 39 female Special Operations Executive (SOE) agents sent overseas during the Second World War to risk their lives on operations in occupied France; notes that Miss Nearne assumed numerous identities to carry out actions including alongside the French Resistance and despite being captured twice, first by the Gestapo and later by the SS, persuaded both that she was an innocent French woman; and further notes that the service she and other SOE agents carried out contributed to the Allied Victory and that Miss Nearne remained tight-lipped about her own contribution, with her remarkable service only coming to light after her death on 2 September 2010, in Torquay, Devon, aged 89.[17]

Torquay council announced that a funeral service was planned to be held at Drakes Chapel, in Torquay, at 11 a.m. on 21 September, but they had to change their mind over the following few days when the world's media started running with her story.

Zoe Brennan, a *Daily Mail* reporter, described this seemingly anonymous woman as 'Agent Rose' and compared her to the character immortalised in Sebastian Faulks' 1999 novel, *Charlotte Gray*, which was turned into a film in 2001, starring Cate Blanchett.

Janey Cruck, of Genes Reunited, and Neil Fraser, who worked on the BBC's popular *Heir Hunters* and for the family firm of genealogists, Fraser and Fraser, managed to identify Didi's nearest relative, but it was Daniel Jobsz of Kin, a London-based firm of investigators, who contacted Odile, who was living in Tuscany, Italy.

Obviously upset on hearing about her aunt's death, Odile immediately made arrangements to fly to Britain. She told a reporter from the *Herald Express*:

I would like to thank everyone for their kind wishes and support at this very sad time. My aunt Eileen was a very private and modest person and without doubt she would be astounded by all the public and media attention. I hope that in death, she will be remembered along with other SOE Agents with pride and gratitude for the work they did both here and behind enemy lines during the Second World War. I have been overwhelmed by all the attention and I would be most grateful if I might be left in peace to mourn the death of my dear aunt.

Following the media coverage, there was a public outcry suggesting a war hero deserved a more fitting send-off. It was the least the country could do. The *Herald Express* had calls and emails from well-wishers from across the country who wanted to attend the funeral. Torbay council said it had received offers from war veterans, historians and members of the public to pay for the funeral. The Torbay and District Funeral Service and Westerleigh Group, which runs Torbay's cemeteries, said they too had received messages from people around the world who had been so moved by Didi's plight that they were offering to pay for her funeral or wanting to send flowers. Their director stepped in to give her a service with the 'dignity and respect she deserves'.

Didi's funeral took place on Tuesday 21 September 2010, at Our Lady Help of Christians and St Denis Roman Catholic Church on Priory Road, Torquay, at 3 p.m. As hundreds were expected at the requiem mass, roads were closed and special parking arrangements were made. There was live coverage of the mass on the 24-hour TV news channels.

When the hearse arrived, the coffin was flanked by 22 standard-bearers from the British Legion and two bagpipers played a lament as it was carried into the church. It was draped in both the Union Jack flag and the Tricoleur, as befitting a hero who was awarded both the British MBE and the French *Croix de Guerre*.

More than a dozen wreaths lay at the gates of the church, some from fellow worshippers and friends who knew her through her work with animal charities in Torquay.

Odile attended the service alongside civic dignitaries, Foreign Office representatives, the Consul General and the Military attaché from the French Embassy in London, the Commander of the FANY and the Chairman of the Special Forces Club.

The *Herald Express* reported military men in uniform occupying the front pews and town councillors filing past wearing their dark suits. The standards of the British Legion were dipped, and among the floral tributes was one from the staff of a national newspaper. It was all done with solemn dignity. It was a poignant service to salute a remarkable woman. Father Jonathon Shaddock, who led the service, commented that, 'Whenever we saw her, she was just very, very quiet and just said her prayers and then slipped away at the end of Mass without having much to do with anybody.' Some were reported saying that, 'It was a pity she never had such recognition in her lifetime, but she never sought such recognition and quite probably would not have welcomed it. Torbay, however, promised to do her memory proud, and yesterday, that is just what it did.'[18]

Odile gave an emotional tribute to her aunt, who she described as 'very modest' about her incredible story:

She sacrificed her private life for the home land. She had a very strong character and was determined in her patriotic views. It is thanks to people like her that we can live peacefully today. She never wanted to speak about what she had done during the war, in fact, she did not want to be famous. People like her just want to forget and not re-live the suffering. Bless her soul. We all loved you. May you rest in peace. My aunt was a lovely person and extremely reserved because of what she had been through during the war. She did many good deeds for animals in distress and those in need. She was a devout Roman

Catholic. Her faith saved her when she was tortured in concentration camps. She was always very modest and I admired her for that. She was very much loved. I am very proud to be her niece.[19]

Adrian Stone, the chairman of the Special Forces Club, gave a eulogy in which he paid tribute to Eileen as 'brave and independent. Her efficiency and courage was shown through her commitment to her story despite going through the German equivalent of water torture. She still stuck to her guns'.

The French Consulate, Edouard Braine, paid tribute to Eileen for her brave service. 'I owe her for the freedom of our country. All my compatriots feel the same. It is important for us to show a message of gratitude for brave people like her who gave us our freedom.' At the end of the service, the last post was played by a French bugler and her coffin was carried from the church to a round of applause from those gathered outside.[20, 21]

John Pentreath, the county manager of Devon's British Legion, said, 'Eileen evaded us in her lifetime, which, of course, was her intention. She lived her life as she had in World War Two, almost covertly. She did not want her story to be known and she succeeded in that quest. It's our regret that we never knew her in her lifetime – that we never knew that we had a heroine in our midst.'[22] In accordance to Didi's wishes, her body was cremated and Odile scattered her ashes in the sea near her favourite spot overlooking Torbay.

In an interview on the BBC's *Heir Hunters* programme about their discovery of Didi's nearest relative, Sister Damien of Our Lady Help of Christians and St Denis Roman Catholic church in Torquay, Sister Damien described her parishioner as 'an enigmatic figure. Eileen always came about an hour before mass, read the paper, slipped up to the Lady Chapel. She was a shadowy little figure going around the church. My first encounter with Eileen was to ask her name, which she sort of fobbed me off and said something to the effect of "That's not important". She didn't invite conversations. She was a mysterious figure because, you realise, you're wondering who is she?' When Sister Damien finally learned about Eileen, she said that she 'fooled all of us. Looking back, I can only explain it that she had never been properly debriefed and that she thought herself as a spy.' According to *Heir Hunters*, Didi's estate was valued at only £13,000, 'not a lot for a fully paid-up war hero' (*Heir Hunters*, BBC, 16 April 2012).

When Odile visited her aunt, she recalled taking her to Teignmouth to see John Keats's plaque, and because of that she knew that Didi would be delighted to have a plaque too, like Keats, so she arranged for one to be put up in her honour. She contacted the Torbay Civic Society and, with the help of Daphne West, paid for a blue plaque to be installed on the front of 2 Lisburne Crescent on 15 March, 2011, what would have been Didi's ninetieth birthday. English Heritage usually do not put up a plaque for anyone until at least fifty years after their death. Didi's was done within a year. She was a truly remarkable woman.

Odile, who travelled from Verona to be at the unveiling, said:

She was a truly wonderful woman. After her death there were so many myths about her. There were reports that she died unrecognised and forgotten by the world. The truth could not be more different. My aunt was much cherished within the community of Torquay, where she lived. She was a brave and loving woman who gave her later years to charitable causes, such as Animals in Distress, about which she felt passionately. But the past, her war experiences, was a place of terrible pain for her and it was her choice not to speak about it.

Her whole life was a sacrifice – a sacrifice to her country, to her Catholic faith and to her ideal of a better world. She was an inspiration to me. I cannot think of a more wonderful way to mark her memory than this blue plaque in the town she loved and where she lived for 20 years.[2]

Appendix:
Report by Miss Eileen NEARNE

On 9th April the SS Commandant of the camp in MARKLEBURG told us that we were going to move 80 kilometres away during the night. The Americans by this time were not far from LEIPZIG so I and two French girls decided to escape. About 11 o'clock we were passing through a forest and I managed to jump out and hide behind a tree and there I met my two French friends. We walked through the town and we hid there in a house, which was bombarded for three days. We then decided to leave and started off through the town. We were stopped by the SS and they asked for our papers. We said we had none as we were French volunteers for work in Germany. Fortunately they let us pass. We slept that night in a garden of a church. Next day we reached LEIPZIG and we were starving hungry having had nothing to eat so we went and asked for help in a German church. They were very good to us and we stayed there for three nights. On 15th April we saw the white flags of the first Americans arriving so we rushed out to meet them. I told them that I was English and asked them if they would show us where the Red Cross was. However, they would not do this but put us in a house for one night. Next morning they put us into a camp. The captain of the camp interrogated us with a lot of SS in the room. When he had heard our story he presented us to the SS and told them that as they had treated us so badly they would have to pay for it but the SS said they knew nothing about us. The next day they moved us to another camp with English prisoners and there I was interrogated by someone in the American Intelligence Service. They asked me my number and I told them I had no number. They asked for my papers and I told them my story how I was arrested and that naturally the Gestapo had taken my papers away. I told then I was a wireless operator and that I knew Colonel Max BAXTER [deliberately avoiding mentioning Buckmaster]. They were not convinced and told me I would have to go through many more camps before I was passed by the British authorities. All this time I had been put in with the Nazis and treated as one of them.

At the last camp I was again interrogated and told them exactly how I was landed in France and arrested by the Gestapo. They expressed great surprise at a plane being able to get there in the night. They were very curious and asked me a lot of questions about the organisation, schools etc. and I did not want to give too much away so they said I was a German agent. They told me they would send a message for confirmation and for the time being I would have to stay in the camp with the Nazi girls. I asked if I could be separated from them and they would not let me so I received exactly the same treatment as the Nazis. They said they were sorry but there were so many German agents they had to be careful. They said even if they did have a message saying I was English it would not prove anything as I might still be a German agent. I stayed here one month. During this time I made a report to the Americans about the Nazi girls saying that they used to ask the Americans for cigarettes and get them to come into their rooms. Next morning one of the Nazi girls had her hair shaved. After this they put me apart with a French girl. Then one day they presented me to an English major who had come to fetch me. He took me to WEIMAR where I was very well treated and we stayed there one night. I explained my story to him and he was extremely nice and sympathetic. The next day I was flown to BRUSSELS where I was again very well treated. I told my story to an English captain and I was then flown over to England.[1]

In Didi's file was the American account of her interrogation:

HEADQUARTERS

FIRST UNITED STATES ARMY

OFFICE OF AC OF S, G-2

INTERROGATION CENTER

2 May 1945

MEMORANDUM:

TO: Officer in Charge, Master Interrogation Center.

SUBJECT: NEARNE, Eileen, alias DUTERTE, Jacqueline, alias WOOD, Alice, alias ROSE.

1. Subject claims to be a British subject by birth and to have worked in France for the British Intelligence Service until she was arrested by the Gestapo on 25 July 1944.

2. Subject stated that she has lived in France with her family since the age of two; that in March 1942 she was issued a passport by the British Consul in Grenoble, France, to return to England; that she went to LONDON via BARCELONA, MADRID, LISBON, GIBRALTAR, and GLASGOW, in company of her sister, Jacqueline NEARNE; that almost immediately after her arrival in LONDON she and her sister joined the Information Service FANY, where she was trained as a W/T operator; that she subsequently entered another Intelligence organization, run by a Col. Max BAXTER (British Army); and that she received training as a W/T operator and cryptographer in a school near OXFORD.

3. In the end of February 1944, Subject stated, she was flown to a field near ORLEANS, France, from where she made way to

PARIS. She was in company of another agent, whose name she does not know, and whom she met twice daily in PARIS in order to obtain from him the reports she had to transmit to England. Those reports were written in clear and Subject encoded them. Subject signed her messages 'ROSE', but claims that she has forgotten her agent's number.

4. In July 1944 Subjects transmitter was detected and Subject was arrested by the Gestapo on 25 July. Subject claims that she was not asked to continue her transmissions. She claims, moreover, that despite being tortured she did not reveal any information detrimental to the British Intelligence Service or its agents.

5. On 15 August 1944 Subject was sent to the Extermination Camp of RAVENSBRUCK (70 kilometre N of BERLIN) where, she stayed for two weeks, from there to TORGAU, then to ABTERRODA, and finally to MARKELBERG near LEIPZIG. From this last camp, Subject claims, she managed to escape on 13 April 1945.

6. Subject creates a very unbalanced impression. She often is unable to answer the simplest questions, as though she were impersonating someone else. Her account of what happened to her after her landing near ORLEANS is held to be invented. It is recommended that Subject be put at the disposal of the British Authorities for further investigation and disposition.

SECRET[2]

NOTES

3 Settling in London & Initial Interview with SOE: Spring 1942

1. Mackenzie, W., *The Secret History of Special Operations Executive 1940 – 1945* (St. Ermin's Press: 2002).
2. Vigurs, K., *The Women Agents of the Special Operations Executive F section – Wartime Realities and Post-War Representations*. PhD Thesis (University of Leeds, September 2011), p. 26.
3. Ibid., pp. 27.
4. Ibid., pp. 30.
5. Email communication with Odile Nearne (January 2012).

4 Training for Work as a Secret Agent: Summer 1942–Autumn 1943

1. TNA HS9 1098/2.
2. Devereaux-Rochester, Elizabeth, *Full Moon to France* (Robert Hale, London:1978).
3. Braddon, Russell, *Nancy Wake: SOE's Greatest Heroine* (Cassell: 1956).
4. Pattinson, J., *Behind Enemy Lines* (Manchester University Press: 2007).
5. Ryder, S., *Child of my Love*, (Collins Harvill: 1986).
6. Alfred Fyffe, (23100) REEL 5 (Thame Park) Imperial War Museum).
7. Marks, Leo, *Between Silk and Cyanide: A Codemaker's Story, 1941–1945* (Harper Collins: 2000).
8. Pawley, M., *In Obedience to Instructions – FANY with the SOE in the Med* (Leo Cooper: 1999).
9. Bailey, Roderick, *Forgotten Voices of the Secret War: An Inside History of Special Operations* (Ebury Press: 2008), p. 55.
10. Stafford, David, *Mission Accomplished: SOE and Italy 1943–1945* (Bodley Head: 2011).
11. Gleeson, James, *They Feared No Evil: The Stories of the Gallant and Courageous Women Agents of Britain's Secret Armies, 1939–1945* (Robert Hale, London: 1976), p. 47.
12. Transcript of Juliette Pattinson's interview with Maisie McLintock.
13. Jones, Liane, *A Quiet Courage*, (Bantam Press: 1990), p. 230.

14. Pawley, M., *In Obedience to Instructions – FANY with the SOE in the Med* (Leo Cooper: 1999).

15. Lord, C. and Watson, G., *Royal Corps of Signals: Unit Histories of the Corps (1920–2001)* (Helion and Company: 2003).

16. Jones, Liane, *A Quiet Courage,* (Bantam Press 1990).

17. Buckmaster, M., 'They went by Parachute,' *Chamber's Journal* (1946-7).

18. Pattinson, J., *Behind Enemy Lines* (Manchester University Press: 2007).

19. Buckmaster, M., 'They went by Parachute,' *Chamber's Journal* (1946-7).

5 Preparations for the Drop into Occupied France: Winter 1943–Spring 1944

1. Foot, M. R. D., *SOE in France: an Account of the work of the British Special Operations Executive in France, 1940–1944* (Frank Cass: 2004).

2. Pierre Tillet's infiltrations and Exfiltrations from France 1941-1945 (www.plan-sussex-1944.net/anglais/pdf/infiltrations_into_france.pdf).

3. Verity, Hugh, *We Landed By Moonlight* (Ian Allan Ltd: 1978, revised 1995).

4. *Archives du Service Historique de la Dèfense, Vincennes : dossier du réseau JEAN MILLET,* cote 17, pp. 28.

5. Marks, Leo, *Between Silk and Cyanide: A Codemaker's Story, 1941–1945* (Harper Collins: 2000), p. 512.

6. Ibid., pp. 512–3.

7. Foot, M. R. D., *SOE in France: an Account of the work of the British Special Operations Executive in France, 1940-1944* (Frank Cass: 2004), p. 189.

8. TNA HS 9/1318/3.

9. Helm, Sarah, *A Life in Secrets: The Story of Vera Atkins and the Lost Agents of SOE* (Little Brown: 2005).

10. Ryder, S., *Child of my Love,* (Collins Harvill: 1986).

11. Vigurs, K., *The Women Agents of the Special Operations Executive F section – Wartime Realities and Post-War Representations.* PhD Thesis (University of Leeds, September 2011), p. 28.

12. Marks, Leo, *Between Silk and Cyanide: A Codemaker's Story, 1941–1945* (Harper Collins: 2000).

13. Ibid.

14. Griffiths, F., *Winged Hours,* (William Kimber and Co. Ltd: 1981).

15. Buckmaster, M., 'They went by Parachute,' *Chamber's Journal* (1946-7).

16. TNA HS 9/1089/2 (26 January 1944).

17. Braddon, Russell, *Nancy Wake: SOE's Greatest Heroine* (Cassell: 1956).

18. Gleeson, James, *They Feared No Evil: The Stories of the Gallant and Courageous Women Agents of Britain's Secret Armies, 1939–1945* (Robert Hale, London: 1976), p. 16.

19. Jones, Liane, *A Quiet Courage,* (Bantam Press: 1990). p. 230.

20. Transcript of Juliette Pattinson's interview with Maisie McLintock.

21. Interview on *Timewatch*, 'Secret memories.', 11 March 1997, BBC 2.

22. Jones, Liane, *A Quiet Courage,* (Bantam Press: 1990), p. 230.

23. Gleeson, James, *They Feared No Evil: The Stories of the Gallant and Courageous Women Agents of Britain's Secret Armies, 1939–1945* (Robert Hale, London: 1976), p. 41.

6 Working for the Resistance in France: 3 March 1944–24 July 1944

1. TNA HS 9/1318/3 (5 Feb 1944)
2. Jones, Liane, *A Quiet Courage*, (Bantam Press: 1990), p. 229.
3. Author's communication with Steven Kippax and Robert Pearson.
4. Tolstoy, N., *Victims of Yalta* (Hodder and Stoughton: 1977), p. 67.
5. Crowdy, Terry, *SOE Agent: Churchill's Secret Warriors* (Osprey Publishing: 2008).
6. Ryder, S., *Child of my Love*, (Collins Harvill: 1986).
7. Foot, M. R. D., *SOE in France: an Account of the work of the British Special Operations Executive in France, 1940–1944* (Frank Cass: 2004).
8. Verity, Hugh, *We Landed By Moonlight* (Ian Allan Ltd: 1978, revised 1995).
9. Jones, Liane, *A Quiet Courage*, (Bantam Press: 1990).
10. Ibid.
11. Ibid.
12. TNA HS9/1089/2.
13. http://www.francaislibres.net/ liste/fiche.php?index=99574.
14. Jones, Liane, *A Quiet Courage*, (Bantam Press: 1990).
15. Interview on *Timewatch*, 'Secret memories.', 11th March 1997, BBC 2.
16. Jones, Liane, *A Quiet Courage*, (Bantam Press: 1990), p. 232–3.
17. Interview on *Timewatch*, 'Secret memories.', 11th March 1997, BBC 2.
18. Jones, Liane, *A Quiet Courage*, (Bantam Press: 1990).
19. Foot, M. R. D., *SOE in France: an Account of the work of the British Special Operations Executive in France, 1940-1944* (Frank Cass: 2004).
20. Verity, Hugh, *We Landed By Moonlight* (Ian Allan Ltd: 1978, revised 1995).
21. The Guardian, Wednesday 30 October, 2010.
22. Jones, Liane, *A Quiet Courage*, (Bantam Press: 1990) p. 234.
23. TNA HS9 1008/6
24. http://redtarget.pagesperso-orange.fr/78%20july%201944.htm
25. Buckmaster, M., 'They went by Parachute,' *Chamber's Journal* (1946-7).
26. Verity, Hugh, *We Landed By Moonlight* (Ian Allan Ltd: 1978, revised 1995), p. 165.
27. Pierre Tillet's infiltrations and Exfiltrations from France 1941-1945 (www.plan-sussex-1944.net/anglais/pdf/infiltrations_into_france.pdf).
28. Ibid.
29. Foot, M. R. D., *SOE in France: an Account of the work of the British Special Operations Executive in France, 1940-1944* (Frank Cass: 2004).
30. Verity, Hugh, *We Landed By Moonlight* (Ian Allan Ltd: 1978, revised 1995), p. 165.
31. http://fr.wikipedia.org/wiki/Ren%C3%A9_Dumont-Guillemet.
32. Richards, Denis, *The Hardest Victory – RAF Bomber Command in the Second World War* (1964), p. 241.
33. TNA HS 9/1089/2.
34. Ibid.
35. Buckmaster, M., 'They went by Parachute,' *Chamber's Journal* (1946-7).
36. Jones, Liane, *A Quiet Courage*, (Bantam Press: 1990).

7 Arrest, Interrogation, Torture & Escape: 25 July 1944–25 May 1945

1. TNA HS9/1089/2.
2. Maisie MacIntosh's interview with Juliette Pattinson.
3. Jones, Liane, *A Quiet Courage*, (Bantam Press: 1990), p. 277.
4. TNA HS9 1089/2
5. Jones, Liane, *A Quiet Courage*, (Bantam Press: 1990), p. 278.

6. Jones, Liane, *A Quiet Courage,* (Bantam Press: 1990), p. 280.
7. Ibid.
8. Jones, Liane, *A Quiet Courage,* (Bantam Press: 1990), p. 281.
9. TNA HS 9/1089/2.
10. Ibid.
11. Jones, Liane, *A Quiet Courage,* (Bantam Press: 1990), p. 283.
12. Imperial War Museum, Yvonne Baseden 6373/2.
13. Tickell, J, *Odette* (Chapman and Hall: 1949).
14. Ibid.
15. Pattinson, J., *Behind Enemy Lines* (Manchester University Press: 2007).
16. Foot, M. R. D., *SOE in France: an Account of the work of the British Special Operations Executive in France, 1940–1944* (Frank Cass: 2004).
17. Pattinson, J., *Behind Enemy Lines* (Manchester University Press: 2007).
18. Ibid.
19. TNA HS9 1089/2.
20. Jones, Liane, *A Quiet Courage,* (Bantam Press: 1990), p. 311–2.
21. Escott, B., *Mission Improbable: A Salute to the RAF Women of SOE in Wartime France* (Patrick Stephens Limited: 1991).
22. Foot, M. R. D., *SOE in France: an Account of the work of the British Special Operations Executive in France, 1940–1944* (Frank Cass: 2004).
23. Jones, Liane, *A Quiet Courage,* (Bantam Press: 1990), p. 313.
24. Ibid.
25. Ibid., pp.14.
26. http://www.fraternite-info.org/fraternite_et_memoire/Files/theme_1_journal_memoire_2010.pdf
27. http://www.leparisien.fr/val-de-marne/tant-qu-on-etait-en-vie-la-resistance-continuait-genevieve-mathieu-80-ans-deportee-du-camp-de-concentration-de-ravensbruck-28-04-2000
28. Helm, *A Life in Secrets: Vera Atkins and the Lost Agents of SOE* (Abacus: 2006).
29. Author's communication with Odile Nearne.
30. TNA HS 9/1089/2.
31. TNA HS 9/1089/2.
32. Buckmaster, M., 'They went by Parachute,' *Chamber's Journal* (1946-7).
33. Jones, Liane, *A Quiet Courage,* (Bantam Press: 1990), p. 316.
34. Ibid.
35. Ibid.
36. TNA HS 9/1089/2.
37. TNA HS 9/1089/2.
38. TNA HS 9/1089/2 (2 May 1945).

8 Life Back in England: 26 May 1945–2 September 2010

1. TNA HS 9/1089/2 (30 May 1945, 15 June 1945).
2. TNA HS 9/1089/2 (The accompanying note in her file read 'Retain or destroy.').
3. Ibid.
4. Ibid.
5. TNA HS 9/1089/2.
6. Email communication with Steven Kippax, 7 March, 2012.
7. http://www.dailymail.co.uk/news/article-1313618/WWII-spy-Eileen-Nearne-died-penniless-British-pension-halted.html#ixzz1hOOarr2Q.
8. Ibid.

9. Author's email communication with Odile, 11 March 2012.

10. http://www.dailymail.co.uk/femail/article-1313039/Charlotte-Gray-revealed-The-truth-British-heroine-died-forgotten.html.

11. http://www.sfclub.org/eileennearne.htm.

12. Author's email communication with Odile, 11 March 2012.

13. http://www.thisissouthdevon.co.uk/Fitting-blue-plaque-tribute-wartime-heroine-Eileen/story-11679160-detail/story.html.

14. http://www.thisissouthdevon.co.uk/Blue-plaque-unsung-hero-spy-risked-life/story-11673938-detail/story.html.

15. Interview on *Timewatch*, 'Secret memories.', 11 March 1997, BBC 2.

16. Author's email communication with Odile, 11 March 2012.

17. www.edms.org.uk/2010-11/724.htm.

18. http://www.thisissouthdevon.co.uk/Recalled-pride/story-11739328-detail/story.html.

19. http://www.thisissouthdevon.co.uk/Heroine-s-send-Eileen/story-11747406-detail/story.html.

20. Ibid.

21. http://www.guardian.co.uk/world/2010/sep/14/wartime-spy-eileen-nearne.

22. http://www.thisissouthdevon.co.uk/Fitting-blue-plaque-tribute-wartime-heroine-Eileen/story-11679160-detail/story.html.

23. Ibid.

Appendix

1. TNA HS 9/1089/2 (30 May 1945).

2. TNA HS9/1089/2.

BIBLIOGRAPHY

Documents and tapes
Imperial War Museum, London.
Yvonne Cormeau, 7385/9; 31572/1 IWM.
Alfred Fyffe, (23100) REEL 5 (Thame Park).

National Archives, Kew.
HS6/437 Eileen Nearne.
HS9/1089/2 Eileen 'Didi' Nearne.
HS9/1089/3 Francis Nearne.
HS9/1089/4 Jacqueline Nearne.
HS9/1318/3 Jean Savy.

Websites
http://www.aapone.com.au/SearchPreview.aspx?url=20100922000256926020&
   section=A&gallery=Eileen+Nearne+funeral
www.abc.net.au/news/2010-09-15/world...eileen-nearne/2260522.
http://news.bbcimg.co.uk/media/images/51675000/jpg/_51675880_eileen_
   nearne_bbc_512.jpg.
http://news.bbcimg.co.uk/media/images/49711000/jpg/_49711145_eileen_
   nearne_bbc_512.jpg.
http://www.dailymail.co.uk/femail/article-1313039/Charlotte-Gray-revealed-
   The-Truth-British-Heroine-died-forgotten.htm.
http://i.dailymail.co.uk/i/pix/2010/09/14/article-1311699-0B2BB500000005DC-
   209_468x705.jpg.
http://www.dailymail.co.uk/news/article-1313618/WWII-spy-Eileen-Nearne-
   died-penniless-British-pension-halted.htm.
http://docs.newsbank.com/s/InfoWeb/aggdocs/UKNB/13AB6052C3102630/
   0F8BFF68D3921800?p_multi=LSTB&s_lang=en-US.
www.edms.org.uk/2010-11/724.htm.
http://www.francaislibres.net/liste/fiche.php?index=99574.

Bibliography

http://www.fraternite-info.org/fraternite_et_memoire/Files/theme_1_journal_memoire_2010.pdf.

http://www.genesreunited.com.au/boards.page/board/general_chat/thread/1240428?d=desc.

http://www.guardian.co.uk/world/2010/sep/14/wartime-spy-eileen-nearne.

http://www.guardian.co.uk/uk/2010/oct/13/eileen-nearne-obituary.

http://hoydenabouttown.com/20101029.8904/an-extraordinary-woman.html.

http://www.independent.co.uk/news/people/news/eileen-nearne-lonely-death-of-a-spy-who-evaded-gestapo-2078548.html.

http://news.blogs.cnn.com/2010/09/23/secrets-of-british-spy-agent-rose-revealed-in-death/.

http://www.npr.org/templates/story/story.php?storyId=130052499.

http://www.paigntonpeople.co.uk/news/Honouring-wartime-heroine-uncovering-lsquo/story-7409373-detail/story.html.

http://redtarget.pagesperso-orange.fr/SOE.htm.

http://www.sfclub.org/eileennearne.htm.

http://www.smh.com.au/world/the-extraordinary-heroism-of-scatterbrained—eileen--the-spy-who-never-came-in-from-the-cold-20101029-176e1.html.

http://www.telegraph.co.uk/news/obituaries/military-obituaries/special-forces-obituaries/8009812/Eileen-Nearne.html.

http://www.theage.com.au/world/unveiling-a-reclusive-heroine-20100924-15qk2.html#ixzz1ikKIBk8G.

http://www.the foxgazette.com/the-secret-life-of-a-lonely-old-lady.html.

http://www.thesun.co.uk/sol/homepage/news/3147632/Sleep-well-Agent-Rose.html.

http://www.thisissouthdevon.co.uk/Secrets-brave-family-spied-Britain/story-13712658-detail/story.html.

http://www.thisissouthdevon.co.uk/Recalled-pride/story-11739328-detail/story.html.

http://www.thisissouthdevon.co.uk/Heroine-s-send-Eileen/story-11747406-detail/story.html.

http://www.vietnamvetssc.org.au/October%202010.pdf.

http://vif2ne.ru/nvk/forum/arhprint/1949404.

http://www.ww2talk.com/forum/special-forces/32813-south-devon-express-eileen-nearne-blue-plaque.html.

Books

Bailey, Roderick, *Forgotten Voices of the Secret War: An Inside History of Special Operations* (Ebury Press: 2008).

Basu, Shrabani, *Spy Princess: The Life of Noor Inayat Khan* (The History Press: 2008).

Binney, Marcus, *The Women who Lived for Danger: The Women Agents of SOE in the Second World War* (Coronet: 2002).

Braddon, Russell, *Nancy Wake: SOE's Greatest Heroine* (Cassell, 1956).

Buckmaster, Maurice, 'They went by Parachute', *Chamber's Journal* (1946–7).

Buckmaster, Maurice, *They Fought Alone* (Popular Book Club: 1958).

Clark, Freddy, *Agents by Moonlight* (Tempus Publishing: 1999).

Cunningham, Cyril, *Beaulieu: The Finishing School for Secret Agents* (Pen & Sword: 2005).

Escot, Beryl, *The WAAF: A History of the Women's Auxiliary Air Force in the Second World War* (Shire: 2003)

Escot, Beryl, *Mission Improbable: A Salute to Air Women of the SOE in Wartime France* (Stephens: 1991).

Foot, M. R. D., *SOE in France: An Account of the Work of the British Special Operations Executive in France, 1940–1944* (Frank Cass: 2004).

Gleeson, James, *They Feared No Evil: Women Agents of Britain's Secret Armies, 1939–45* (Robert Hale: 1976).

Griffiths, F., *Winged Hours* (William Kimber and Co. Ltd.: 1981).

Helm, Sarah, *A Life in Secrets: The Story of Vera Atkins and the Lost Agents of SOE* (Little Brown: 2005).

Hue, A., *Next Moon: The Remarkable True Story of a British Agent Behind the Lines in Wartime France* (Penguin: 2005).

Jones, Liane, *A Quiet Courage* (Bantam Press: 1990).

Mackenzie, William, *The Secret History of SOE: The Special Operations Executive, 1940–1945* (St Ermins: 2002).

Marks, Leo, *Between Silk and Cyanide: A Codemaker's Story, 1941–1945* (Harper Collins: 2000).

Mackenzie, William, *The Secret History of Special Operations Executive 1940–1945.* (St Ermin's Press: 2002)

Ottaway, Susan, *Violette Szabó* (Pen and Sword: 2002).

Overton-Fuller, Jean, *Noor-un-nisa Inayat Khan (Madeleine)* (East-West Publications: 1971).

Pattinson, Juliette, *Behind Enemy Lines* (Manchester University Press: 2007).

Rigden, Denis, *SOE Syllabus Lessons in Ungentlemanly Warfare: World War II,* Public Record Office (Kew: 2001).

Stafford, David, *Mission Accomplished: SOE and Italy 1943–1945* (Bodley Head: 2011).

Tickell, Jerrald, *Odette: The Story of a British Agent* (Chapman & Hall: 1995).

Verity, Hugh, *We Landed By Moonlight* (Ian Allan Ltd.: 1978, revised 1995).

Vigurs, K., *The Women Agents of the Special Operations Executive F section – Wartime Realities and Post-War Representations.* PhD Thesis (University of Leeds, September 2011).

Television
Heir Hunters, BBC, 16 April 2012
Timewatch, 'Secret memories.', 11 March 1997, BBC 2.

Newspapers
News Chronicle, 9 June 1945.

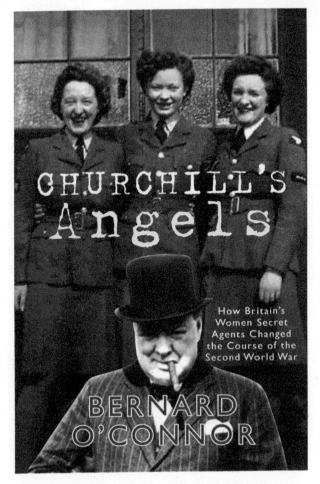

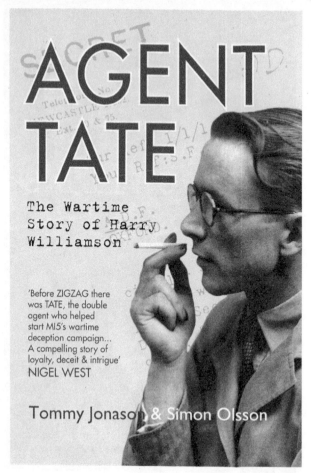

Also available from Amberley Publishing

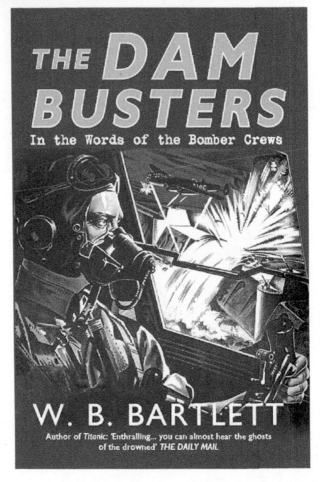

The story of the legendary bouncing-bomb attack on Germany's dams

The Dam Busters raids have gone down as perhaps the most famous air-strikes in history. Yet behind the story of courage and determination there lies another, darker side, both for the aircrews – 40% of whom died in the mission – and for those who lived below the dams in the path of the flood, many of whom were not even German. This new account tells the story of those dramatic events through the eyes of those who were there.

£20 Hardback
66 illustrations (32 col)
352 pages
978-1-4456-0382-7

Available from all good bookshops or to order direct
Please call **01453-847-800**
www.amberleybooks.com

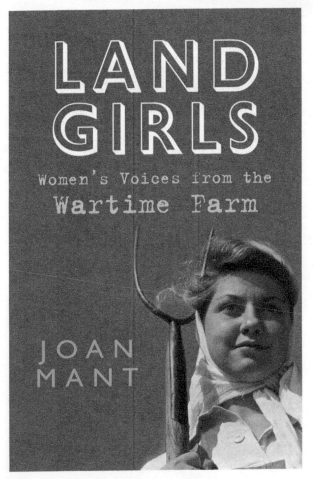

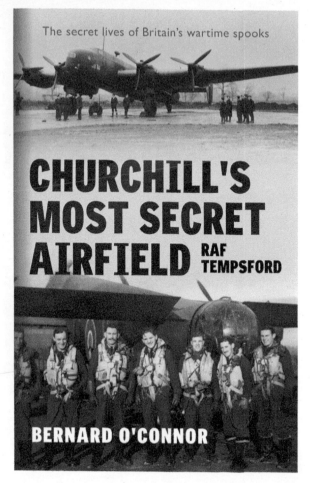

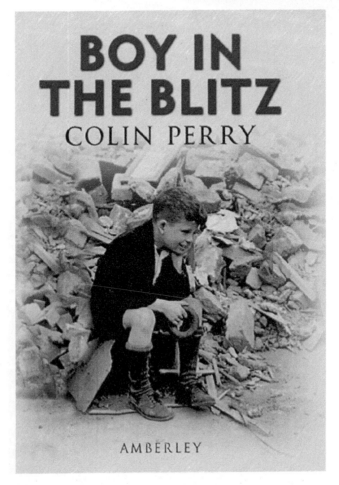

Also available from Amberley Publishing

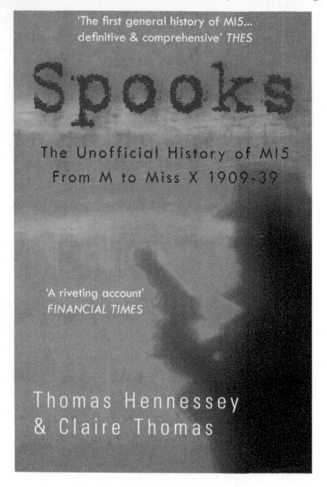

'The first general history of MI5...
definitive & comprehensive' *THES*

Spooks

The Unofficial History of MI5
From M to Miss X 1909-39

'A riveting account'
FINANCIAL TIMES

Thomas Hennessey & Claire Thomas

The real history of MI5

'PO Box 500, London W2' – the nondescript address from behind which one of the world's most famous secret services hid: MI5. Drawing on previously secret sources, this book lifts the lid on Britain's Security Service in its battle against German and Soviet espionage. It tells the sensational stories of the officers and agents and the enemies they confronted, from MI5's creation in 1909 under the direction of Vernon Kell, Britain's first spymaster.

Building on the service's wartime success, Maxwell Knight ('M'), MI5's charismatic and eccentric agent runner, penetrated Soviet and Fascist spy networks during the 1920s and 1930s. His agent, 'Miss X', was instrumental in breaking the Percy Glading spy ring run by the Soviets, while the beautiful Joan Miller and 'Miss Z' helped bring to justice Tyler Kent, who was passing information to the Axis powers.

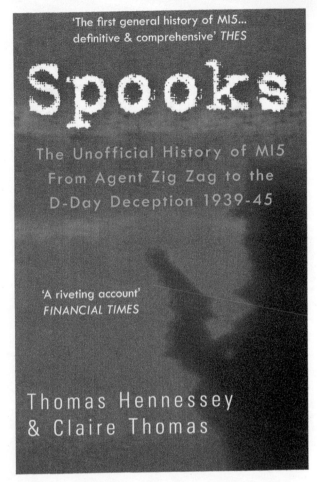

Also available from Amberley Publishing

How to fly the legendary fighter plane in combat using the manuals and instructions supplied by the RAF during the Second World War

'A Must' *INTERCOM: THE AIRCREW ASSOCIATION*

An amazing array of leaflets, books and manuals were issued by the War Office during the Second World War to aid pilots in flying the Supermarine Spitfire, here for the first time they are collated into a single book with the original 1940s setting. An introduction is supplied by expert aviation historian Dilip Sarkar. Other sections include aircraft recognition, how to act as an RAF officer, bailing out etc.

£9.99 Paperback
40 illustrations
264 pages
978-1-84868-436-2

Available from all good bookshops or to order direct
Please call **01453-847-800**
www.amberleybooks.com

Aavailable September 2012 from Amberley Publishing

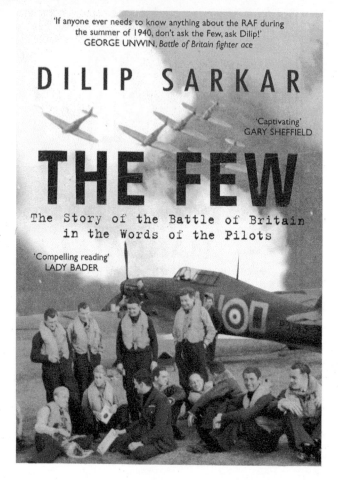

'If anyone ever needs to know anything about the RAF during the summer of 1940, don't ask the Few, ask Dilip!'
GEORGE UNWIN, *Battle of Britain fighter ace*

DILIP SARKAR

'Captivating'
GARY SHEFFIELD

THE FEW

The Story of the Battle of Britain
in the Words of the Pilots

'Compelling reading'
LADY BADER

The history of the Battle of Britain in the words of the pilots

'Over the last 30 years Dilip Sarkar has sought out and interviewed or corresponded with numerous survivors worldwide. Many of these were not famous combatants, but those who formed the unsung backbone of Fighter Command in 1940. Without Dilip's patient recording and collation of their memories, these survivors would not have left behind a permanent record.' LADY BADER
'A well-researched detailed chronicle of the Battle of Britain'. HUGH SEBAG MONTEFIORE

£9.99 Paperback
129 photographs
320 pages
978-1-4456-0701-6

Available September 2012 from all good bookshops or to order direct
Please call **01453-847-800**
www.amberleybooks.com

Also available from Amberley Publishing

An extraordinary true story of combat in the Battle of Britain

SPITFIRE PILOT

ROGER HALL, DFC

The intensely evocative memoir of one of 'the Few',
Spitfire pilot Roger Hall

The Battle of Britain memoir of Roger Hall, a Spitfire pilot in 152 Squadron based in the South East of England, the heart of the fighting during the epic battle. Roger recounts in exhaustive detail his own experience of air-to-air combat with Me109s and Me110s (he shot down three enemy aircraft during the Battle of Britain), and that of his fellow pilots. Hall had no compunction in revealing his fear of wartime flying. He strips away the veneer of glory, smart uniforms and wild parties and uncovers the ordinary, very human young men who lived a life in which there was no tomorrow. There is no nostalgia here.

£20 Hardback
50 photographs
224 pages
978-1-4456-0557-9

Available from all good bookshops or to order direct
Please call **01453-847-800**
www.amberleybooks.com

INDEX

Abteroda 201-2

Agazarian, Francine 87

Anderson, F/L Murray 7, 172-3, 218

Antelme, France 86-90, 94, 173-4, 177

Arisaig 79, 136

Atkins, Vera 41-3, 61-4, 94-5, 97-8, 160, 163-4, 167, 170, 210-11, 218-19,

Azay-sur-Cher 89

Baseden, Yvonne 44, 98, 107, 133, 191, 215, 218-9,

Beaulieu 79, 94, 110, 116, 132-3, 160, 195, 205

Belin 87

Belleuse, Colonel 180

Belsen 200

Bochler, Herr 181

Bodington, Nicholas 89

Bordeaux 18, 86

Borrel, Andrée 86

Boulogne-sur-Mer 15, 39

Bourg-la-Reine 175, 177, 184

Brierley, Ron 71

Brussels 209, 231

Buchenwald 200

Buchwald 202

Buckmaster, Maurice 36-7, 60-65, 79, 83, 89-90, 95, 97, 107, 110, 153, 162, 166-7, 170, 180, 182, 185, 202, 210, 230

Caldwell, F/L 90

Chambord 86

Chartres 90

Châteauroux 8, 82, 180

Chaumont-sur-Tharonne 88

Churchill, Peter 192

Clermont-Ferrand 82-3

Cooper, Mrs 212

Corbin, Charles 180

Couture-sur-Loir 89

Crouy-sur-Cosson 86

Dachau 94, 200

Damerment, Madeleine 90, 94

Darnard, Joseph 120

de Baissac, Claude 86-7

de Baissac, Lise 86-9, 94-5, 180, 218

de Vomecourt, Philippe 180

Denise Bloch 199

Déricourt, Henri 89

Deux Poiteaux 87

Devereux-Rochester, Elizabeth 51, 53

Dowlem, R. 87

Dumont–Guillemet, Réne 177, 179-81

Dunbar 76

Durieux, Maurice 172–3
Fawley Court 66, 71, 96
Flower, Raymond 87
Fourcard, Pierre 200
Frager, Jacques 84
Gaynes Hall 79, 171
Gieules, Robert 88, 88
Goldsmith, John 87
Gouin, Mme 89
Grendon Hall 66, 70, 75, 77, 91
Grenoble 18–19, 21–2, 39, 83, 129,
    218, 231
Hankey, F/L 28, 166–7
Haslam, E. 211–2
Hayes, Victor 87
Herriot, Éduoard 87–8
Heslop, Richard 180
Holmewood Hall 171
Hysing-Dahl 180
Jacquet, M. 181
Jepson, Selwyn (E. Potter) 37–9,
    41–2
Jones, Sydney 177
Khan, Noor Inayat 88, 90–2, 215
Large, Bob 180
Lee, Lionel (Daks) 90–2, 94
Lefort, Cécile 197
Leipzig 204–6, 211, 229, 232
Lejeune, Pierre 87
Le Mans 90
Leprince, M. 84
Le Vernet 20
Le Vésinet 124
Les Lagnys 7, 172
Les Tronchay 177
Lévy, Alexandre 84
'Louise' 174, 176, 182
Lovinfosse, George 172–3
Luzillé 180
Lyon 83, 149, 200
Marignac 87
Marnay 87
Markkleeburg 204–5, 229
Marks, Leo 68, 72–4, 90–4, 100–4,
    164, 175, 219
Matthieu, Geneviève 199–204, 218
Maury, Gerard 179
McCairns, 'Mac' 89

McLintock, Maisie, 'Mac' 66, 75–6,
    79, 161, 194, 216
Ménétréol-sous-Vatan 167
Milar, M. 185
Milsted, Capt. 171
Mizrahi, Colonel 180
Mouy 163
Murray-David, Beryle 164
Nearne, Francis 14, 16, 19, 22, 33,
    45, 83–4, 160–3, 218, 185
Nearne, Frederick 14, 16, 33, 160
Nearne, Jacqueline 14, 16, 18, 20–
    22, 26–7, 33–4, 37, 42, 44–5, 62,
    65, 79, 81–4, 86, 89, 98, 108–9,
    161, 185–6, 210–19, 222, 231
Newman, Isidore 89
Nice 15, 18–21, 39, 129
Noble, George 90, 92
Nouan-sur-Loire, 86
Orleans 174, 208, 231–2
Paris 23, 31, 82, 85–91, 148–9,
    153, 163–4, 173–4, 177–9, 182–4,
    186–7, 194, 200, 207, 210, 214,
    218, 232
Patriotic School 24, 27, 37, 40
Pau 83
Peleuve, Harry 86
Philby, Kim 111, 114
Ployet, Maurice 163
Poitiers 83, 86–7, 89
Poundon House 66, 77
Quatre Pavillions 87
Rake, Denis 180
Ratcliff, Leonard 180
Ravensbrück 196, 198–202, 204,
    211, 216, 219, 232
Régis, M. 180
'Renée' 205, 207
Reynaud, Paul 88
Ringway aerodrome 79–94
Ruffec 89
Rymills, 'Bunny' 87
Sainville 90
Sansom, Odette 192, 218–9
Savile Row 165
Savy, Jean, (Millet) 85–9, 94, 161,
    163, 165–8, 171–4, 177–81, 183
Sceaux 173, 213

Skilbeck, Major 110, 114
Soucelles 84
Southgate, Maurice (Hector) 82–3, 180
Southgate, Josette 180
St Egrève 19, 83–4
St Laurent Nouan 83
St Leu d'Esserent 179, 214
Suttill, Francis 88, 118
Szabó, Violette 199, 201–2, 220
Tangmere, RAF 32–3, 87, 89, 146, 167, 180
Taylor, F/L Robert 180
Tempsford, RAF 12, 29–33, 79, 87–8, 90, 167, 171, 177
Thame Park 66–95, 98, 104, 114, 161, 175–6
Thatched Barn 27, 175

Torgau 201–2, 232
Torquay 9, 219–28
Toulouse 83
Trotobas, Michael 180
Vaughan-Fowler, F/L. 87
Vendôme 89
Vichy 19, 23, 35, 83, 112, 119–20, 130, 149–50, 154
Villers-les-Ormes 180
Wake, Nancy 53, 56, 110
Wanborough Manor 37, 44, 79
Weimar 208, 230
Wheatley, F/S 87
Wilson, Jimmy 135
Winterfold 13, 44–60, 62, 64, 67, 98, 114
Whitaker, Capt. 172
'Yvette' 205, 207